THE COMPLETE BOOK OF BASEBALL SIGNS AND PLAYS

2ND EDITION

STU SOUTHWORTH

FOREWORD BY "ROD" DEDEAUX
HEAD COACH, U.S.C. TROJANS 1941-1986

COACHES CHOICE™   SPORTSMASTERS

ISBN: 1-58382-001-9

Library of Congress Catalog Card Number: 98-89415

Cover Design: Julie L. Denzer
Cover Photos: Courtesy of David Gonzales
Production Manager: Michelle A. Summers

a **SPORTS**MASTERS book, published by Coaches Choice

Coaches Choice Books is a division of: Sagamore Publishing, Inc.
P.O. Box 647
Champaign, IL 61824-0647
Web Site: http//www.sagamorepub.com

Dedicated
to
Coach Bob Webster
first varsity baseball coach
Pacific High School
San Bernardino, California (1953-1955)
and
University of Southern California
"Trojans" pitcher (1945-1947)
Pacific Coast Conference champions

and to
Fred R. Pettengill
Pacific High School's
first all-CIF (first team)
baseball player (1960)
varsity third baseman (1958-1960)
and
varsity third baseman
University of Oregon "Ducks" (1961-1962)
Pacific Coast Conference

in memoriam
and
with pride
from
Pacific High School's "Pirates"

Acknowledgments

There are many friends, coaches, colleagues, family, storytellers, typists, research aides, umpires, and many others who have given of their time, interest, expertise, stories, and suggestions to complete a baseball text of this type and complexity. A complete listing of every contributor would be virtually impossible.

To all of those who contributed in any way toward the completion of this volume, the author extends a hearty "Thank you."

First and foremost, thanks go to Pam Crosson and Cecille Watkins, typists, whose excellent work in preparing the chapters of the original manuscript was difficult and time-consuming.

Chief contributors to Chapters 3 and 4 were two excellent baseball men from the city of San Bernardino, California. Coach Jim McGarry spent more than a month in assisting the author in formulating, organizing, and checking Chapter 3. Chief Umpire Charlie Lewis, a premier baseball umpire from the Inland Empire assisted the author in formulating, organizing, and checking Chapter 4.

The field diagrams found in the text were done by John Evanko, commercial artist for the Altoona, Pennsylvania, school district. The quality of his work and his understanding of the complex points in the game of baseball are remarkable.

So many baseball coaches, at all levels of the game, contributed. The University of Arizona's head coach, Jerry Kindall, himself a great teacher and author of several volumes, deserves many thanks for his interest in this text on baseball signs. Some parts of his book *Baseball* are found in several chapters.

Thanks to Coach John Monger, formerly from the Chino High School district, Don Lugo High School, for his story contribution, "The Grand Slam Triple Play."

Thanks so much, Claude Anderson, former sportswriter for the *San Bernardino Sun*, for his interest and support to the author and his texts on baseball since 1981.

Without the sketches and explanations in Chapter 2, "Offensive Plays and Signs," used with permission of the Human Kinetics Publishers, Champaign, Illinois, this vital portion of the book would have been most difficult to do using only portions of the author's first book, done in 1988, *High Percentage Baserunning*.

Parts of the baseball texts *The Art and Science of Aggressive Baserunning*, by Coach Cliff Petrak, Brother Rice High School, Chicago, Illinois; and *Baseball, Signs and Signals*, by Coach Tom Petroff, University of Iowa, were used with the authors' permission.

The author extends his sincere thanks to dear Ella Kennedy Penny, retired English teacher, Liberal High School, Liberal, Kansas, who encouraged the author, in that sophomore class in 1940, to be a writer of books. She is still one of the author's main sources of advice and encouragement.

I express gratitude to my family for its support and interest along the way since 1981, in writing five baseball volumes. To Thelma Southworth, my wife, and Michael, Kathy, and Michelle, our children, who spent hours listening and contributing to the progress of each chapter.

Chapter 4, "Umpires' Calls and Signs" was given a final check by two excellent umpires in the Inland Empire. We are grateful to both NCAA Umpire Phil Meyer, of Yorba Linda, California, and Umpire Gene Cestaro, of San Bernardino, California.

Many thanks to Coach "Rod" Dedeaux, Head Baseball Coach at University of Southern California, 1941-1986, for contributing the Foreword for this book.

Thanks to Senior Editor John Douglas, Avon Books, publishers of this work, for accepting the manuscript to publish, and for his months of inspiration, guidance, and work to assemble this complex work into an informative and enjoyable baseball text. And thanks, John, many thanks, for being baseball's "in-house" champion from the beginning.

HAROLD S. SOUTHWORTH

Foreword

It is a very special honor for me to be asked to comment on this wonderful work of my good friend, Harold Southworth, because it is dedicated to one of my very favorite people, Bob Webster.

Bob was truly a student of the game. He excelled in pitching for the University of Southern California Trojans, ranking alongside many players who achieved great fame in the major leagues. His most promising professional career was untimely cut short, but he went on to become one of the finest high school coaches in the glorious history of baseball development in Southern California.

Baseball—The Greatest Game.

The subtle complexities of this sport relate so intimately to our everyday lives. It appears so simple that to the uninitiated, it can have a "ho-hum," existence, but as those persons mature and begin to learn its many facets, they fall in love with the game and yes, to some of us, it becomes *almost* a religion.

There is the physical: Can he run? Can he throw with velocity, with accuracy? Hit? Hit with power? Field?

There is the mental: Is he intelligent? Can he think while doing the physical? Is his approach to the game positive? Is he coachable? And does he have enough self-discipline to take direction from his manager and others?

Yes, we're talking about baseball signs. This facet of the game just might be one of the most neglected elements in developing the strategies of the game. For signs to be useful, they have to be appreciated. So, the first step is making the player understand what is the purpose of the play to be called. Then, he will be looking for it with enthusiasm.

The peculiar characteristics about signs are that they *must be complicated* or else they can be deciphered and turned into a negative. And add to that, the *good* sign stealers will never let you know that they do have your signs. On the other hand, the signs *must be simple*, so that in the heat of battle, they can be recognized and implemented without distracting from the physical job that has to be done.

What appeals to me about this book is that its author, Harold Southworth, clearly shows that he is a student of the game. He has had the great advantage of experience gained by being involved with all levels of players. He takes great pains to explain in detail the strategies themselves and seems to bring to life every situation.

You'll enjoy this book for happy reading far beyond its technical advice.

—ROD DEDEAUX

Contents

Preface

It's mid-July as we find ourselves sitting in those hardwood folding seats out at the ballpark of our favorite professional baseball team. The game hasn't started yet, but we are already becoming acclimated to the sights and sounds around us.

However, upon close scrutiny of this familiar scene, in which we have found ourselves many times, we realize something very interesting. What we discover is that, as we take in the sights and listen to the sounds of the game, the importance of the sights will far outweigh the significance of the sounds. We discover that the sounds add very little to our understanding of the game. Of course, some of the very important sounds of a ball game do have a bearing on our understanding of what is happening; I'm talking about the words of the coaches, players, and umpires. Unfortunately, these people are usually too far away for us to hear what they are saying, and the roar of the crowd fails to make these sounds any clearer.

Fortunately for the fan, the players, coaches, and umpires also find it difficult to communicate verbally, either because of the difficulty of hearing one another or because, in many cases, they would prefer that their opposition not be aware of their words to each other. *So it is, then, that most of the communication that goes on in a ball game is of the nonverbal variety. Consequently, just as a deaf person must learn to read lips, so, too, must the dedicated fan learn to "read" the body language exhibited by the people on the field.* This means careful observation of the signs, signals, gestures, and gyrations of the umpires and players, the latter in both offensive and defensive situations. This holds true for the coaches, too, who communicate not only from the coaching boxes but also from the dugout when their players are out on the field on defense. The degree to which we can correctly interpret the meanings behind these body movements will determine the degree to which we find ourselves involved in this summer pastime.

Umpires' signals, players' offensive and defensive gestures, and coaching gyrations make for a game within a game. Sometimes they are simple, sometimes they are complex, sometimes they are subtle, and sometimes they are as exciting and dramatic as Babe Ruth's legendary pointing to the right-field bleachers in the 1932 World Series at Wrigley Field. As most people know, that gesture was followed by one of the most exciting encores in entertainment history.

While the body language of baseball is usually simple, subtle, and often of a secret nature, so much more enjoyment can be received from the game when it is watched with this nonverbal communication in mind.

All of the information relating to signs and signals throughout the twelve decades of baseball's history has been preserved, passed down mainly by word of mouth. Perhaps this is easily explained when we realize that signs are very secret to a baseball team, so the coaches and managers do not wish to place this knowledge on paper during their active careers, and none of them yet have been moved to give away their secrets after their retirement from baseball. This skill has therefore remained unwritten; to thousands of people it is a deep, dark secret.

Since I am a retired baseball coach with over thirty years of experience, and because I did use an excessive number of signs in those years of my coaching tenure, I feel a great need to lay out in front of the baseball world this text on the subject.

Could any reader, or baseball coach for that matter, tell us the name of every one of the possible offensive plays or maneuvers for which a sign can be given? Similarly, could a baseball player or manager recite every defensive trick for which names are given and for which signs are given and rehearsed? It is probable that many in baseball could not. The author freely admits that he would be hard-pressed to do the same. But this game of baseball has a considerable number of plays for which signs are given to players. I will make every effort to bring each of them to the reader of this book.

We find a great deal of controversy and confusion in regard to signs and body language among players and coaches. I hope that this volume will clear up and organize in the minds of baseball people the points that cause their misunderstanding. We find poor communication on the field, but more than this, we find *incomplete* communication. So many more plays could be run if only the coaches and players knew them and would practice them. Would an admiral or general go into battle with only a portion of his arsenal? Of course not. And yet, how many coaches go into a baseball game with no sign for a given situation or play or are guilty of having never rehearsed it?

This text will clearly show readers that there is a definite need for clear signs from coaches to players for every situation in a baseball game, offensive or defensive.

Does the reader realize that baseball teams steal each other's signs? The dark secrets of how this is done border on a tale of counterintelligence in warfare. The thinking and clever tricks involved in this process will amaze all who see exactly how it is done.

The author wishes you an interesting journey in exploring the mysteries of baseball's silent communication system.

HAROLD S. SOUTHWORTH

San Bernardino, California

Chapter 1

THE HISTORY, PHILOSOPHY, AND EVOLUTION OF PLAYS AND SIGNS

The Unusual History and Evolution of Baseball's Offensive Plays (Hitting, Bunting, Running)

CAST OF CHARACTERS

1. Ned Hanlon (1857-1937)

2. John McGraw (1873-1934)

3. Wee Willie Keeler (1872-1923)

4. Hughie Jennings (1869-1928)

5. Dan O'Rourke (1868-1898)

6. Harold S. "Stu" Southworth

These six baseball men fit into one of baseball's, if not all of athletics', most interesting stories. For these are six of the most noteworthy contributors to what we know as "offensive baseball"—how to move men around the bases and score runs. Travel with us now back to the year 1890, that baseball season when our modern game was formed. Its rules and structure have really changed little since that year, and there have been very, very few changes in strategy. Between 1869 and 1890, a period of twenty-one years, baseball's offensive game was experiencing many confusing changes, and the professional leagues needed some measure of standardization in strategy and execution of their offensive plays. Finally this came in the person of Ned Hanlon, major league manager from 1892 to 1898.

At that time, signs and plays were only developed as a primitive art, but Ned and his players set the pattern for all of baseball to come. It was these men, including such players as Wee Willie Keeler, John McGraw, Wilbert Robinson, and Hughie Jennings, who devised the first bits of "inside baseball strategy," making it one of the parts of today's national sport that is a true art form.

We are told that Ned Hanlon would sit at his kitchen table at home, a diagram of the baseball field in front of him with little cut-out squares and circles of different colors on it representing men on the diamond, then play mental strategy games with these men (much as today's coaches play with their X's and O's in their "chalk talks"). He would go to bed at night and dream of new plays, see men running around on his "dream diamond." When a new idea roused him from sleep, he would get out of bed and light the kerosene lamp, jotting down the play just revealed to him. The next day he would take his drawing to the "laboratory," the diamond with its living models, and his professional team would practice, rehearse, and time the play until they were letter-perfect in its execution. Thus, baseball's first real "plays" were perfected—those that are known today as the various types of bunts, the hit-and-run play, the run-and-hit play, the squeeze bunt, and the double and triple steals.

Let's pause in this fascinating early story to remind the baseball reader that the author, in his 1984-88 research book, *High Percentage Baserunning*, discovered that, from 1869 to 1988, baseball's offensive experimenters devised and discovered more than two dozen of these offensive maneuvers. Although Ned Hanlon and his players were the first truly successful inventors of baseball plays, they still left something to be desired, for they ended their careers having uncovered less than half of the possible plays.

Well, who uncovered the other offensive plays, which they never touched upon? Why, of course, the coaches and managers and baseball minds who closely followed upon these men in time. They gradually visualized and tried successfully, one by one, from 1900 to 1990, the remainder of the plays of which you are about to learn.

The plays that Ned Hanlon conceived and taught his team to execute left the rest of his league reeling, because baseball, as it was then played, was basically a "pitch-hit-catch game" with no real strategies attached. Your team either hit the ball or lost the game. It is too bad that, in this 1990 decade, almost one hundred years later, many coaches and managers still try to win ball games the same way, defying the odds all the way. When they play this way, the percentages are against them!

The story is told of how Ned Hanlon's team executed thirteen hit-and-run plays in sweeping a four-game series against the New York Giants. Manager John Ward of the Giants threatened to haul Hanlon before the baseball commissioner, on the grounds that "he wasn't playing baseball"; rather, it was some "new game that he invented." (The author of this text recalls having the same charges leveled at him in his various levels of coaching, both by fans and managers alike. My reply to these criticisms was always the same—"If you object to those tactics, then go out on the practice field and learn how to stop them.") Of course, there is a way to stop nearly every one of those new strategies, but the fielding team must study the offensive maneuvers and take time to practice the counters to them. Even after teams copied Ned Hanlon's plays, and this author's plays, we devised ways to work options of them—always one jump ahead of the defense.

McGraw, Jennings, and Robinson later became great managers in the major leagues early in the twentieth century. The tricks they had learned soon became commonplace with their teams, and hence, throughout all of organized baseball to this very day.

To make the story of the history and evolution of baseball plays much more interesting to the baseball coach and reader, perhaps we should create an interesting and unusual parallel between two coaches of different eras. The two men to whom I refer are Coach Dan O'Rourke, the big redheaded Irishman, from Midvale, New York, who was manager of the Adams Mill Lumber Company team, an Industrial League semipro coach who had that team from 1895 to 1898; and Coach Harold S. "Stu" Southworth, who coached the game from 1947 to 1984, a high school and American Legion baseball man (only) in the states of Washington, Oregon, and California.

COACH DAN O'ROURKE—PLAYING AND COACHING SUMMARY

- Played sandlot and school baseball—Middleburg, New York 1885-1895

- Played and managed the Adams Mill baseball club 1895-1898

- Born in Elmira, New York, November 12, 1868

- Died in Midvale, New York, August 3, 1898

COACH STU SOUTHWORTH—PLAYING AND COACHING SUMMARY

- Player, 1936-1940, playground and recreation

- Player, 1941-1947, Grossmont High School

  San Diego Summer League

  University of Denver

  Whitman College

  University of Washington

  U.S. Navy service ball

- Head baseball coach, 1949-1953, Silver Lake, Washington American Legion Jr. Baseball, Eugene, Oregon

  Davenport High School, Davenport, Washington

  American Legion Jr. Baseball, Davenport, Washington

- Various coaching positions, 1954-1984, Pacific High School,

  San Bernardino, California

  Eisenhower High School, Rialto, California

  San Gorgonio High School, San Bernardino, California

- Born in Dallas, Texas, April 19, 1925

- Coach Southworth retired from active teaching and coaching of athletics in 1984 to become a writer of baseball textbooks

If we were to search baseball history for the answers to the following questions, what would we find?

- What is the total number of baseball plays, both offensive and defensive, that have been designed, tried, and tested through the decades? (We can answer that one. There are definitely more than two dozen such plays.)

- Who discovered each of these plays? How were they learned by the originators?

- What signs were first used for each of these plays? How have these signs changed?

- What was the evolution of all these plays? Which came first, what then followed, and so forth?

- Where was each of the plays discovered? What were the dates and places of their first trials?

- Is there actually a record of all the above questions and answers to which we could refer?

If we earnestly set out to research all of the above questions, it is highly unlikely that we could find exact dates, names, places. Even if it were possible to do so, the time and cost would be prohibitive for our purpose.

We know that the plays of offensive baseball are broken down into seven main categories:

- Steals (before the pitch)

- Steals (on the pitch)

- Delayed steals (after the pitch)

- Hit-and-run/run-and-hit

- Fake steal play

- Bunts

- Fake bunt/fake bunt and slash

Add the wipeoff sign and the take sign, which are vital to coaching baseball but are not really plays.

We shall not only journey into "play evolution" by year and place, but will also show the reader how various persons, in a field of endeavor, discover, associate, and thus go on to discover more. We have already seen how those old-timers discovered possibly fourteen baseball plays by 1895. We shall now follow two later coaches as they found the remaining plays, and discuss their logical approach to something drastically new to everyone about them.

In the early years of their coaching careers, O'Rourke and Southworth knew nothing but "hit away" as a tactic. This is where all novices who learn baseball begin their thinking as far as strategy is concerned. This concept states that you get on base with a base hit, then you just stand safely near that base until a teammate hits you around to score. Very simple baseball, eh?

When coaching began, however, they soon discovered that a carefully laid down bunt can get a man on base as easily as a hard line drive base hit. We then imagine both coaches drilling teams by the hour on bunting. This play is called the drag bunt, and we will begin numbering our plays here (we don't actually include the hit away maneuver as a "play"). Dan and Stu soon learned that a bunt will also advance all runners to the next base. With practice they perfected the sacrifice bunt to move runners one base along. The teams of the two coaches had now learned two plays, plus hit away. (Hit away, of course, will always remain baseball's premier maneuver. Really, no planned play can replace the base hit.) From this point on in the two coaches' lives, the learning and progression of plays increased in tempo.

One day these two fine coaches asked themselves, "Why give up an out on a bunt when we can advance the runner two bases instead?" Be greedy, of course. It is not that difficult a play, moving the runner from first base to third base, just have him stealing on the pitch. Thus was born the next play, sacrifice bunt to move a runner two bases along.

These coaches had, earlier in their careers, seen the suicide squeeze bunt executed successfully. This play scores one run on the bunt. With lots of rehearsal this became their next play. Their repertoire was growing fast.

The logical next step in redheaded Dan O'Rourke's and blonde headed Stu Southworth's minds was this—"Why score just one man on a suicide squeeze bunt?" Be greedy and score two. How is this possible? Easy. Just have the very fast second base runner stealing on the pitch. This became the suicide squeeze bunt to score two runs. It was practiced and honed to perfection. Before long, the coaches' teams had two types of squeeze plays.

Both coaches had toyed with the percentages of success when they called the steal-on-pitcher plays. They rehearsed their teams diligently in executing these plays, beating the catcher's throw down to that next base. This could be used for any runner, at any time, at first, second, or third base.

The next play was added to the coaches' selection when they thought, "On the suicide squeeze bunt to score one run, why sacrifice the runner, the out, and the run on a bad bunt or a missed bunt?" And so was born in their minds a new creation with a new title—the safe squeeze bunt. The third base runner tries for home only on a very good bunt. He is not committed to come home as he is on the squeeze bunt.

The fake bunt and slash was created a few days later when the first and third basemen moved in on a bunt and the other infielders shifted. But this time, the batter, in bunting stance, changed his hand position on the bat and punched a soft hit over the drawn-in field. A clever play.

(The number of offensive plays is growing, isn't it? Soon they would have all of them. They needed only to keep on thinking, imagining, and building on existing plays that were tried and proven.)

These two innovative coaches then saw that there were times when they should signal batters not to swing at the next pitch, let the pitch go by, for various strategic reasons. This play became the take. Really, this one is a sign, not an actual play. It may help a play succeed, however. Of course, these two enterprising young coaches were teaching communications (signs or signals) as they introduced each new play.

It was necessary to call several plays on defense. There was the intentional walk to the batter, for instance. The coach merely pointed to first base, thus indicating "Walk the next batter."

Brainstorms hit every coach at the most unexpected times. They are triggered by a previous observation or series of events. One day in the careers of both Southworth and O'Rourke this occurred. Listen to this thought: "Why give up an out at all on a sacrifice bunt? Instead, have the batter stick the bat out in a bunting pose while the runners are stealing the next bases. If they steal the bases, then we haven't had to give up an out to advance them." A new creation—the fake bunt—came into being.

After all of these events, what is the next logical thought that might enter the brain of any baseball coach? If you can pull a fake bunt on the other team, why not a fake steal? That's logical. Have your runners fake steal often, but not in a definite pattern. The defense yells, "There he goes," except that he doesn't—on that pitch. If the runners did this often, defense would never know on which pitch the runners were going to steal, much the same as in the story *The Boy Who Cried Wolf*.

The repertoire of plays had swelled. This select "bag of tricks" caused a team to win much more frequently than before. Runs came faster. Why? Because they were getting more varied weapons in their arsenal, of course.

Just as old Ned Hanlon had done in the 1890s, so also at some time early in their careers, Dan and Stu found baseball's "gem" play, the hit-and-run. On the pitch, the batter must swing and the runners must steal, and the batter tries to hit the ball toward a hole vacated by a shifting infielder or hit it over an infielder's head. This play had been used against both their teams—and with resounding success. So they adopted it and placed it in their prize collection of plays. Coaches so often do this. They are real copycats. Now why hadn't these two young mentors thought of that play themselves? Who knows? Sometimes good ideas escape us.

In a few weeks the coaches had reversed the hit-and-run and created another maneuver, the run-and-hit. Two different plays from the same idea. They didn't realize it, but their greatest fun was still to come—and some mighty new discoveries as well.

They suddenly, one day, noticed the frequency with which they had men on first and third bases (only those bases). Very, very often in games. They called this situation "men at the corners." They pondered, "How can I steal home while my first base runner is stealing second base?" To their great amazement, after trying various plays with live players on their "living laboratory," they uncovered several different plays that would allow the double steal with men on first and third. Each of the plays worked with wild success—all were timed a little differently. They found that some plays could be done before the pitch, some could be done on the pitch, and some could be executed after the pitch. Good heavens, had any baseball coach ever possessed so many offensive play gems with which to trick the opponent? Not even those 1891-1898 teams had all these weapons to use, those collected by Dan O'Rourke and Stu Southworth in the years 1897 and 1956.

But there were still more good plays hidden away, waiting to be unearthed by those enterprising experimenters.

At about the same time in each of their careers, Stu and Dan realized that there was only one way they were going to keep "sharp," as coaches and team players alike, on this growing arsenal of plays. The great idea struck them one day: Why not have one practice every week on nothing but baserunning and offensive plays? Bunting, stealing, running, team play—all offense. Another idea they kicked themselves for not having done before. At this practice they brought out sliding pads, gloves, and nothing else. Bats were brought out only for bunting and hit-and-run plays. No other batting practice.

They did this for the remainder of their coaching careers—and won and won and won.

Sometime in the latter parts of the careers of these coaches, the last major play type entered into their thinking. Perhaps it came from seeing an opponent use a unique style of steal play. This discovery is the delayed steal. Now, Dan and Stu had, for years, stolen most of their bases on the pitch, beating the pitcher's slow delivery, the catcher's weak throw down—or both. Later on, with men on first and third bases, the coaches had devised the early steals.

Gradually an absolutely essential thought grabbed them. It went like this—"Why not steal the next base either on the catcher's return to his pitcher or on the catcher's pickoff attempt at any base?" This would be a whole new class of steals—always stealing after the pitch has reached the catcher's glove. A great idea, for the defense expects all steals to be done on the pitch—not before or after.

Coaches Dan O'Rourke and Stu Southworth completed their lifetime repertoire of offensive baseball plays by inventing the various types of these delayed steals. In each of these plays timings are varied; no two are alike at all. Refer to Chapter 2 of this text for complete descriptions of these delayed steal types.

Both coaches, very late in their careers, completed the last play with the delayed steal while the bases are loaded. It is the weirdest play ever devised for baseball, but these coaches found that it always worked, never failed to score a run.

And now we come to the end of this baseball tale—the discovery of baseball's offensive plays (1869- 1990). We have heard of the valuable contributions to baseball understanding of Ned Hanlon, his players, Coach Dan O'Rourke, and Coach Stu Southworth. What eventually happened to Hanlon, McCraw, Jennings, Keeler, Robinson, O'Rourke, and Southworth?

Ned Hanlon managed professional baseball teams every year from 1889 to 1907.

John McGraw became a very famous manager. Most noteworthy was his 1902-1932 stint with the great New York Giants. He was inducted into the Baseball Hall of Fame at Cooperstown in 1937.

Hughie Jennings also became a very famous manager, serving with the Detroit Tigers from 1907 to 1920. He was inducted into the Baseball Hall of Fame at Cooperstown in 1945.

Wee Willie Keeler played for many teams from 1892 to 1910. He was inducted into the Baseball Hall of Fame at Cooperstown in 1939.

Wilbert Robinson played and managed in the major leagues from 1886 to 1902. He managed the Brooklyn Dodgers from 1914 to 1931.

Coach Daniel O'Rourke, it is sad to relate, died at the end of the 1898 season, in Midvale, New York, at age thirty, from a strange malady. He had only managed for four years at Midvale. What is really incredible is his having discovered, by himself, practically all of baseball's plays in only four years as a small-town coach. He was a true genius.

Coach Stu Southworth, your author, is the only one of this collection of innovators to be alive today. He lives with his wife, Thelma. After college graduation in 1947, he coached a number of high school baseball teams and American Legion clubs in Washington, Oregon, and California until 1984, a thirty-seven-year span. Having never played one inning of professional baseball, he will obviously not land in any Baseball Hall of Fame. However, he believes his contributions to the game of baseball to be important. Coach Southworth does believe that a "mere handful" of baseball players and managers, from all who have been in the game these many years, know of the facts or events of our story just unfolded.

The following charts show the entire pattern of plays, by title (and the signs chosen for those plays), which baseball coaches discovered, rehearsed, and executed on the diamond. Notice that only two of these plays are of a defensive type. They are the intentional walk and the four options the defense chooses from to stop the opponent's double steal play with men on first and third bases.

Baseball's unspoken language has been a part of the game for nearly a century. It was the original professional teams, with such players as John McGraw, Hughie Jennings, Wilbert Robinson, and Wee Willie Keeler, who devised the first bits of truly "inside baseball strategy." This group first perfected such maneuvers as the bunt, the hit-and-run play, the squeeze, and the double steal.

However, most baseball historians credit a man named Ned Hanlon, who was a manager in the later 1890s, as the creator of all of these tricks. So you see, neither Dan O'Rourke nor Stu Southworth dreamed these up.

Baseball's Most Important Bunting Plays

Name of Play	Visual	Verbal	The Signal	Special Tips
Take sign	X	None	Coach folds arms across chest	Same sign to runners and batters
Hit-and-run play	X	None	Coach crosses legs—sitting or standing—*to batter* Coach puts hand in face area *to runners*	This play requires 2 signs

Baseball's Bunting Plays

Name of Play	Visual	Verbal	The Signal	Special Tips
Drag bunt or sacrifice bunt (move runner only 1 base)	X	None	Coach puts 1 hand on 1 knee Hand on left knee—bunt left side of diamond Hand on right knee—bunt right side of diamond	Same sign to batter and runners
Safe squeeze bunt	X	None	Coach tugs at his belt with 1 or 2 hands	Same sign to batter and runners
Suicide squeeze (score 1 run)	X	None	Coach puts 1 hand on 1 knee	Same sign to batter and runner
Suicide squeeze (score 2 runs)	X	None	Coach puts 2 hands on 2 knees	Same sign to batter and 2 runners
Sacrifice bunt (move man from 1st base to 3rd base)	X	None	Coach puts 2 hands on 2 knees	Same sign to batter and runner

Baseball's Fake Bunting Plays

Name of Play	Visual	Verbal	The Signal	Special Tips
Fake bunt and steal 2nd or 3rd base	X	None	Coach puts hand to face area—*to runners* Coach shows closed fist—*to batter*	The play requires 2 signs
Fake bunt-slash (man on 3rd base)	X	None	Coach moves hand from neck to crotch, straight down	Same sign to batter and runner
Fake bunt-slash (man on 1st or 2nd base)	X	None	Coach moves hand from neck to crotch, straight down	Same sign to batter and runners

Baseball's Steal and Fake Steal Plays

Name of Play	Visual	Verbal	The Signal	Special Tips
Fake steal	X	None	Coach kicks the dirt with either foot	Batter and runner get same sign
Single steal on pitcher	X	None	Coach puts hand to face or neck area	Same sign for all these 4 plays—and batter picks up same sign
Double steal on pitcher	X	None	Coach puts hand to face or neck area	
Triple steal on pitcher (man on 3rd base)	X	None	Coach puts hand to face or neck area	
Steal home on pitcher	X	None	Coach puts hand to face or neck area	
Delayed steal (man on 2nd base only)	X	None	Coach waves arm in front of him horizontally as if indicating to runners "No, no"—to the runner	Batter is not involved (hit away)
Delayed steal (men on 1st and 2nd base only)	X	None	Coach waves arm in front of him horizontally as if indicating to runners "No, no"—to the runner	Batter is not involved (hit away)
Delayed steal (men on 2nd and 3rd base only)	X	None	Coach waves arm in front of him horizontally as if indicating to runners "No, no"—to the runners	Batter is not involved (hit away)
Delayed steal (bases loaded)	X	None	Coach waves arm in front of him horizontally as if indicating to runners "No, no"—to the runners	Batter is involved (take)
Delayed steal (man on 3rd base only)	X	None	Coach waves arm in front of him horizontally as if indicating to runners "No, no"—to the runner	Batter is not involved (hit away)

The Special Defensive Plays

Name of Play	Visual	Verbal	The Signal	Special Tips
Intentional walk	X	None	Coach points to 1st base	Same sign for pitcher and all of the team
Infield cutoff play/ pitcher cutoff throw	None	X	Coach yells, before the pitcher is in stretch, last name of the catcher	Catcher keeps throw very low and hard
Infield cutoff play/ catcher fake throw (fires to 3rd base)	None	X	Coach yells, before the pitcher is in stretch, last name of the catcher	Catcher full-arm fake, step out and step back
Infield cutoff play/ 2nd baseman cutoff throw	None	X	Coach yells, before the pitcher is in stretch, last name of the 2nd basemen	Catcher keeps throw very low and hard
Infield cutoff play/ let throw go to 2nd base	None	X	Coach yells, before the pitcher is in stretch, last name of shortshop	Catcher keeps throw very low and hard

The Special Double Steal Plays
-or-
7 offensive options (runners on first and third)

Name of Play	Visual	Verbal	The Signal	Special Tips
Before the pitch (men on 1st and 3rd base, 0 or 1 out)	Coach will motion	X	Coach yells "OK" and the last name of 1st base runner. He then yells the correct number of outs.	Batter is not involved
Before the pitch (men on 1st and 3rd base, 2 outs)	3rd base runner off base a little	X	Coach yells "OK" and the last name of 1st base runner. He then yells "two away."	Batter is not involved
Before the pitch (man on 3rd and batter at plate)	X	X	In time-out, coach tells batter, who walks, to jog to 1st, say "1001," adjust belt, dash for 2nd Coach motions 3rd base runner off the base a little	2 signs are required for this play. One is a verbal discussion between batter and coach
On the pitch (men on 1st and 3rd base, 2 outs)	X	None	Coach puts hand to face or neck area—*to 1st base runner* Coach motions 3rd base runner off the base a little	2 signs are required for this play
On the pitch (men on 1st and 3rd base, 0 or 1 out)	X	None	Coach puts hand to face or neck area—*to 1st base runner* Coach motions 3rd base runner off the base a little	2 signs are required for this play
After the pitch (men on 1st and 3rd base, 0 or 1 out)	X	None	Coach gives delayed steal sign to 1st base runner—moves hand across body horizontally Coach motions 3rd base runner off the base a little	2 signs are required for this play
After the pitch (men on 1st and 3rd base, 2 outs)	X	None	Coach gives delayed steal sign to 1st base runner—moves hand across body horizontally Coach motions 3rd base runner off the base a little	2 signs are required for this play

MYTHS AND FALLACIES OF BASERUNNING

Fallacy number 1: The bat should be used to score men on base who got there with the use of the bat. The bunt and stolen base are "too risky."

Fallacy number 2: Teaching running plays takes too much time and will just confuse the average player.

Fallacy number 3: Coaches don't want to make baserunning "so special in the minds of the players" that they minimize the other parts of the game mentally.

Fallacy number 4: Most players on most teams are not intelligent enough to learn and *memorize and instantly recall* all of these plays when called for in a particular situation in a game.

Fallacy number 5: "We can win by keeping it simple" is the cry from coaches. Don't get too complicated. Too many plays will confuse the mind of a player, whether he is smart or dumb.

Fallacy number 6: You must be a bunch of "speed demons" on the base paths to make all those possible plays work.

Fallacy number 7: "We won the league title back at good old State University by not using all of those fancy running and bunting plays. So why use them now? I am going to coach the rest of my life just exactly like my old coach did."

Fallacy number 8: Fancy baseball is not "good" baseball.

Fallacy number 9: "The fans and players will think I am crazy to try these weird plays." Peer pressure, eh?

Fallacy number 10: Practice time spent on these baserunning plays will not pay off.

THEORIES ON BASEBALL SIGNALS

Philosophy of the Running Game and Signs Used

There are so many schools of thought on the exact methods of teaching signs that they could not all be mentioned here. In thirty years of coaching baseball, I have found more men who favor using very few signs than those who use a lot. *I have tried my best to probe into this and find out why they don't want to use more than a few baseball signs.*

Reason 1: "My players are so dumb that they can learn only four or five signs." I feel that if you have speed on your team, and you really do have "dumb kids," then you are not going to win that many ball games anyway. They may be fine hitters and have speed, but they will lose their share of baseball games on poor running. *Remember, it is one thing to get a man on base, and it is quite another to get him around to home.* They are quite different skills. When a coach gives you this "dumb kid" bit, he is resigning himself and his team to defeat with a negative attitude. It has been my experience that a boy of baseball playing age can learn just about anything he really wants to learn. Would a high school boy, age sixteen, have any trouble learning the names, addresses, phone numbers, and main personality traits of the twelve best-looking girls in his class? Then why would a boy, vitally interested in being a ball player, have trouble with a dozen or more signals in a practice or a game? The secrets to teaching a lot of baseball signs are to *do it in an interesting manner,* incorporate it into practice well, and keep a repetitive barrage at him until he learns them. He will learn them if he wants to play ball.

Reason 2: "I can win with only four or five signs. I don't need more than five." Well, would a football coach or basketball coach use only five plays in a season? Obviously not! Right here, let me inject my belief that you must have a sign for every play that *you may want to use.* Otherwise, how would you ever be able to communicate? *The coach who uses the excuse that he wants to use just four or five signs all season is not aware of the fact that in all of baseball you perhaps need only twelve or thirteen signs at the most!*

Reason 3: "Oh, that's fancy baseball," or, "What would my fans and players think if I used all those signs and plays?" If a coach is not innovative and daring and willing to experiment with the possibilities of the game, should he be coaching? If he is willing to coach only one-half the game, then is he going to win? If a coach is going to be intimidated by players, fans, moms and dads, and alumni should he be coaching? In other words, shouldn't a baseball coach constantly expand and grow in the game by adding plays to his repertoire, and learn to move away from the mainstream of the game he coaches? He should be contributing his thought and creativity to his total game. These coaches who pattern their baseball after what they see on TV are forgetting that *they are not managing in the professional ranks- yet!*

How Many Signs Should You Use?

My basic philosophy is that you must have a different sign for every play you want to use. You never know when you will have to use these, so you had better be ready at any time.

If you go on the field with only a few signs, *you are cheating your team.* You are asking them to go out to face the enemy with only a fraction of the possible arsenal of weapons available to you.

I group my signs, however, so that all the bunt signs look alike. But even the bunt signs have one little difference in each that distinguishes it from the rest. *My steal signs are of three different types, so I want my signs for stealing to be very different.* This keeps the player from being confused when a steal play is on. He has a chance to think about the timing before he has to go into the play and execute. You may use some signs three or four times in a row, and you may not use a sign for several weeks. Lack of use does dull the memory. To keep sharp on sign giving, sign taking, and sign interpretation, it is imperative that you practice them as often as you can. *A very good method for doing this is to give your players a wallet-size card with the names of all the plays on it.* Have them pair off in twos or threes and recite each play and its sign to each other. One player can call out the sign and the other ones give the play, or vice versa. Never put your plays and signs together on the same paper. They can easily get lost and fall into the wrong hands.

Methods of Relaying Signs

The main consideration here is not to make signs so secret that the opponent can't pick them up. Rather, it is to make them so simple that your team should never miss one. Remember, a missed sign can cause you to lose an out, an inning, a key game, or a championship.

This is another part of baseball that is done in many ways. In the major leagues, the coach giving signs will usually give several, one right after the other. One sign may be the "indicator." On a particular night, you may agree to execute the third sign shown, say, out of a series of five given. On another night, perhaps, the second one shown. Or you may agree on the first sign shown after the indicator sign. There are many systems. A very excellent system of sign relaying that some teams use is to have the wife of a coach, or even someone in the stands, give the signs. The following two chapters discuss all of these systems.

Would you believe me if I told you that in my thirty-three years of coaching high school, junior high school, and American Legion summer baseball, I can only remember three teams out of probably three hundred and fifty who stole my signs at times? All of them were kind enough to come over and tell us so, after the games. Of course, there may have been isolated instances when other teams stole a sign here or there, but if they did, it had no drastic result in the outcome of the game.

In my coaching, I have used two systems.

System A: I start out in a season using only a one-sign system. I flash one sign for what I want. I hold it on until the runner and batter see it. Believe it or not, most teams are so poor at picking up my signs that all I need to show is one sign at a time. Sometimes I find that the other team is not even trying to steal my sign. Here's another fact to remember: *When you use twelve or thirteen signs instead of four or five, it makes it much more difficult for the opposing team to steal any sign you have.*

System B: If I find that I am playing against very alert opponents, or that they are intentionally looking for signs on every pitch, *then we huddle with the team and go to a four-sign or five-sign system.* I usually give four or five signs in a row. On that day, the rule may be to execute the third sign I give.

Usually, if I use the one-sign system, then giving no sign at all means "Hit away." If I use the many-sign system, then we have to have a sign for the hit away.

THE ELEMENT OF SURPRISE IN THE GAME OF BASEBALL

One incident recorded in major league baseball history tells of a player who became so confused by the yelling and all of the activity around him that he finally took the ball and threw it wildly high into the air; it landed in one of the decks of the grandstand. He still has no idea why he threw it or where it landed.

Another case is that of a base runner who was picked off first base, managed to elude the tag and the overthrow, ran to second and slid, beat a close play there, got up and ran to third base, slid there, beat a close tag, kicked the ball into the dugout area, and then became so disoriented that he got up and broke for second base, slid, and got up, satisfied that he had reached home safely. He stepped off the base and was finally tagged out.

Surprise, confusion, yelling, unusual situations—all can combine to break down logic or previous learning patterns in the human mind. *Baseball running plays can actually be created and staged to create this confusion in an opponent.*

In the case of a baseball team, which involves nine persons, rather than one, if one of the nine reacts incorrectly, then the other eight men are helpless to rectify the situation, and they all fail together to stop the play. Therefore, be assured that *the prime target in this war is the catcher.* Most running plays are designed to fool him. The catcher is the only team member who faces the entire field and can see the whole picture. As the catcher goes, so goes the team. He guards the only thing important in the game—*home plate.*

The opposition knows just about what a team is going to try in a given situation; they defense accordingly, practicing these old standard plays on practice days. But how many teams have you seen who practice against the unusual plays and know how to react? Of course, very few teams do, and this is precisely why they look foolish on the diamond when another team pulls an unexpected move. It is because they have been coached for only the expected moves.

So, coaches and players, isn't it about time to mix the old standard plays with some of the unusual ones and make a real game out of it? *Let's entertain our club, their club, and the fans, and let's win while we do it!*

Practicing Signs

Practice—the manager or coach should not be satisfied just to go over the signs with his team and let it go at that. Sufficient practice time should be devoted to executing them until they are well understood. They should be used in all intrasquad games, with the coaches performing their duties on the baselines under typical game conditions.

Major league players have a chance to practice their signs all through spring training. The signs are basically the same as those used the previous year, but there might be a change in the key or in the yes or no part of it. In a meeting, we will go through them quite thoroughly. Then we have a coach stand up and give the men a sign. I will pick out somebody and ask, "What sign is *that*?" We will go through them until we have them down quite well.

BASEBALL OFFENSE, ADDING THE FOURTH DIMENSION TO THE GAME

Offensive baseball usually has three main dimensions. First, the batter hits to get on base. Eventually, he must *hit* the ball to force an error or to get a base hit. Second, the batter bunts the ball. Eventually, every batter may be called upon to *bunt*. Now the batter becomes a runner. The third dimension of the game is *running*. But this is referred to as "individual baserunning."

A player can learn some baserunning from his own observation and basic logic. Some running, of the "individual type," must be taught. The reasoning behind this may not be so obvious to the player.

The "fourth dimension" is where most ball clubs, *on all levels, are lacking*. Most of them will admit it. This skill is called "team baserunning," as opposed to "individual baserunning." A real fan of baseball will tell you that not only are teams not knowledgeable in this dimension, but that this part of the game is that "extra skill" that gives polish to the offensive team. Men working together on bases as a team or as batter and runner coordinating their efforts are what we mean by the "missing dimension" in baseball today.

This book is written and presented to make baseball coaches and players aware of team running, and is dedicated toward the elimination of one of the game's worst statistics, the LOB (men left on base).

Chapter 2

OFFENSIVE PLAYS AND SIGNS

Introduction to Offensive Plays and Signs in Baseball

This chapter will break offensive plays into these categories: stealing on the pitch, stealing before the pitch, stealing after the catcher has received the pitch, the hit-and-run play, the run-and-hit play, the fake steal, the drag bunt, the sacrifice bunt, the safe squeeze play, the suicide squeeze play, the fake-bunt-and-slash play, the fake bunt, the fake steal, the take sign, and the wipeoff sign.

With so many kinds of offensive plays to choose from, not mentioning the hit away, certainly any imaginative baseball coach who knows the weaknesses and strong points of his batters and runners very well should increase run production greatly. The coach and his team must spend more time practicing, and the coach who does this will become infinitely more versatile in proper play selection. The coach will also find himself using more and more of the plays. Remember that these plays were all invented, tried, and found to confuse opponents between 1880 and 1900. Yet over one hundred years later we find baseball coaches who either never heard of them or saw them run, or who do know about them but stubbornly refuse to play baseball with more than a few of the possible plays.

PROPER RUNNING FORM

It's very simple: Effective running requires good technique from every muscle in your body. A swimming coach would never tell his team, "Forget technique. Just get from one end of the pool to the other as fast as you can." Wildly thrashing your arms and legs is not going to help you win a swimming race any more than poor running form will help you stretch a double to a triple, or score from first base on a long single.

It is an unhappy fact that we cannot increase our running speed significantly after the age of sixteen or eighteen. But remember, all we are hoping to do is pick up one extra foot in ninety—and that can, with effort, be done. Furthermore, in the early developmental years of a person's body—from ages eight to sixteen—even more improvement will be seen with the practice and utilization of the following techniques.

- Run with your head up, your eyes on the target, and a "loose" chin. When you grit your teeth and tighten your jaw, that tension transfers down the cords of the neck into your shoulders and restricts necessary shoulder work. Do not bob your head up and down, or from side to side, or in any way divert the head's position from a straight line toward the target.

- Run with your shoulders level and allow your arms to pump freely straight ahead and back from the shoulder. The arms act as pistons that drive the upper body and should form approximately a ninety-degree angle at the elbow. As your arms pump rapidly ahead and back in a push-pull movement, your elbows should remain close to your sides to prevent your arms from flapping. As your arms go forward, your hands should go no higher than the shoulders; if your hands proceed up past the shoulders, part of the momentum generated by their pistonlike pumping is dissipated upward rather than continued forward. As your arms pump backward, your hands should go no farther than the hips before they begin their forward thrust. Both hands should be loosely cupped rather than tightly clenched. This prevents tension and tightness from being transferred up the arms to the shoulders and upper body. The hands should not swing past the midline of your body, and all action should be directed forward, not sideways, so that the upper body doesn't zigzag. The faster and more efficiently your arms pump, the more your legs do the same.

- Your hips should be level throughout the running action. Keep your knees bent and lift them high—up to the level of the hips, then extend each lower leg as far as possible toward the target. By lifting your knees high, you can lengthen your stride and cover more ground. Your legs should not leap and glide but rise, stretch, and thrust forward powerfully.

In baseball, the runners must react to two distinctly different types of situations. First are all of the team running plays. These would be the possible plays on the diamond in which the runner and batter or multiple runners would work as a team within a team. Actually, in most of these plays, *a ball is not hit at all*; the batter usually takes the pitch, although not necessarily. Second are the plays accompanied by a hit ball.

Following is a list of all the situations with runners or combinations of runners on base. There are only eight of these possible in baseball. They are:

- No one on
- Man on first only
- Man on second only
- Man on third only
- Men on first and second only

- Men on second and third only

- Men on first and third only

- Bases loaded

I constructed a miniature diamond and placed it in front of my desk in my study so it would be easy to refer to. Then, for each of the hitting and bunting situations, I looked at the eight possible men-on-base combinations. What I actually did was to *define exactly what each runner on each base would do in each situation for every type of ball hit in baseball*. These have been carefully checked for correctness by other coaches. This task was one of the main objectives of this baseball text, for I don't believe this has ever been done in the history of the game.

Now, the question arises, "How would a baseball coach use this information?" I had the following uses in mind:

- *Excellent for use in practice.* You could put runners on the bases and practice one of these plays per day, thus going through every possible hit-ball situation with your runners in a very short time.

- *Very good for helping a coach to check his runners to see if they ran the bases correctly.*

- *Excellent for study by a young coach.* If he keeps studying these, he will develop a good "mental image" of runners.

This is a first in baseball literature. We have captured, in reference form, the exact moves that all runners must make when balls are hit in baseball.

WHY DO WE NEED A MANUAL OF ALL THE BASERUNNING PLAYS?

Baseball has developed to its present form over a period of more than one hundred years. During the earlier years of baseball, different baserunning plays were tried and either adopted or rejected. Articles and books have been written on each play or on several such plays, but no authoritative text has ever brought them together into one manual.

This is an attempt to collect all the running plays in baseball, sort them out, categorize them by types, and present them in an organized manner suitable for any player, coach, or manager to use easily and quickly.

To my knowledge, this manual contains every known running play ever used in baseball. If it does not, then subsequent printings of this volume will include them until the number is complete. A sign is also given for each play.

It is my intention to give coaches and players, from Little League up to and including the professionals, a reference to study and rely upon in this part of the game. I realize that Little League coaches will be restricted in their use of a manual such as this, for the strict rules relating to leading off a base reduce the number of plays usable by them. But from the Pony League age group and on up, the art of baserunning is wide open, and all the plays in this book will apply.

A manual on baserunning is also needed to give baseball another dimension. So many coaches rely on the hitting and/or bunting game. In other words, their coaching surely gets runners on base, but too many teams leave too many men on base. These plays are offered in an attempt to encourage teams to run more, to force their opponents' errors, and to adopt the philosophy of making things happen.

OFFENSIVE SIGNAL "MESSAGES"

- Take
- Green light (hit away)
- Bunt
- Fake bunt
- Fake-bunt and-slash hit
- First-and-third walkoff
- First-and-third runoff
- First and third, runner on first slides into second
- First and third, runner on first stops short of second and gets in a rundown
- Signal system in which a runner on second relays to the batter the catcher's signals
- To the batter: "What's the count on you?"
- To the batter: "Try to get catcher interference"
- Suicide squeeze
- Delayed squeeze
- Sacrifice squeeze
- Slide
- Keep going on to score
- Stop at this base, although you may round it
- Stop at this base and do not round it
- Ball 4 steal (with runner on third only) if batter gets a walk
- Feed the kitty (if a player misses a signal or otherwise messes up) (we have a system of fines for such occurrences)
- The batter's or runner's signal to the coach if his signal must be repeated
- Extend your lead
- Shorten your lead

- Steal

- Delayed steal

- Switch positions in the batter's box

- To the batter: "Bend down for dirt while the pitcher is in his windup" (trying to get a balk call)

- Indicator for signal

- Indicator "wipeoff"

- Acknowledgment signal by batter on squeeze play

- Verbal signal to the batter whenever I can pick up the catcher's signals from my position at third base

CATEGORIZING BASEBALL'S RUNNING PLAYS

There are individual and team-type running plays in the game of baseball. There may be some variations of these, or coaches may have tricks or offshoots of them, but, basically, *all of them are contained in this text.*

In attempting to break down all possible plays, I chose three categories:

Type 1: Plays broken down by the various positions of base runners on those plays. The various positions are: no one on, man on first, man on second, man on third, men on first and second, men on second and third, men on first and third, and bases loaded.

Type 2: Plays broken down by timing. In other words, does the play operate before the pitcher's delivery, during the pitcher's delivery, or after the pitcher's delivery?

Type 3: Plays broken down by types of offensive men involved. In other words, is the batter alone in the play, is the runner alone in the play, is the runner working with another runner, or is the batter working with the runner?

Tables with a complete listing of these plays are on pages 22-24.

BASE RUNNER RESPONSIBILITIES

In the Dugout

Review the team signal system, as well as the meaning of the various arm gestures of the base coaches for rounding a base, sliding, taking a turn, and so forth.

Watch for special pickoff plays, the frequency of pickoff attempts, the usual depth of the infielders, and the types of pickoff moves employed by the pitcher. It is especially important to determine tipoffs on the pitcher's move to first before arriving at first later in the game. The team that has the first base dugout has an advantage in determining such tip-offs due to the angle created between the pitcher and dugout. Those watching for the pitcher's pickoff characteristics should position themselves near the first base end of the dugout.

Baserunning Plays Broken Down by the Positions of Runners on Various Bases

Special Situation	Name of Play	Man on 1st	Man on 2nd	Man on 3rd	Men on 1st and 2nd	Men on 2nd and 3rd	Men on 1st and 3rd	Bases Loaded	Nobody on Base
Before pitcher delivers	Double steal (0 or 2 outs)						X		
	Double steal (2 outs)						X		
	Double steal, Batter walks (any number of outs)						X		
While pitcher is delivering	Single steal	X							
	Double steal				X				
	Triple steal							X	
	Single steal			X					
	Double steal (0 or l out)						X		
	Double steal (2 outs)						X		
After the pitcher has delivered (catcher has the ball)	Double steal (0 or l out)						X		
	Double steal (2 outs)						X		
	Delayed steal-man on 2nd		X						
	Delayed steal-men on 1st and 2nd				X				
	Delayed steal-men on 2nd and 3rd					X			
	Delayed steal-based loaded							X	
	Delayed steal-man on 3rd			X					
None	The take sign	X	X	X	X	X	X	X	X
None	Hit-and-run play	X	X		X	X	X		
None	Intentional walk	X	X	X	X	X	X		X
None	The fake steal	X	X	X	X	X	X	X	
Batter has intention of bunting	Drag bunt for base hit	X	X	X	X	X	X	X	X
	Sacrifice bunt to move runner 1 base	X	X		X				
	Sacrifice bunt to move runner 2 bases	X			X				
	Safe squeeze bunt			X		X	X		
	Suicide squeeze to score 1 run			X		X	X	X	
	Suicide squeeze to score 2 runs					X	X	X	
None	Fake bunt, steal 2nd base	X							
	Fake bunt, steal 3rd base		X						
	Fake bunt and slash				X				
	Fake bunt and slash	X		X					

Baserunning Plays Broken Down by Timing

Special Situation	Name of Play	Before Pitcher Delivers	During Pitcher's Delivery	After Pitcher Delivers (Catcher has the Ball)
None	Double steal, men on 1st and 2nd	X		
	Double steal, men on 1st and 3rd	X		
	Double steal, man on 3rd, batter walks	X		
None	Single steal, man on 1st		X	
	Double steal, men on 1st and 2nd		X	
	Triple steal, bases loaded		X	
	Single steal, man on 3rd		X	
	Double steal, men on 1st and 3rd		X	
None	Double steal, men on 1st and 3rd			X
	Delayed steal, man on 2nd			X
	Delayed steal, man on 1st and 2nd			X
	Delayed steal, men on 2nd and 3rd			X
	Delayed steal, bases loaded			X
	Delayed steal, man on 3rd			X
None	The take sign	X		
None	Hit-and-run play		X	
None	Intentional walk	X	X	X
None	The fake steal		X	
Batter has intention of bunting	Drag bunt for base hit		X	
	Sacrifice bunt to move runner 1 base		X	
	Sacrifice bunt to move runner 2 bases		X	
	Safe squeeze bunt		X	
	Suicide squeeze to score 1 run		X	
	Suicide squeeze to score 2 runs		X	
Batter has no intention of bunting	Fake bunt, steal 2nd		X	
	Fake bunt, steal 3rd		X	
	Fake bunt and slash, man on 3rd		X	
	Fake bunt and slash, man on 1st		X	

Baserunning Plays Broken Down by Types of Offensive Men Involved

Special Situation	Name of Play	Runners are Alone	Batter is Alone	Runner and Batter Cooperating
Before pitcher delivers	Double steal, men on 1st and 2nd	X		
	Double steal, men on 1st and 3rd	X		
	Double steal, man on 3rd, batter walks			X
While pitcher is delivering	Single steal, man on 1st	X		
	Double steal, men on 1st and 2nd	X		
	Triple steal, bases loaded	X		
	Single steal, man on 3rd	X		
	Double steal, men on 1st and 2rd	X		
	Double steal, men on 1st and 3rd	X		
After the pitcher has delivered (catcher has the ball)	Double steal, men on 1st and 2nd	X		
	Double steal, men on 1st and 3rd	X		
	Delayed steal, man on 2nd	X		
	Delayed steal, men on 1st and 2nd	X		
	Delayed steal, men on 2nd and 3rd	X		
	Delayed steal, bases loaded	X		
	Delayed steal, man on 3rd	X		
None	The take sign		X	X
None	Hit-and-run play			X
None	Intentional walk		X	
None	The fake steal	X		
Batter has intention of bunting	Drag bunt for base hit		X	
	Sacrifice bunt to move runner 1 base			X
	Sacrifice bunt to move runner 2 bases			X
	Safe squeeze bunt			X
	Suicide squeeze to score 1 run			X
	Suicide squeeze to score 2 runs			
Batter has no intention of bunting	Fake bunt, steal 2nd		X	
	Fake bunt, steal 3rd		X	
	Fake bunt and slash, man on 3rd		X	
	Fake bunt and slash, man on 1st		X	

In the On-deck Circle

After a ball has been hit that will bring one or more runners across the plate, the next hitter should position himself behind home plate, out of the way of the catcher and umpire. Yet he must remain in line with third base, where advancing runners on the line can see him clearly. He should also move any loose equipment out of the way. Thus, any runners trying to score can be given the arm signal to slide or come in standing. Once the runner passes the third base coach, that runner must pick up the on-deck hitter for instructions. Otherwise, anything else he might hear from the coach could be intended for a following runner.

In the Batter's Box

The batter must be ready to advise quickly any runner on third following a pitch that gets away from the catcher.

Getting Out of the Batter's Box

Whether the batter be left-handed or right-handed, his first step out of the box should be made with his rear foot. This would be the right foot for the right-handed batter and the left foot for the left-handed batter. When this is not happening, it is usually the result of poor weight distribution, hitting off the heels, or swinging too hard.

On a questionable ball hit down the third base line, the batter should begin running immediately. He doesn't wait for an umpire's call. If it is ruled a fair ball, the umpire wouldn't make a verbal call anyway. He only calls out when the ball is foul.

On a bunt, the bat must not be dropped in fair territory, where the ball might roll up against it. This would result in an offensive interference call. The bat must be dropped behind the plate.

When hit by a pitch or when receiving a walk, the batter should sprint to first. It is not just a matter of hustle; it provides a greater amount of time to pick up the signals from the third base coach and to look over the infield defense.

On a third-strike pitch that is in the dirt or that is dropped by the catcher, the batter should take off for first. He might also consider doing so even with first base occupied and less than two out. This is because, occasionally, the catcher will unnecessarily throw to first anyway. In the process, he may throw the ball away, thus allowing for the advancement of another runner or two.

Maximizing Speed Down the Line

Coming out of the batter's box, a low start with rather pronounced body lean is best. This body lean diminishes quickly as the body arrives at its maximum speed in close to an upright position. The lean continues to exist at an angle of about twenty-five to thirty degrees from the vertical position.

After Running Through the Bag

The stop shouldn't come too quickly, since a stumble or fall could easily result. The runner shouldn't allow himself to run too far down the line either. In case of an overthrow, the increased distance to second might make a try to second impossible. *A slight glance to the right after having passed the bag informs the runner of an errant throw and chance for advancement a split second sooner than hearing it from the first base coach.*

In returning to the bag after having overrun it, the turn back to the infield can be made in either direction. He knows whether he will be running through the bag or taking a turn, and there certainly is a correct way of doing each. Just rounding a base takes a lot of thought, study, and practice if it's to be done in the most efficient manner.

Finally, in continuing to follow a philosophy of aggressive and daring baserunning, the runner who knows he has first must be thinking of the possibility of going to second even before he rounds the bag. He must be aware of the conditions that would warrant such a try just as well as those that would prohibit a try for the extra base.

SLIDES: TYPES, EXECUTION, AND STRATEGY

The head-first slide is a very aggressive type of slide that seems more often than not to gain the close call of the umpire. It is not to be used when a force play is involved or when the base is being blocked.

The knees and hands should hit the ground simultaneously, with the chest very close behind. This is important, since to do it otherwise will result in a painful belly flop fall.

Because the runner's upper body is already leaning forward, no reversal of the body angle becomes necessary to go into the slide. For this reason, many feel that the head-first slide gets the runner to the base quicker than does any variation of a feet-first slide.

So as to provide the smallest possible tag area, the slide should be executed to the outside of the bag, with the left hand grabbing out for just a corner of the base. The exception to this rule, however, would be when the runner sees the baseman moving off the bag to take a wide throw or jumping high to get a very high throw.

In this instance, the runner decides (well ahead of the bag) to slide away from the diamond. The baseman cannot take a high or wide throw and reach down and tag the sliding runner at the same time.

With any slide on a tag play, make as little contact as possible with the bag so as to present a small target, as well as less opportunity for an injury.

How much distance must be allowed for the slide will depend on the speed of the runner, his height, field conditions, and the type of slide to be used. Usually, for a feet-first slide, one to one and one half body lengths (or five to ten feet) is about right.

With any feet-first type of slide, the back of the shoulders should be parallel to the ground, with the arms and hands back.

HOW TO STEAL FIRST BASE

For the first few years of your playing baseball, you hear the familiar expression "You can't steal first base." Actually, there are several ways to "steal" first base.

I recall a young boyhood friend at Golden Hill Playground in San Diego during the summers of 1938 to 1941. Does the name Solly Hemus ring a bell? Solly and I would gather with other kids and play "over the line" for hours at a time. But on Saturday mornings we played in the city's American Legion "B" league's games. Solly was a leadoff man. He would pull on his shirt at the belt so it puffed out. Then he would crowd the plate so far that the shirt would get hit by an inside pitch. Solly would appeal that the ball had hit him and he would look somewhat injured. I don't know how many times I saw the umpires award him first base. *Solly had "stolen" first base.* Of course, with today's tight-fitting uniforms, this might not be so easy to do. Oh, incidentally, Solly went on to become second baseman for the St. Louis Cardinals (and their manager for several years).

Another technique for stealing first base is to take your position at home plate before the pitcher delivers, let us say with men on base, come around early, and fake a bunt very early. This will cause the catcher to move his body and glove up closer to the plate. Then, bring the bat back to batting position, sliding your hands back into their hitting position. Your bat will invariably touch the catcher's mitt. *Appeal to the umpire for catcher interference.* He may award it to you. This has happened many times in baseball. So you see, in a sense, this too is "stealing" first base.

Whenever a batter draws a walk, a pitcher makes him a 1.000 hitter. The batter really hasn't had to prove himself. The greatest hitter in the history of baseball never hit over .370 lifetime. So, a walk gives a hitter almost three times the advantage of the greatest hitter. When a batter carefully watches a pitcher's offerings and lets the bad ones go by, even the very close ones, and draws a walk, he has done his team a great service. In a sense, such a batter has also "stolen" first.

Then there is the switch-hitter or switch-bunter. He places himself on the right side of the plate and bats left-handed. This gives him a step-and-a-half head start down the first base line, which translates into quite a few tenths of a second. If he hits a ground ball into the hole, if he dumps a quick drag bunt in front of the third baseman or down the first base line, that runner is going to beat it out if he has any speed at all. Here is a clear-cut example of a player able to "steal" first base.

HOW TO STEAL SECOND, THIRD, OR HOME

So, you have reached one of the bases safely, eh? You no doubt walked to first, or perhaps you got a two-base hit and reached second, or maybe you were on first base and were moved to third base on a well-executed hit-and-run play. Anyhow, you are standing on a base.

But now, ball player, you are on your own! *You are going to steal a base all by yourself.* No help from anyone in the ball park—except yourself. Are you up to it? How do you perform this feat? How do you, all alone, outwit and outplay the entire defensive team and actually "steal" right out of their pockets? You will be safe or out by just a split second.

In the earlier days of baseball, this was not something that was foremost in the minds of ball players. Their emphasis was on hitting the ball and not taking chances. As the game rolled toward the year 1900, more and more players were coming to realize that stealing a base was not that difficult. Really! They started studying every aspect of the pitcher, the catcher, the infielders, and better and better base stealing emerged.

The name Ty Cobb, of course, comes to the fore in this category. Ty Cobb not only studied the requirements of stealing first, second, third, and home, but he also added one more vital ingredient. That was real intimidation. People never got excited about base stealing until he did. He challenged them, and so have the other great ones down the line. Pepper Martin, Jackie Robinson, Maury Wills, Rod Carew, Lou Brock, Tim Raines, and Rickey Henderson, to mention just a few, really put the pressure on the defense, and the crowds love it!

In this section of the text, we shall attempt to break down the factors that can help a runner steal a base. Basically, there are six main factors in base stealing.

- You, the runner/stealer, and psychological factors
- The condition of the playing field
- The pitcher's characteristics
- The catcher's characteristics
- Which of the three bases you are attempting to steal
- The count, number of outs, and score of the game

We shall now break each of these into its components.

You, the Runner/Stealer

Experiments have been made to see if a base stealer's speed can be increased with practice over a period of time. Sad to relate, speed increases very little. Oh, you can improve your initial step, your slide, and other factors of your run, but a person is born with a certain "speed afoot." You must know how relatively fast you are. *Don't overestimate or underestimate your speed.* The other factor here is psychological, which will include your alert thinking and awareness, your intimidation of and challenge to the defense, and your daring. These factors can all be improved with experience. Your willingness to slide, to contact a defensive man, your lack of fear, increased aggressiveness—all of these can sure help make up for lack of speed.

The Condition of the Playing Field

Obviously, a field not in good condition, or wet or cold weather conditions, can all work against a base runner's stealing time. The runner would be at the disadvantage. A field that has muddy spots, holes, or pits near a base will not be ideal for stealing a base. A cold day, compared to a very warm one, could also slow down a runner A base runner must weigh all of these factors when he decides to attempt a steal. Of course, weather conditions could work against the defense as well. Certain field conditions could prevent the pitcher or catcher from throwing down to a base against a steal.

The Pitcher's Characteristics

These include:

- Can he throw a fastball (a vital factor)?
- Is he a curveball or knuckleball pitcher?
- Does he have a good move to your base?
- Does he have a high or slow leg kick?
- Does he look over to your base very often?
- Does he throw over to your base very often?
- Does he pitch quickly from the stretch position?
- Does he throw many pitchouts?
- Does he give his pickoff throw away with head and shoulder?
- Does he give his pickoff throw away with knee and leg?

The Catcher's Characteristics

These include:

- How good is his arm?
- How quickly does he get the throw away?
- How accurate is his throw?
- Does he try the pickoff at your base?
- What pitch does he call for with two strikes?
- Does he dig out balls in the dirt well?
- Does he stay in front of wide pitches?
- Does he drop to the ground immediately to block low bounces in the dirt?
- Does he call for many pitchouts?

Which of the Three Bases You Are Attempting to Steal

How you steal and when you steal also depend on which base you are stealing. The amount of lead allowed to you is different at each bag. The score, the number of outs, and the count on the batter all go into determining whether you can steal a particular base at that time.

Some base runners feel that stealing third base is easier than stealing second base, for several reasons. Of course, the steal of home is one of athletics' most difficult feats. No one steals home who is not extremely fast and quick on the base paths. Also, it is a rare play. Very rare!

The Count, Number of Outs, and Score of the Game

"Getting into the game" means knowing the number of outs, the count on the batter, and the score of the game—a smart base runner is "into the game" at all times. He knows the characteristics of pitcher and catcher as well. Experience tells him when and when not to steal. He may be lucky enough to outguess the defensive team on a certain pitch. The bases are no place for a "baseball dreamer," a man who is asleep. Knowing when to stretch a hit into the extra base is necessary, so that a rally is not cut short by poor baserunning. These things are all gained from experience.

WHAT EVERY BASE RUNNER SHOULD KNOW

There are some tenets of good baserunning that can't be singled out for use between two particular bases only. Instead, they must be applied at every base. There are guidelines, for instance, that every runner is encouraged to follow while perched on a base and still others that must be remembered while in a long lead. A few rules also apply to all runners as they begin their advance to the next base as a ball is hit. All of them, in one way or another, are more examples of those important characteristics of good baserunning at work: aggressiveness, daring, alertness, signal knowledge, and deep involvement in the game.

Some strategic guidelines will be found here. They should be used to guide the actions of multiple runners, regardless of the bases they occupy.

Standing on a Base

Before every pitch, the runner looks to the coach for a sign. If doubt exists, the runner calls for time rather than trying to guess. However, this means that an offensive conference is being used unnecessarily. Ideally, a signal should exist for just this situation. Such a prearranged signal from the runner to the coach asks the coach to give or repeat a signal.

Every runner's mind should be like a computer stored with vital information. He should know the score, inning, number of outs, other runners on base, and the positioning of the infielders and outfielders, along with the strength of their arms. He should also be fully aware of the meaning and execution of the various signals that may be flashed his way.

Gambling on the bases is aggressive baserunning when your team is ahead. However, discretion is the main characteristic of a good base runner when his team is trailing, especially late in the game.

A runner never begins his leadoff if the pitcher's foot isn't on the rubber, much less if he is off the mound. Also, he locates the ball. Who has it?

In the Primary or Secondary Leadoff

With every pitch, anticipate a passed ball or wild pitch. Be ready to jump upon such a gift opportunity. Anticipation is the key word.

In the absence of a batted ball, wild pitch, or passed ball, the runner must hustle back quickly to the bag. He shouldn't get caught sleeping by underestimating the strength of the catcher's arm or his willingness to throw to the bag in an attempted pickoff.

Be watchful for a bad throw back to the pitcher from the catcher. Notice which infielder, if any, guards against such an overthrow after every pitch.

The runner must freeze in his tracks whenever a line drive is seen coming off a bat with less than two out, unless it can be immediately determined whether the ball will be caught. Double plays resulting from this situation should be the exception, not the rule.

Whenever the pitcher carelessly goes into a full windup, the runner should always be ready to advance to the next base (other than home).

A runner must go on a hit-and-run play, but following a normal steal sign he should not go through with the steal if he falters on his first step or is fooled by a pitcher's motion. There is no sense in chalking up an easy out for the opposition just so you can say that the signal given was seen and executed.

Before Stepping off the Bag

Be aware of the game situation, including the score, inning, number of outs, and any other men on base. If necessary, get help from the first base coach. Know the location of the ball, always being on the lookout for a hidden-ball trick. Seeing the pitcher off the mound area (as is required by the rules) might be an indication that someone else has the ball.

Don't get into a conversation with the first baseman or even your own first base coach, so as to remain entirely focused on the game and your purpose on base.

To prevent scraping a hand or jamming a finger on a slide, some runners like to hold grass or dirt in their hands. When sliding, they will, therefore, keep their fists closed. However, the runner must be consistent with this habit, being careful not to do it only when a steal or hit-and-run signal is on.

Look for a signal after every pitch, standing with the left foot on the bag. Continue to watch the third base coach until he has concluded giving all gestures, both meaningful and otherwise. This makes it more difficult for the opposition to steal any signals.

Following a long foul ball, the runner is wise to pick up the next signal while returning to the bag. This gives the runner more time to assume his next leadoff after retouching the bag.

AGGRESSIVE BASERUNNING—THE MENTAL PERSPECTIVE

In studying the various techniques and strategies of baserunning, players must become enthusiastic about their purpose. There is so much to gain, but so much to learn, too. They must become convinced that what they are being taught will affect the play of the opposition. Even more important is the realization that the effect will be felt across all nine positions on the field. The defense's great awareness of the team's baserunning intentions will create in them considerable pressure. That kind of pressure leads to both mental and physical mistakes. The base runners must really believe this.

If they do, their beliefs will lead to a strong team attitude toward aggressive and daring running.

Important, too is the realization that such exciting baserunning is not reserved for just the one or two fastest players of the club. Even average-speed players can learn and contribute greatly when they are willing to dedicate their efforts to a thorough study of baserunning.

Besides, speed by itself isn't enough. Knowledge of the team's signal system and strategies, along with the incorporation of such abstract concepts as alertness, daring, and involvement, are all very important. All too often, these components don't get the credit they deserve as vital characteristics of good base runners. But once their importance is realized by each player, a unifying team attitude will develop. From that point on, the team's baserunning alone will take it a long, long way.

THE INGREDIENTS OF SUCCESSFUL BASERUNNING

Individual Players' Traits

- Average to better-than-average speed
- Aggressiveness without foolhardiness
- Confidence with no fear of failure
- Alertness and quick reflexes
- A deep involvement in the game
- Sliding ability
- A working knowledge of the fundamentals of good baserunning techniques
- A thorough familiarity with the team's signal system and arm gestures of the coaches

Team Attitudes

- We will control the game with aggressive but intelligent baserunning.
- We will be daring whenever the situation calls for such action.
- "We will accept our mistakes positively and turn them into constructive learning experiences."
- "We will be so aggressive that our runners won't have to be coaxed or encouraged by our coaches to run. Rather, we would like our coaches to hold up only those occasional runners who may tend to become overly aggressive to the point of foolhardiness."

- "We don't get credited with a run when one of our players becomes a base runner, only after he successfully circles those bases. Therefore, we won't sit back until our base runners have successfully completed their tasks."

Baserunning's Two Knockout Punches

- A strong feeling of awareness of our presence on the bases

- Pressure and more pressure brought on by that awareness

The Mental Aspects

The mental prerequisites to good baserunning are desire and confidence. The runner should realize that the lower the level of play, the poorer will be the skills of the pitcher in holding him on base and the poorer will be the quickness, strength, and accuracy of the catcher's arm. Helping, too, will be the runner's confidence in his own speed. Often, it will be close to or even equal to that of his professional counterpart. Acquiring confidence is the most challenging part of the battle. The player must constantly assure himself of his knowledge of the pitcher and his moves, his own reflexes and speed, his ability to get a good lead, and his mastery of the techniques of sliding.

The runner must put any fear of failure completely out of his mind. If he ever does get thrown out, he won't get "down." In fact, he won't even be afraid of being thrown out or picked off, although he will naturally try always to avoid these mishaps. When these things happen, he will just work all the harder on his next attempt. He will continue to tell himself that his ability to run the bases far surpasses the abilities of the pitcher and catcher to keep him planted.

THE STEALS

If a team can use the steal successfully, it can eliminate the sacrifice. A steal is not only a great asset to the offensive club, it also rattles the pitcher and his fielders.

The Single Steal

The single steal is usually tried when a team is ahead, tied, or no more than one run behind. *A team usually does not attempt a steal when it is more than two runs behind.*

The Double Steal

There are various types of double steals. With runners on first and third, some are: the straight steal from first base; the runner on first breaks before the pitch to cause a balk or get caught in a rundown and the delayed steal. If successful, the last play can result in one run scored and a runner on second base.

The Triple Steal

The triple steal must be baseball's premier "risk play." It is electrifying to the team executing it, the defense, and the crowd. *It is an unusual gamble.*

The advantages of the triple steal are:

- It has a devastating psychological effect in favor of the team that executes it successfully.

- One run scores (free) without using a batter.

- Three bases are credited as stolen.

- The force plays and the double play have been removed at every base. First base is open.

- Whether successful or not, all runners are now in scoring position for the next batter.

The disadvantages are:

- If unsuccessful, the psychological disadvantage is not that devastating. You still have two more runners in scoring position.

- You have lost an out.

Compare the advantages to the disadvantages. Does the reader still believe the triple steal is such a risky maneuver? How about it, Coach?

PLAY 1:　DOUBLE STEAL WITH MEN ON FIRST AND THIRD, NONE OR ONE OUT

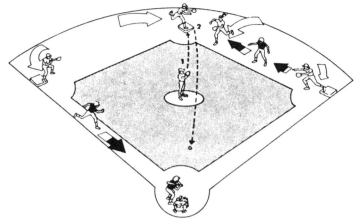

This play is designed to steal home and second base without giving up any outs. The psychological advantage is tremendous because the defense expects a steal play on or after the pitch—not before. Based totally on the element of surprise, the success rate is 80 percent or more.

Play Progression and Analysis

- Coach yells "OK," then shouts last name of first base runner, followed by the number of outs. Third base runner and batter hear this sign.

- First base runner waits until the pitcher is in the stretch. Just before the delivery, runner breaks hard toward second base. Everyone sitting on the bench yells "Balk!"

- With none or one out, the runner keeps going hard and slides into second base; if ball is thrown to first, the runner gets into a trap.

- The instant the pitcher throws to the area around second base, the third base runner breaks for the plate, sliding hard.

- As the throw goes home, the first base runner then steals second.

Single Sign or Holding Sign

Verbal sign: "OK, [last name of the first base runner], [and] none [or one] away." Third base runner ready to break for home on the same sign.

PLAY 2:   DOUBLE STEAL WITH MEN ON FIRST AND THIRD, TWO OUTS

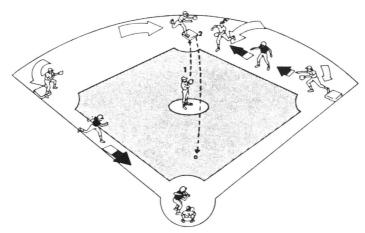

This play is designed to steal home and second base without giving up any outs, but it may only score a run before the third out, ending the inning. As in Play 1, the psychological advantage is tremendous. The defense will not expect this attempt with two outs, nor will it expect this play before the pitch. The success rate for this play is at least 80 percent because it is based completely on the element of surprise.

Play Progression and Analysis

• Coach yells "OK," then the last name of the first base runner, followed by "two away."

• Third base runner and batter hear the same sign.

Single Sign or Holding Sign

• First base runner waits until pitcher is coming down in the stretch. Just before the delivery, first base runner breaks hard for second base, then suddenly stops halfway.

• Runner forces a rundown between first and second base. The third base runner breaks for the plate at just the correct instant—the moment second baseman throws to first baseman.

• With two outs, be certain that the trapped runner does not allow himself to be tagged out until the third base runner crosses the plate. Otherwise, the run does not count, and the inning is over.

Verbal sign: "OK, [last name of the first base runner], [and] two away." Third base runner ready to break for home on the same sign.

PLAY 3:   DOUBLE STEAL WITH RUNNER ON THIRD AFTER THE BATTER HAS WALKED TO FIRST

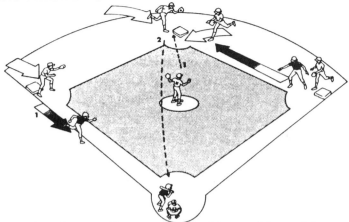

This unusual play is designed to steal home and second base without giving up any outs. The psychological advantage of the play is great; the defense is totally surprised because the play begins with the hitter walking to first base rather than being there earlier. This is one of the best running plays in baseball, with a success rate of 80 percent or better.

Play Progression and Analysis

- With a two- or three-ball count, call for a time-out and tell the batter, "If walked, jog to first base, stop on the bag, and wait for the pitcher to rub the ball or take his eyes off you. Be sure to act casual. Then break hard for second base."

- If there are no outs, instruct the player to slide into second base. If there are two outs, instruct the player to stop halfway between second base and first base and get into a rundown.

- The runner on third base leads off slightly as the batter jogs to first base. Then, the third base runner breaks for home plate when the pitcher actually throws to the shortstop or second baseman to tag the runner coming from first.

Single Sign or Holding Sign

Verbal signs given by coach during a conference with the batter (see instructions).

With a 2-ball or a 3-ball count on the batter, the coach calls him away from the plate and tells him: "If you walk, trot down to first base casually, step on the base, tug at your belt one or two times, don't be in a hurry, count a slow '1001.' Then break fast for second base. Go all the way, unless two are out. If two are out, stop halfway to second base for a rundown, and don't get tagged unless the run scores first."

PLAY 4:   SINGLE STEAL ON THE PITCHER

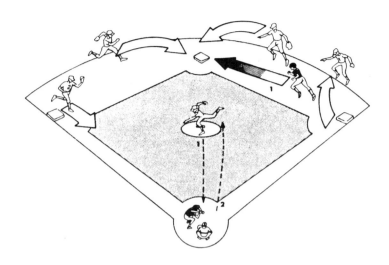

The purpose of this play is to steal second base from no help from the batter. There is no element of surprise because this play is anticipated by all defenses. If successful, the play creates some psychological advantage, for the runner moves into scoring position. A team, if stealing with its fastest men only, usually expects 50 percent success from this play.

Play Progression and Analysis

- Runner receives the steal-on-pitcher sign.

- Runner takes maximum lead, on each pitch, at all times.

- Runner must be sure pitcher has started to commit himself to the plate.

- Runner needs quick first step to get maximum acceleration. Slide hard.

- Runner should get up fast and be ready to advance on an overthrown ball.

Single Sign or Holding Sign

Coach touches any part of his head, from top of cap down to his neck, glasses, etc., with one hand.

Multiple Sign System (Series of 5 Signs)

Indicator sign

Indicator sign is coach holding up a fist and also touching any part of his head area.

Sign to be used is the first one flashed after the indicator. This is also called the "hot sign."

Hot sign

PLAY 5:   DOUBLE STEAL ON THE PITCHER

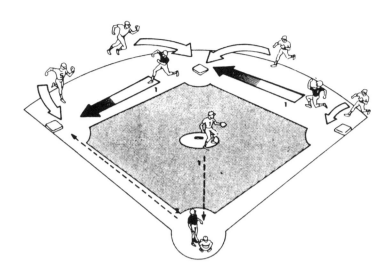

The purpose of this play is to advance men from first and second to second and third while the pitcher delivers. The runners get no help from the batter. This tactic advances both runners into scoring position and removes possible double plays at second and first base. The success rate of this double steal is 50 percent with a fast lead runner.

Play Progression and Analysis

- Both runners get the steal sign from the coach.

- First base and second base runners take maximum leads.

- Both runners must be sure pitcher has committed delivery to the plate.

Single Sign or Holding Sign

Coach touches any part of his head, from top of cap down to his neck, glasses, etc., with one hand.

Multiple Sign System (Series of 5 Signs)

Indicator sign   *Hot sign*

Indicator sign is coach kicks dirt with one foot.

Sign to be used is the first one flashed after the indicator, also called the "hot sign."

PLAY 6:   TRIPLE STEAL ON THE PITCHER

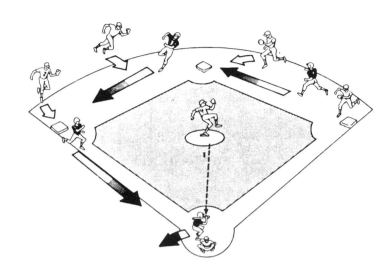

The purpose of this play is to advance three men to the next bases, stealing home while the pitcher delivers. This is one of baseball's most difficult and daring running plays. Psychologically, to be the victim of a triple steal is devastating to a team's morale. The success rate is, obviously, very low (10 percent). The lead runner must be incredibly swift, and all other necessary factors must be perfect, working together for the running team.

Play Progression and Analysis

- Man on third base is the key here. This runner must be extremely fast and get maximum jump on the pitcher.

- Pitcher must wind up and not take usual stretch.

- If pitcher takes the stretch, all runners know the play is off. This play will fail if pitcher is in the stretch.

- Runners on first and second bases take a big lead. They do not slide at next bases, but take big, wide turns, ready to steal another base if the ball gets away from the catcher.

- All runners make sure pitcher winds up before they go.

- All three runners must beware of pickoff plays. This is when the opponent will try them.

- Third base runner should slide hard and low, away from pitcher's throw and tag by catcher.

Single Sign or Holding Sign

Coach touches any part of his head, from top of cap down to his neck, glasses, etc., with one hand.

Multiple Sign System (Series of 5 Signs)

Indicator sign   *Hot sign*

Indicator sign is coach holding up a fist and also touching any part of his head area.

Sign to be used is the first one flashed after the indicator.

PLAY 7:   SINGLE STEAL OF HOME ON PITCHER

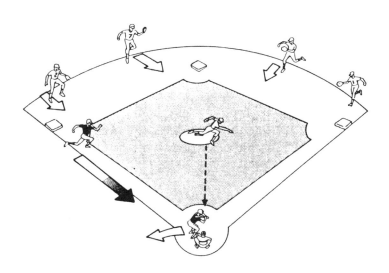

The purpose of this play is to steal home and score a run while the pitcher is in the windup—thus performing one of baseball's most difficult and daring running plays. Psychologically, to be the victim of a steal-home play is devastating to a team's morale. The success rate is obviously low (10 percent). The runner must be incredibly swift, and all other factors must be perfectly together for the running team.

Play Progression and Analysis

- Man is on third base with no other runners.

- Runner must be extremely fast and get a maximum jump on the pitcher.

- Pitcher must wind up, not take his stretch.

- If pitcher takes his stretch, runner knows the play is off. This play will fail if the pitcher is in his stretch.

- Third base runner makes sure pitcher has started the motion and is committed to the plate.

- Runner must beware of a pickoff play.

- Runner should slide hard and low in a hook slide away from the pitcher's throw and tag by the catcher.

Single Sign or Holding Sign

Coach touches any part of his head, from the top of cap down to his neck, glasses, etc. with one hand.

Multiple Sign System (Series of 5 Signs)

Indicator sign

Indicator sign is the coach putting two hands on his belt.

Sign to be used is the first one flashed after the indicator.

Hot sign

PLAY 8:   DOUBLE STEAL ON THE PITCHER WITH MEN ON FIRST AND THIRD, NONE OR ONE OUT

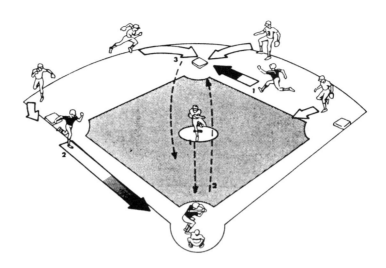

The purpose of this play is to steal home and second base and have no one put out. The psychological advantage of this play is not too great, because this is one play that all teams spend a great deal of time practicing. Even though it is difficult to defense, the defense is ready for it, so the element of surprise is lacking. Surprisingly, though, if used sparingly this play should still give the running team a 70 percent rate of success.

Play Progression and Analysis

- Coach gives steal sign to first base runner. Coach indicates to third base runner that a double steal play is on.

- First base runner steals on the pitch. Third base runner edges off as pitcher delivers. Runner must have a good lead.

- Catcher now has the ball. Catcher fires to second base to infielder covering the base.

- The instant the third base runner sees the ball go past the pitcher on the mound, runner breaks for the plate and slides.

- As the runner going to second base sees the throw going back to the plate, runner steals second base, sliding.

- Only your fastest runners will be able to make it from third base to home on this play against good catcher and infield arms.

Single Sign or Holding Sign

Coach touches any part of his head, from the top of cap down to his neck, glasses, etc., with one hand (with the other hand he motions third base runner off base).

Multiple Sign System (Series of 5 Signs)

Indicator sign   *Hot sign*

Indicator sign is the coach folding his arms in front of his chest.

Sign to be used is the first one flashed after the indicator.

SPECIAL STEALS OF THIRD

Delayed Steal from Second Base on Catcher

The runner takes a very long lead as the pitch is thrown. The catcher, knowing that he has got the runner picked off, throws down to second hurriedly. At this point, the runner breaks for third. He stands a good chance of making it, since the throw is long and no prearranged cut by the pitcher will be coming. A left-handed batter adds further to the chances of success for this play. Of course, the runner must have quick reflexes. Sometimes, too, the runner may find himself caught off the bag accidentally as a result of overaggressiveness. By first faking hard back toward second, he can diminish the chances of the catcher's running out toward him before throwing. It is a good idea to use this ploy even when the special play is on.

Delayed Steal from Second Base on Pitcher Pickoff

Another special steal of third involves the runner's intentionally getting picked off by a right-handed pitcher's move. It is very risky, though, and should be attempted only by very fast runners and only when playing with a comfortable lead. Of course, the runner's lead must be a long one, and his initial move to third comes the instant the pitcher begins his pickoff move. The runner is banking on the hope that the pitcher will go through with his throw to second even though the runner is running toward third at the time. The smart pitcher will usually not go through with the throw, but will run at the runner.

One type of delayed double steal might be used against a rookie pitcher, especially a left-hander. As he comes down and gets set, the man on first base should start to run. I do not want him simply to jog, because if he starts jogging, it will look too much like a trap. I want him to break as though he were actually going to steal.

Although the pitcher knows there is a man on third base, if he is not concentrating at that particular moment, his first impulse is to back off, *and he will likely throw to second base.* The runner on third base knows this play is on, too, *so he is creeping off;* then, *as soon as the pitcher backs off, he starts to go.* Many times, if the pitcher makes only a motion toward second, the runner on third has a good chance to score before the pitcher can recover and throw to home.

The delayed steal should work particularly well at the college and high school levels. (In fact, the delayed double steal is at times tried in the major leagues, and it has proven to be a daring, tricky play that works. However, a manager has to know how to pick his spots and situations.) I do not think it should be used against a veteran pitcher, though, because he will step off the rubber and look to third before he commits himself to second base.

The natural impulse of many pitchers is to follow the runner. "There goes that runner!" Because he wants to do something about it, he will step off the slab and start his motion to second or throw to get the runner in a rundown. *Before the defense knows it, it is too late to stop the runner going home. If the pitcher does not step off, he will very likely balk.*

PLAY 9: DOUBLE STEAL ON THE PITCHER WITH MEN ON FIRST AND THIRD, TWO OUTS

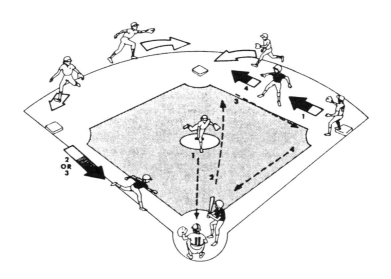

The purpose of this play is to score a run from a steal home and to steal second with no one put out. If the third out is made on the second base play, the runner must cross home plate first. The psychological advantage of this play is not too great because this is another play that all defenses spend a great deal of time practicing. Even though it is difficult to defense, the defense is set for it, so the element of surprise is lacking.

Play Progression and Analysis

- Coach gives steal sign to first base runner. Coach also yells the number of outs: "Two." Coach indicates to the third base runner that a double steal is on.

- First base runner steals on the pitch. Third base runner edges off as the pitcher delivers. Runner must have a good lead.

- Catcher has the ball and fires to second base area, but the first base runner stops halfway to second base. Now a rundown starts on the first base runner.

- The instant the third base runner sees the ball sail beyond the pitcher toward second, runner breaks for the plate and slides.

- As the trapped first base runner sees the ball thrown to the plate, runner proceeds to steal second base. Trapped runner must not be tagged out before the run scores.

- Only the fastest runners can make it from third base to home.

Single Sign or Holding Sign

Coach touches any part of his head, from the top of cap down to his neck, glasses, etc., with one hand (with the other hand he motions third base runner off base).

Multiple Sign System (Series of 5 Signs)

Indicator sign   *Hot sign*

Indicator sign is coach bends down and puts one hand on one knee.

Sign to be used is the first one flashed after the indicator.

PLAY 10:   DOUBLE STEAL ON THE CATCHER'S THROW BACK TO THE PITCHER WITH RUNNERS ON FIRST AND THIRD, NONE OR ONE OUT

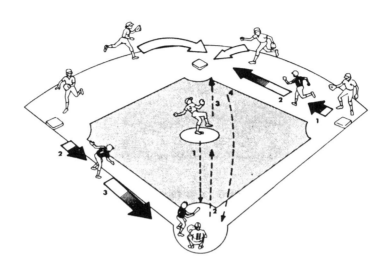

The purpose of this play is to steal home and second base with no one put out. The psychological advantage of this play is very great. Opponents do not expect a steal play after the catcher receives the ball. Success rate of this play is very high (75 percent).

Play Progression and Analysis

• No verbal sign is given. Coach gives delayed steal sign. This play is a form of delayed steal.

• First base runner leads off a normal amount and comes back only one half a step. Be sure first base runner does not lean toward second base. This will give the play away.

• The instant the first base runner sees the ball leave the catcher's hand to return to the pitcher, runner takes off in a sprint, keeps going, and slides.

• Third base runner takes a lead as the pitcher receives the catcher's return toss.

• The instant the third base runner sees the ball leave pitcher's hand for second base area, runner breaks for the plate and slides.

• First base runner steals second on the throw to home plate.

Single Sign or Holding Sign

Coach waves one hand in front of his body horizontally. He also moves his head back and forth, indicating "No" (with the other hand, coach motions third base runner off base).

Multiple Sign System (Series of 5 Signs)

Indicator sign   *Hot sign*

Indicator sign is the coach kicking dirt with one foot.

Sign to be used is the first one flashed after the indicator.

PLAY 11:   DOUBLE STEAL ON THE CATCHER'S THROW BACK TO THE PITCHER WITH RUNNERS ON FIRST AND THIRD, TWO OUTS

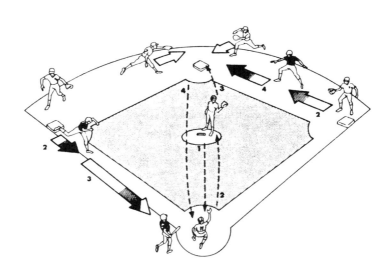

The purpose of this play is to steal home and steal second base with no one put out. The psychological advantage is very great. Opponents do not expect a steal play after the catcher receives the ball. Success rate of this play is very high (75 percent).

Play Progression and Analysis

• No verbal sign is given. Coach gives delayed steal sign. This play is a form of delayed steal.

• First base runner leads off a normal amount and comes back only one half a step. Be sure first base runner does not lean toward second base. This will give the play away.

• The instant the first base runner sees the ball leave the catcher's hand to return to pitcher, runner takes off in a sprint. Runner suddenly stops halfway to second base.

• Third base runner leads off as the pitcher gets the return toss.

• The instant the third base runner sees the ball leave the pitcher's hand for the second base area, runner breaks for the plate and slides.

• First base runner steals second on the throw to home plate.

Single Sign or Holding Sign

Coach waves one hand in front of his body horizontally. He also moves his head back and forth, indicating "No" (with the other hand, coach motions third base runner off base).

Multiple Sign System (Series of 5 Signs)

Indicator sign

Indicator sign is the coach folds arms in front of chest.

Sign to be used is the first one flashed after the indicator.

Hot sign

PLAY 12: DELAYED STEAL ON THE CATCHER'S THROW TO SECOND BASE WITH RUNNER ON SECOND BASE

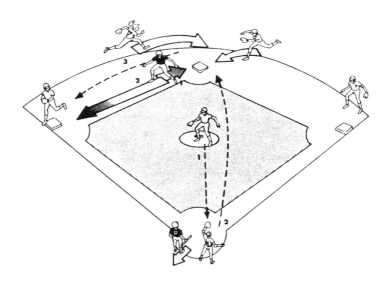

The purpose of this play is to steal third base by fooling the catcher, drawing his throw to second base. Any delayed steal play has a great psychological advantage because the timing of the play is different from what the defense expects. The success rate for this steal is 30 percent, unless the second base runner is extremely swift.

Play Progression and Analysis

- Runner on second base receives delayed steal sign from the coach.

- As the pitch is made, second base runner dashes off second base about thirty to thirty-five feet.

- Runner acts as if to head back to second base.

- If the catcher fires a pickoff throw to second base, the runner breaks for third base. Runner slides hard.

- Runner actually is beating two throws (from catcher to second and from second to third).

Single Sign or Holding Sign

Coach waves one hand in front of his body horizontally. He also moves his head back and forth, indicating "No."

Multiple Sign System (Series of 5 Signs)

Indicator sign   *Hot sign*

Indicator sign is the coach tugs at his belt with two hands.

Sign to be used is the first one flashed after the indicator.

PLAY 13: DELAYED STEAL ON THE CATCHER'S THROW TO FIRST BASE WITH RUNNERS ON FIRST AND SECOND

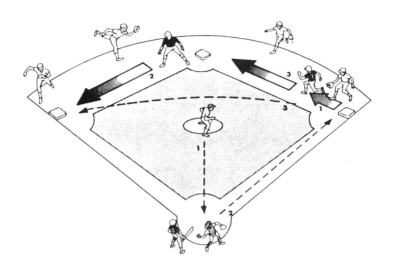

The purpose of this play is to double-steal second and third bases by fooling the catcher into throwing to first base. The success rate for this particular delayed steal is quite high, 50 percent, or much higher if the second base runner is extremely swift.

Play Progression and Analysis

- Both runners get delayed steal sign from coach.

- Man on first base breaks off the base about thirty-five feet. Man on second base edges off the base a maximum lead, around twenty to twenty-five feet.

- Suddenly, catcher fires a pickoff throw to first base. Runner is now trapped off first base.

- Just as the ball leaves the catcher's hand, the second base runner goes to third base, sliding hard.

- First baseman will throw too late to third base to get the runner there.

- As the ball leaves first baseman's hand, first base runner steals second base.

Single Sign or Holding Sign

Coach waves one hand in front of his body horizontally. He also moves his head back and forth, indicating "No."

Multiple Sign System (Series of 5 Signs)

Indicator sign   *Hot sign*

Indicator sign is coach moving one hand up and down in front of body from neck to waist.

Sign to be used is the first one flashed after the indicator.

PLAY 14:   DELAYED STEAL ON THE CATCHER'S THROW TO SECOND BASE WITH RUNNERS ON SECOND AND THIRD

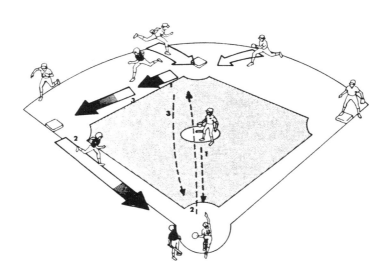

The purpose of this play is to double-steal two bases, including home, by fooling the catcher into throwing to second base with a runner on third base. Success rate on this play for stealing both bases, including home, is 40 percent.

Play Progression and Analysis

• Runners on second and third get delayed steal sign from coach.

• Man on second base breaks thirty-five feet toward third base on the pitch. Man on third base edges slowly off third on the pitch.

• Catcher fires a pickoff throw to second base. As the ball leaves the catcher's hand, man on third base breaks hard for the plate, slides hard.

• Second baseman fires home to throw out the runner at the plate.

• As second baseman releases the ball for home plate, the second base runner steals third base easily.

Single Sign or Holding Sign

Coach waves one hand in front of his body horizontally. He also moves his head back and forth, indicating "No."

Multiple Sign System (Series of 5 Signs)

Indicator sign   *Hot sign*

Indicator sign is coach holds one fist in front of body and other hand touches a part of his head.

Sign to be used is the first one flashed after the indicator.

PLAY 15: DELAYED STEAL ON THE CATCHER'S THROW TO FIRST OR SECOND WITH BASES LOADED

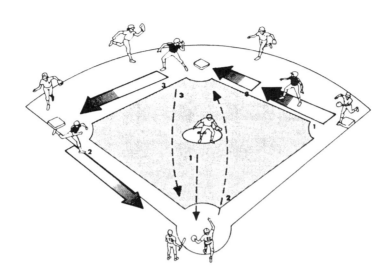

The purpose of this play is to steal three bases, including home, by fooling the catcher into throwing down to first base or the second base area. No play in baseball offers your running team more of a psychological advantage than this one. It is so unusual that you have the element of complete surprise in your favor. Success rate is very high, around 75 percent, for stealing all three bases, including home, without giving up even one out.

Play Progression and Analysis

- All three runners receive delayed steal sign from their coach.

- As the pitcher delivers, first base runner breaks for second base, as if runner forgets a man occupies that base. He stops twenty feet from second base and looks startled. (The batter has been given the take sign.)

- Second base runner stands on second base and yells loudly, "Get back," to the first base runner. Third base runner edges off his base cautiously, watching the scene.

- Catcher throws ball to first base or down to the second base area. As the catcher releases the ball, the third base runner breaks for home and beats the throw home from the baseman. As the throw goes home, the other two base runners steal their next bases.

Single Sign or Holding Sign

Coach waves one hand in front of his body horizontally. He also moves his head back and forth, indicating "No."

Multiple Sign System (Series of 5 Signs)

Indicator sign   *Hot sign*

Indicator sign is coach bends over and puts one hand on one knee.

Sign to be used is the first one flashed after the indicator.

PLAY 16: DELAYED STEAL ON THE CATCHER'S THROW TO THIRD WITH A RUNNER ON THIRD

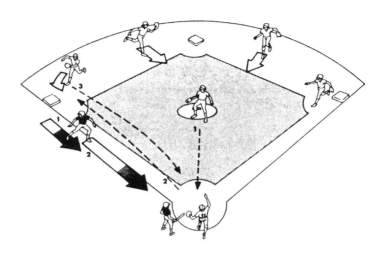

The purpose of this play is to steal home by fooling the catcher into throwing down to third base. Success rate on this play, unless the runner is extremely quick and fast, will be only 20 percent.

Play Progression and Analysis

- Man on third base gets delayed steal sign from the coach.

- As the pitcher delivers, third base runner yells, makes a lot of noise, and leans toward home, thirty-five feet off the base. Runner then fakes a lean back to third base.

- Catcher fires ball to third base; he thinks he has the runner picked off because the runner appears to be heading back in a dive to the base.

- The instant the third base runner sees the ball leave the catcher's hands, he breaks for the plate.

- Runner then beats the throw from third baseman back to the catcher.

Single Sign or Holding Sign

Coach waves one hand in front of his body horizontally. He also moves his head back and forth, indicating "No."

Multiple Sign System (Series of 5 Signs)

Indicator sign   *Hot sign*

Indicator sign is coach puts hand on head area and also crosses legs.

Sign to be used is the first one flashed after the indicator.

THE HIT-AND-RUN PLAY

The hit-and-run is one of the most exciting plays in baseball. The runner breaking from first must be protected; therefore, the batter must be capable of getting a piece of the ball on any given pitch. *His main concern is to hit the ball on the ground and, hopefully, toward the area vacated by the middle infielder who is covering second base.* While the runner at first can be bunted over, the right type of hitter can accomplish more by hitting the ball into right field, thereby ending up with men on first and third.

The purpose of the hit-and-run is to advance the runner an extra base and to protect him from the double play. It is often used in the middle or late stages of a game and is a good play when the pitcher is behind the batter, especially on a three-and-one count. With a runner on first base, the right-handed hitter will try to hit the ball behind the runner, because the second baseman will be covering the bag when the runner breaks toward second. The batter must swing at the ball wherever it is pitched. *If the catcher guesses the play and calls for a pitchout,* the offense, of course, is in trouble. If a wild pitcher is on the mound, a manager is a little reluctant to put on the hit-and-run.

THE RUN-AND-HIT PLAY

Instead of hitting behind the runner here, the batter simply tries to hit the ball, which, for young, inexperienced players, is an easier skill to execute. *The run-and-hit can cause many problems for the defense, such as breaking up a double play when there is a slow runner on first.*

A good time to call for a run-and-hit is when the pitcher is behind in the count (2-0, 3-1, or 3-2), because he must come in with the pitch. The runner should be on the move, and the hitter is instructed to go for the ball, *if it is in the strike zone.* The run-and-hit is used more with a fast runner on base, so if the pitch is out of the strike zone, the runner has a chance to steal a base.

The hitter should know that the runner is going, and if the pitch is in the strike zone, he must swing. *The worst thing that can happen on a run-and-hit is to have the runner go and then have the hitter take a pitch right down the middle.*

THE HIT-AND-RUN WITH MEN ON FIRST AND THIRD

Very similar to the regular hit-and-run play, this one is even better. Normally, the break by the runner at first will find one of the infielders moving toward second to take a throw from the catcher. However, because the defense will be suspecting the double steal, both infielders will be moving toward second, one to take a possible throw and the other in an attempt to cut off the throw and relay it to the plate. This means that 50 percent of the infield will be opening up for the batter to punch the ball through. If that does happen, the back runner will be able to advance to third. Of course, on the pitch, the runner on third takes his normal leadoff, but he doesn't break for home until he sees the ball hit someplace other than in the air. Even if the ball is hit on the ground to the pitcher, it is smarter to break for the plate than to allow the defense to turn a double play at second and first. If the third base runner sees that he is going to be a sure out at the plate, he gets himself into a rundown; the runner from first tries to advance to third if the rundown can be made to last long enough.

A good contact hitter who can hit to the opposite field is really needed here, but the contact itself is more important than hitting to the opposite field, since portions of both sides of the infield will open for the batter.

In case the pitch is not hit, the runner at third must have prior instructions from the coach as to what his reaction is expected to be if a throw is made to second. Should he fake a break and return to protect the back runner, or should he react by breaking for the plate? He must know. The instructions of the coach will surely depend on the running abilities of the runner at third, as well as on the score and the inning.

So, we have learned a most important coaching technique—that is, calling for the hit-and-run with men at first and third is a smart move.

PLAY 17:   HIT-AND-RUN

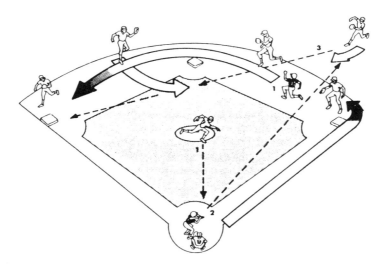

The purpose of this standard play is to move a runner up one or two bases, with the runner going and the batter swinging. Ideally, the ball will be hit through the hole vacated by the second baseman; the runners will end up at third and second bases at the completion of the play. It can be worked with one runner on first, runners at first and second, or runners at first and third.

Play Progression and Analysis

- Men on base get the steal-on-pitcher sign from the coach.

- Batter gets a separate hit-and-run sign from the coach. We assume a right-handed batter at the plate.

- Runners break with the pitch and steal the next bases.

- Hitter must swing at the pitch. If it is a terrible pitch, he merely fans the air with the bat, but does not hit the ball. Hitter tries to hit the ball on the ground through the hole vacated by shortstop or second baseman.

- Runner on first base rounds second base and watches third base coach's sign. Runner usually slides into third base.

- As the first base runner steals, the second baseman covers second base to take the throw from the catcher.

- The right fielder will have to play the hit ball. He will throw to third base in an attempt to get the runner there.

- When the hitter rounds first base and sees the ball thrown all the way through to third base, he then heads for second base, slides, and beats the third baseman's throw back to second base.

Single Sign or Holding Sign

Coach crosses legs as sign to hit any pitch and he puts hand on any part of head or hat or neck area as runner's sign to steal on the pitch.

Multiple Sign System (Series of 5 Signs)

Indicator sign

Indicator sign is coach gives the hand on head area.

Sign to be used is the first one flashed after the indicator.

Hot sign

PLAY 18:   THE FAKE STEAL

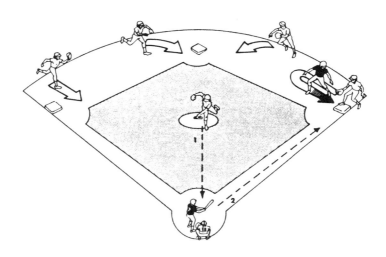

The purpose of this play is to set up the real steal play and/or to cause a bad pickoff throw at that base by the catcher. After this play has been used, the defense won't be able to distinguish a real steal from the fake steals. Great psychological damage can be done with this tactic. It worries the pitcher and catcher on every pitch, and the defense has to shade over, opening up defensive holes when a steal is bluffed by the running team. The success rate on this play is 100 percent, for no runner showing just a bluff or a fake steal should ever be picked off even by the best catcher's throw to a base.

Play Progression and Analysis

- Runner on base receives a fake steal sign from the coach.

- Runner takes the lead, always leads off the maximum amount each time, and always leads off the same distance.

- As pitcher delivers, runner breaks down two steps hard and returns fast to base, ahead of the pickoff throw.

- All the offense will yell, "There he goes," on each fake steal maneuver.

- Catcher will usually fire a pickoff throw to the runner's base.

- Runner must judge distance so that he gets a maximum lead toward the next base in case of a hit ball and still prevents a pickoff from catcher's throw.

Single Sign or Holding Sign

Coach kicks the dirt with one foot.

Multiple Sign System (Series of 5 Signs)

Indicator sign   *Hot sign*

*Indicator sign is the coach waving
one hand in front of the body in a
horizontal movement.*

*Sign to be used is the first one
flashed after the indicator.*

BUNTING

Sacrifice Bunt

The key rule in executing the sacrifice bunt is to have the hitter give himself up. On the straight sacrifice, the batter attempts to bunt the ball only if the pitch is a strike. He should concentrate on bunting the ball on the ground.

Late in the ball game, with the score tied or the team one run behind, the runner on first must be moved to second. The hitter should bunt the ball down the first base line because the first baseman will be holding the man on. Besides, the third baseman usually plays shallow in this situation. With runners on first and second, the bunt should be down the third base line so that the third baseman has to field it. In this situation, the first baseman is charging and is right on top of the bunter.

Bunt for a Hit

In bunting for a base hit, the hitter must know where the first baseman and third baseman are playing. Are they playing deep or shallow? Are they expecting the play?

Some pitchers fall off the mound, and if a right-hander falls off toward first, the bunt should be down the third base line. If the pitcher is a left hander and he falls off toward the third base line, the bunt should be down the first base line.

Fake Bunt on Fake Bunt and Slash

In the hope that the first and third basemen will charge in toward the plate, the hitter assumes a bunting position. *Then, if the infielders charge, the batter will try to slap the ball past them. This is a good tactic against the charging bunt defense.*

The batter may wish to fake a bunt when a runner is trying to steal a base. This action may disrupt the catcher's effort to throw out the runner.

In still another situation, the batter will fake a bunt attempt when he is taking a strike. In this instance, it is intended to draw in the infielders, especially the third baseman. If successful, the infielders' range will be limited.

THE SQUEEZE PLAYS

The safety and suicide squeeze plays are usually tried in the late innings with a runner on third base, one out, and the team at bat ahead, tied, or no more than one run behind.

The Suicide Squeeze

The runner should wait until the pitcher's arm is at the top of his delivery. One of the dangers of the suicide squeeze is that, if the runner leaves too soon or otherwise gives away the play, the pitcher will knock the hitter down. The hitter then does not have a chance to bunt the ball, and the runner will very likely be tagged out at the plate. If the runner waits, then it is up to the hitter to bunt the ball on the ground. *It does not have to be a good bunt, but merely on the ground, not too hard, and toward the pitcher.*

Many hitters in this situation try to lay down a perfect bunt. The ball rolls foul and it defeats their purpose. If the runner starts at the proper time, all that is necessary is for the ball to be bunted on the ground. *It is essential that the hitter attempts to bunt the ball wherever it is thrown.*

The Safety Squeeze

The runner at third base should make his move only if the ball is bunted on the ground. If the ball is popped up or missed, the runner does not go. There should be a speedy runner on third because he must not start too soon—*he waits to see where the ball is bunted and then takes off.* The ball is not bunted unless the pitch is a good one. The runner will try to score only if he thinks he can make it. A quick start is essential for the runner from third base. Always use this bunt when a tag at the plate is necessary.

THE RUN-AND-BUNT PLAY

This play is a variation of the sacrifice bunt in which the base runner attempts to steal the next base. To protect the runner, the hitter must bunt the ball regardless of where it is pitched. On occasion, the run-and-bunt play is used more or less as a surprise tactic. With the bunt in order, the first baseman charges in and, as he moves in quickly, the runner attempts his steal. This can be dangerous if the hitter pops the ball up, misses it completely, or is thrown a bad pitch. Therefore, it is necessary that the person at bat be a good bunter.

PLAY 19: DRAG BUNT FOR A HIT

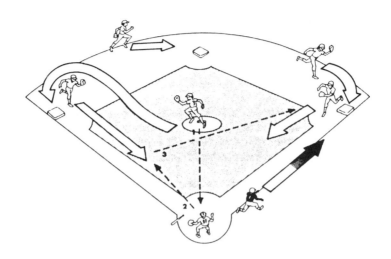

The purpose of this play is for the batter to lay down a perfect, slow-rolling bunt anywhere in fair territory, then beat the throw to first base. If the bunter performs this maneuver batting left-handed, he has the jump of a step or a step and one half toward first base. The psychological advantage is great. Execute this play when the defense isn't expecting it. A success rate of 30 percent is good for drag bunting.

Play Progression and Analysis

- Batter gets the sign from the coach.

- If batter is right-handed, drag ball slowly to third baseman or first baseman.

- If batter is left-handed, drag ball slowly to third baseman.

- In either case, at the time of contact with the ball, batter must get a good jump toward first base.

- Batter has to run at top speed. It is always a close play.

- Batter should bunt only if the pitch is good.

- Be sure batter does not square around and show the bunt too soon. He wants to keep the infielders away from the plate.

Single Sign or Holding Sign

Coach bends down slightly and places one hand on one knee. Right hand on right knee indicates to bunt to right side of infield. (Left hand means bunt to left.)

Multiple Sign System (Series of 5 Signs)

Indicator sign

Hot sign

Indicator sign is coach places hand on his glasses or any part of his head area.

Sign to be used is the first one flashed after the indicator.

PLAY 20:   SACRIFICE BUNT THAT MOVES RUNNERS ONE BASE

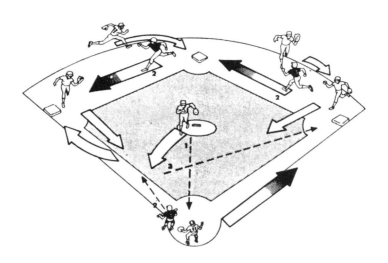

The purpose of this play is to move runners from first to second base or from second to third. We are willing to give up an out to do this. This tactic may also put two runners in scoring position and take double play chances off at third and second base. The psychological advantage is not great on this play. Every team does it, expects it, and practices it. Success rate on sacrifice bunts should be 75 percent.

Play Progression and Analysis

- Batter and runner must both get the sacrifice bunt sign from the coach.

- Runners may or may not be given the steal sign by the coach.

- If steal is given, hustle to next base and slide, whether bunt is a success or not, unless ball is popped up.

- If steal is not given, runner must be able to get to next base after the bunt is down. Runner must also be able to get back to the base if the bunt is missed.

- Usually the batter should bunt only strikes or close pitches.

- When executing a sacrifice bunt, batter should make his moves early enough to get bat out and make a good bunt.

Single Sign or Holding Sign

Coach bends down slightly and places one hand on one knee. Right hand on right knee indicates to bunt to right side of the infield. (Left hand and knee means to bunt to left.)

Multiple Sign System (Series of 5 Signs)

Indicator sign   *Hot sign*

Indicator sign is coach tugs at belt with two hands.

Sign to be used is the first one flashed after the indicator.

PLAY 21:   SACRIFICE BUNT THAT MOVES RUNNER TWO BASES

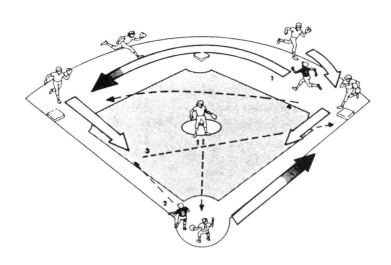

The purpose of this play is to place a sacrifice bunt on the ground in such a way that the first base runner can be advanced all the way to third base. This is a shocking play. The defense never expects a runner to try for two bases on a bunt; the play depends on their neglect of third base. Success for this bunt play should be 50 percent if the first base runner is very fast.

Play Progression and Analysis

- First base runner knows he is going from first to third on the bunt. Special sign is given.

- Batter gets the "sacrifice two bases along" sign. Batter must bunt the ball thirty feet in line with third base. A slow, soft bunt is required. Batter hopes for a pitch slightly inside.

- Runner on first base is also given the steal-on-pitcher sign from the coach. This is a stealing play, too. Runner must have a big lead and a big jump to make it from first to third base.

- Bunt dies in the grass. Third baseman comes in to field the ball. As the throw is made for the out at first base, the runner rounds second base. Third base is not guarded by anyone. First base runner sees this and does not slow down.

- He makes it into third base easily. Even if third base is guarded, the throw from first will arrive too late.

Single Sign or Holding Sign

Coach bends down slightly and places both hands on both knees, indicating that every runner is trying to advance two bases.

Multiple Sign System (Series of 5 Signs)

Indicator sign   *Hot sign*

Indicator sign is coach will hold fist up in front of body and touch head area with the other hand.

Sign to be used is the first one flashed after the indicator.

PLAY 22:   SAFE-SQUEEZE BUNT

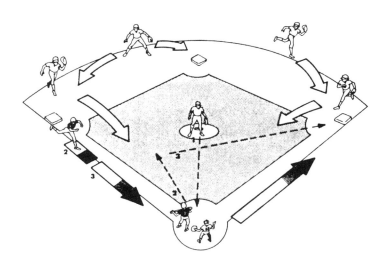

The purpose of this type of bunt is to score a run from third base by bunting without making an out. The runner will come home, but only if it is a good bunt the runner thinks he can beat. This play does not have much element of surprise. All teams know it and expect it. Many teams use it as a part of their bunting repertoires. The success rate should be 60 percent if the third base runner is fast and the batter is a good bunter.

Play Progression and Analysis

- Batter gets safe-squeeze sign from the coach. Third base runner sees the same sign.

- Do not give the third base runner any kind of suicide squeeze or steal sign. It isn't a suicide or a real steal.

- Third base runner goes home fast only if ball is slowly bunted between the pitcher and first base or between the pitcher and third base.

- If ball is bunted badly, third base runner should come very far off third and bluff a break home. If infielder throws to first base to get the bunter out, third base runner has the option to either try to make it to the plate or go back to third.

Single Sign or Holding Sign

Coach tugs at belt with both hands. He also indicates that ball is to be bunted in a certain area (but runner is not committed to come home unless it is a good bunt).

Multiple Sign System (Series of 5 Signs)

Indicator sign   *Hot sign*

Indicator sign is coach puts one hand on one knee.

Sign to be used is the first one flashed after the indicator.

PLAY 23:   SUICIDE SQUEEZE BUNT TO SCORE ONE RUN

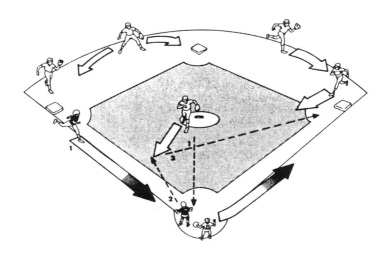

The purpose of this play is to score only the third base runner. He breaks for home on the pitch, and the batter must lay down a fair bunt. The defense feels helpless as the bunt is laid down fair, for there is no defense against the unexpected suicide squeeze. If the bunt is good, the run scores. This is simply a steal home with help from the bunter. Success rate on suicide squeeze bunts is 75 percent.

Play Progression and Analysis

- Tell the third base runner not to commit himself down third base line until the pitcher has committed himself to the batter. Keep the pitcher guessing.

- Batter and runner must both see and understand both signs given to them by the coach. Batter gets suicide sign from coach.

- Runner gets steal-on-pitcher sign from the coach.

- Batter must bunt softly anywhere in fair territory.

- Batter should square around to bunt just as pitcher is coming down in his delivery.

- If bunt is missed, third base runner must take out the catcher.

- If pitcher is in stretch, avoid a third base pickoff and have runner shorten his lead before breaking for the plate.

Single Sign or Holding Sign

Coach bends down slightly and places one hand on one knee. This sign tells the third base runner to come home on the pitch, tells batter he must bunt the ball.

Multiple Sign System (Series of 5 Signs)

Indicator sign   *Hot sign*

Indicator sign is coach folds arms in front of chest.

Sign to be used is the first one flashed after the indicator.

EXECUTING THE DOUBLE SUICIDE SQUEEZE BUNT

This play does the same amount of damage to an opponent as does a home run over the fence with one man aboard. But the play uses a ball that is bunted no more than thirty feet from the plate.

Now, how do you score two runs on a ball hit no more than thirty feet from home? Is that possible? It sure is! When this play starts, runners must be either on second and third or be on all three bases. In either of these situations, the coach may flash the signal for a double suicide squeeze play. This special sign means that you want two runs to score on the bunt. Here are the things that make this unusual play work:

- Third base runner need not be fast at all.

- Second base runner needs to be very fast.

- Bunter must get the ball down on the ground somewhere. He must not miss the ball or foul it off or pop it up.

- Preferably, bunter gets the weak bunt in line with the third baseman coming in, but it must die thirty feet from home plate.

- Third base runner and second base runner both must be stealing.

- The third baseman must pick up the bunt and actually throw to first base for the out.

- Second base runner must not try to score if pitcher fields the bunt or if ball is bobbled at all!

Do these things in exactly the way described:

Signal is given to third base runner, second base runner, and batter. They get the one sign, the same sign. They all must be sure that they understand what is being called for.

As the pitcher goes into his stretch, runners take a normal lead. They don't give the play away by taking too much lead. On the pitcher's delivery, the two runners steal and are coming hard.

Batter gets his bat on the ball. Ball is bunted fair somewhere on the ground. It dribbles straight for the third baseman fielding it, but it dies thirty feet from the plate. The third baseman must pick up a dead ball and make a very difficult play.

Make sure that the third baseman actually throws the ball to first base. We do not want the catcher or pitcher to field the ball.

By this time, the third base runner has scored. One run is in now. As that runner scores, he immediately lines up behind home plate in line with the third base line to assist the next runner coming in. He will definitely tell him to slide hard, for this is always a close play. He yells loudly and signals downward with the hands and arms.

Now the third baseman is throwing the ball to first base to try to get the bunter out. From the time the third baseman stoops over to pick up the ball until he gets rid of the ball toward first base, he has no idea where the runner who started from second base could be. *His back is completely to the runner rounding third base.* As the third baseman releases his throw, the second base runner "steps on the gas" and heads for home plate. He never breaks stride from second base to home.

The second base runner should beat the throws from the third baseman to the first baseman and back to the catcher. It will always be a close race, but the fast runner should always win it, if he does not slow down along the way.

Usually, the first baseman will hesitate slightly on the play. This slight hesitation is just enough to assure that the throw to the plate will be somewhat late.

What are the best times to use this play? I will mention a few choice ones. First, try it with one out. This is a "copout," perhaps, but you are assured that you will never get wiped out of an inning by a triple play.

One word of warning. Everything has its price or risk. If the bunter pops the ball into the air and it is caught, the defense could throw to second base and third base and get a triple play on you. *So, don't use this play with none away.*

The play is equally effective whether a team is ahead or behind. It is so great a surprise that the defense never expects anything this daring. If you are ahead, say 4-2, and you can get more runs on this play, you now are ahead 6-2. The opponent now has to score five runs to beat you. In other words, this is an excellent way to "pad" a lead and put a game out of reach.

If you are behind, say 4-2, this is the last thing the defense expects a trailing team to do. If it is early in the game and you are willing to try this play, you could tie up the game 4-4, and you are back in the ball game with two outs and no one on base.

PLAY 24:   SUICIDE SQUEEZE BUNT TO SCORE TWO RUNS

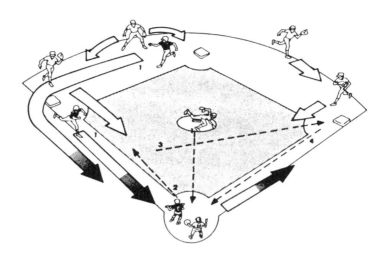

The purpose of this play is to score the runners on second and third bases. Both runners break for the next base on the pitch, and the batter must lay down a fair bunt. This is baseball's premier running play. It shocks the minds of the opponents. Scoring two runs on one bunt is almost unheard of in the game, but it is not that difficult to do. The success rate for this double suicide play is 60 percent, high enough to the play more often than it is attempted.

Play Progression and Analysis

- It is important that the second and third base runners do not commit themselves to steals until the pitcher brings his arm down to deliver.

- Both batter and runner must see and understand both signs given by the coach. Batter gets a special "suicide squeeze, score two runners" sign from coach. Both runners get steal-on-pitcher sign and see the sign to the batter.

- Batter must try to place a very soft, dead bunt in a particular spot, on a line to third base and thirty feet from the plate.

- Batter should square around to bunt just as pitcher is coming down in the delivery.

- If the bunt is missed, third base runner must take out the catcher and second base runner must stop at third base.

- If bunt is good, but bobbled or not hit to third baseman, the second base runner stops at third base.

Single Sign or Holding Sign

Coach bends down slightly and two hands are placed on two knees. This indicates that both the second and third base runners are to try to score on a good bunt.

Multiple Sign System (Series of 5 Signs)

Indicator sign   *Hot sign*

Indicator sign is coach kicks dirt with one foot.

Sign to be used is the first one flashed after the indicator.

PLAY 25:   FAKE BUNT AND SLASH WITH A MAN ON FIRST OR SECOND

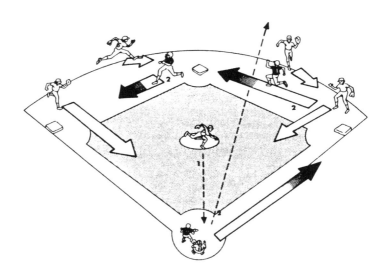

The purpose of this play is to swing at a pitch with a slash motion, a reluctant half-swing. It looks like a bunt or fake bunt play at first; then the bat is drawn back as the ball is pitched. Finally, the batter punches at the ball, attempting to get good contact. Advantages of this play are several. The infield is drawn in by the batter's fake bunt stance, but the fielders then find the ball popped over them for a lazy base hit. This can move an alert base runner two bases along if the ball is well placed. Since bat control is especially difficult to teach younger players, a success rate of only 25 percent can be expected.

Play Progression and Analysis

- Batter gets the sign from the coach for the fake bunt and slash.

- Batter squares around to bunt very early, with his bat out level to the ground. He grips the bat in such a way that his hands are also ready to use the bat to hit.

- Just as the pitcher's arm comes down in his delivery, the batter draws bat back to a hitting position, but keeps it in front of his body. He is going to punch the ball.

- Runners on base watch the hit ball, but they do not steal on the pitch. However, if the ball clears the infield on the fly or is a slow roller, runners slide into the next base.

Single Sign or Holding Sign

Coach moves one hand up and down in front of his body from neck to waist. He tells batter to fake bunt, then slash ball through or over the infield. No steal sign.

Multiple Sign System (Series of 5 Signs)

Indicator sign   *Hot sign*

Indicator sign is coach puts two hands on two knees.

Sign to be used is the first one flashed after the indicator.

PLAY 26: FAKE BUNT AND SLASH WITH A MAN ON THIRD

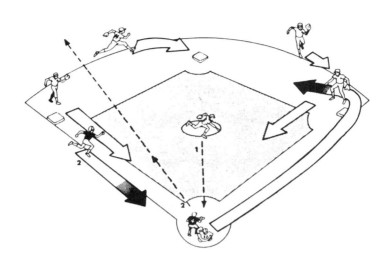

The purpose and technique of this play are identical to Play 25, except that this one scores a run. Because bat control is difficult for younger players, a success rate of only 25 percent can be expected.

Play Progression and Analysis

- Batter gets the sign for the fake bunt and slash. Runner gets the same sign. This is not a steal play.

- Batter squares around to bunt very early, holding the bat out level to the ground. He must grip the bat, however, so his hands are also ready to use the bat to hit.

- Just as the pitcher's arm comes down in his delivery, batter draws bat to a hitting position, but keeps it in front of his body. He is going to punch the ball.

- Runner on third base watches the hit ball. If it clears the infield on the fly or is a slow roller, he comes home.

- Batter does not have to swing at a bad pitch.

Single Sign or Holding Sign

Coach moves one hand up and down in front of his body from neck to waist. He tells batter to fake bunt, then hit ball through or over the infield. No steal sign.

Multiple Sign System (Series of 5 Signs)

Indicator sign   *Hot sign*

Indicator sign is coach puts hand on glasses or any part of head area.

Sign to be used is the first one flashed after the indicator.

PLAY 27:   FAKE BUNT WITH A MAN ON SECOND

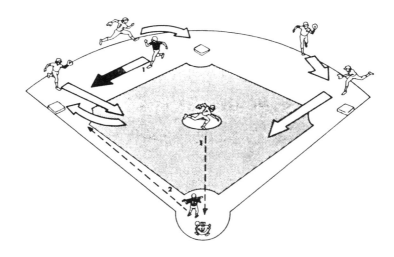

This play is a clever way to assist the second base runner to steal third base. The batter assists his teammate in this effort. The play is designed to fool the third baseman who likes to creep in too far to get an edge on the bunting play he believes is coming up. He moves in too far and cannot get back to cover his base when the catcher tries to throw out the stealing runner. The second base runner must have a good lead. Successful execution not only results in a stolen base, it often causes the errant catcher's throw to sail into left field, allowing a run to score. Success rate on this play is 50 percent.

Play Progression and Analysis

- Batter gets sign for fake bunt.

- Runner gets the steal-on-pitcher sign.

- Both the runner and the batter must see both signs.

- Batter squares around to bunt very, very early. Batter puts the bat out and levels it to the ground. Batter watches the ball sail past the bat, but doesn't let it touch the bat.

- Batter brings the bat in from the bunting position, but rather slowly. He doesn't want to physically interfere with catcher. The bat will create a visual hazard for the catcher, and it may slow down his throw to the base.

- Runner takes off with the pitch, slides hard into the next base, and gets up fast.

Single Sign or Holding Sign

Coach holds one fist in front of his body, telling batter to fake bunt. Hand on head area is steal sign (bunter wants to fake the bunt toward third).

Multiple Sign System (Series of 5 Signs)

Indicator sign   *Hot sign*

Indicator sign is coach folds arms in front of his chest.

Sign to be used is the first one flashed after the indicator.

PLAY 28:   FAKE BUNT WITH A MAN ON FIRST

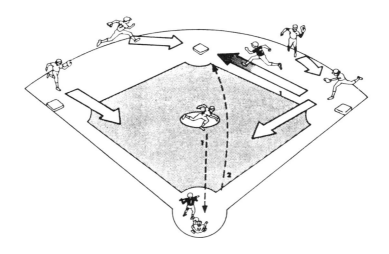

This play is a clever way to assist the first base runner to steal second base. The batter assists his teammate in this effort. The opponent must guess whether the team will bunt or fake bunt. This play is designed simply to get the bat in the eyes of the catcher in order to slow his throw or cause it to be off target. This is definitely a steal play. The first base runner is going on the pitch. He must have a good lead. The running team will advance a runner without sacrificing an out. Success rate is high at 60 percent.

Play Progression and Analysis

- Batter gets the sign for fake bunt, and the runner gets the steal-on-pitcher sign.

- Both runner and batter must see each other's signs.

- Batter squares around to bunt very early. He puts his bat out and levels it to the ground.

- Batter watches ball sail past the bat, but he doesn't let it touch the bat.

- Batter brings the bat in from his bunting position, but rather slowly. He doesn't want to physically interfere with the catcher. The bat will give a visual hazard to the catcher and may slow his throw to second base.

- Runner takes off with the pitch, slides hard into the next base, and gets up fast.

Single Sign or Holding Sign

Coach holds one fist in front of his body, telling batter to fake bunt. Hand on head area is steal sign (bunter wants to fake the bunt between pitcher and first).

Multiple Sign System (Series of 5 Signs)

Indicator sign

Hot sign

Indicator sign is coach placing hand on head area and crossing his legs.

Sign to be used is the first one flashed after the indicator.

PLAY 29:   THE WIPEOFF SIGN

The wipeoff sign is very important to the coach and players who are on offense. It can be given for several reasons. Following are several:

- The coach may have had second thoughts. He may have made a "dumb" mistake and does not want the team to go through with a play. He made a mental error.

- The coach or someone on the team may detect that the opposing team has picked up one of the signs. When the opponent "steals" one of your signs and moves in such a way that the play you are trying surely would fail, then the wipeoff sign is imperative.

- The coach may have given a sign and his team members picked it up and are ready to execute it. But the coach suddenly remembers another play that will work even better. Coach then wipes off the old play and will give the signs for the new play.

- The wipeoff sign should be very fast and simple. I usually wipe my hand across the letters on my uniform, as if I were wiping dirt off my hands.

- A very important point in giving signs: Whenever a sign is given, as soon as the pitch is made (and the batter does not hit the ball and the runners do not move) another sign must be given to batters or runners. Do not assume that a sign given is given for the duration of that batter's time at bat! A new sign must be given to the batter and each runner *after each pitch.* For this reason, it is vital that batter look for a sign after every pitch and that runners go back to their bases and take a long, hard look before moving off their bases.

PROPER PROCEDURE FOR A BATTER AND/OR RUNNER WHO MISSES OR MISUNDERSTANDS A SIGN

If, at any time, a baseball player feels that he does not understand a sign given by a coach, he immediately yells "Timeout." As soon as he is given a timeout by the umpire, he and the coach meet and the coach gives the sign to him quietly by word of mouth, using as much time as is allowed. If, however, the person giving the sign, or the person responsible for sign origin, feels that the runner's or batter's calling a timeout might tell the defensive team what is coming next, then the wipeoff sign will be given or the coach will simply say to the player during the timeout that the sign is off.

However, when the runner and batter return to their positions, before the umpire yells "Play ball," the person giving the signs may give another sign and a new play may start after the old one was called off.

PLAY 30:   THE TAKE SIGN

Of all the signs of baseball, perhaps the take sign is one of the least understood and the most poorly executed. It is certainly a most important sign. The take sign means that the batter will intentionally let the ball go by. He has no intention of swinging at it. The take may be given for several reasons. Some of those reasons are:

- The pitcher may be weakening; his control is getting bad. Perhaps the batter can work the pitcher for a base on balls.

- Your team may be several runs behind late in the game. Your best chance of loading the bases is to take the first few pitches to a batter to get ahead of the pitcher on every batter.

- Your team may have a tricky running play called that requires that the catcher have the ball to start the play. In such a case, the batter takes the pitch.

- Your team may have a steal play on with its runners. The batter is to take the pitch while a runner steals a base.

- In rare cases, a fast base runner may steal home by himself. The batter takes the pitch.

HOW DOES A BATTER EXECUTE THE TAKE SIGN?

First, the batter sees the take sign given by the coach. He steps into the batter's box and takes his practice swings. The batter must give every indication that he intends to swing. He does not stand there and silently watch the ball whistle by into the catcher's glove. Instead, he takes a stride. He then brings the bat around halfway. This fakes out the opposing team. If there is a man on base, and if he is stealing, the batter's fake half-swing and stride into the ball could possibly cause the catcher to drop the ball, or it could cause him to slow up his throw to the base or make an inaccurate throw.

If the batter stands and is motionless on taking a pitch, he gives the catcher full view of the field and does not assist his runner at all.

SIGNALS

The secret language of baseball is signals, and no team gets very far without them. If a team is to win, a simple but effective system of communications must be set up. Flashing his signals from the bench or from the coaching lines, the manager or head coach can coordinate individual efforts into team action.

The signals flashed to the batter are certainly one of the two most important types of body language exhibited in a ball game, along with the signals that a catcher will give to his pitcher.

The signs given to a batter are more often than not flashed by the third-base coach, rather than the first-base coach, whose function and signal-giving assignments will be discussed later. Everyone knows how important the signs of the third-base coach to the batter happen to be. That includes the defense, who will often be trying to steal those signals by either breaking down the code in its entirety or by at least anticipating a particular play coming up as a result of a poor cover-up by either the coach or batter.

The degree of complexity with which the signals are given varies from team to team and also depends upon the level of ball being played. In the major leagues, for instance, Willie

Mays explains what we might see: "The third-base coach might hitch up his pants, stamp his feet, twist his cap, then touch his belt buckle, clap his hands, and keep right on going by wiping his fingers across his chest, kicking the dirt with his left foot, and so on. The player at the plate, who has stepped out after each pitch to look at what the coach is doing, knows how to pick out the sign from all the rest of the fooling around."

On the other hand, some feel that this is a bit too much. College coach Joe Russo states: "Keep the signals simple. Concealment isn't as important as having your players pick them up quickly and accurately."

On the high school level, Coach Cliff Petrak distributes to his players a sheet of 32 signals, of which 23 are of the offensive variety, which means that he might be flashing as many as 23 different signals to batters and base runners from his place at the coach's position at third base. Eight of those signals call for eight different alternative strategies to impose when their team has runners on first and third bases.

Mickey McConnell, Director of Training for Little League baseball, believes in simple signals for the younger players: "Some players tip off the signs by looking away the moment they read the signal.

The player should keep his eyes on the coach for several moments after the sign has been flashed, and the coach should continue to give dummy signals to avoid detection. Signals and signs should be held to a minimum with young players. Don't confuse or overburden them with wigwagging that would startle the Signal Corps."

On most college ball clubs and, certainly, with the major league teams, the signs are, indeed, many and do require serious study and concentration by the players. Fans at major league games would also do well to watch the manager, usually seated or standing near one end of the dugout, for it is he who normally calls the shots. To do so, he must also have a separate set of signals worked out with his third base coach. In other words, the third base coach is only the middleman.

While the actual meaning of each of the signs given to the batter from the third base coach is beyond the scope of this book, the manner in which the sign is communicated is within its scope.

TYPES OF SIGNALS

The most common types of signals given by a coach or manager are: flash signals, holding signals, block signals, combination signals, rub-off signals, and word signals.

Flash Signals

Flashing signs is a common method used to make them harder to detect. Actually, they are just what the name implies. They are "flashed" to the players through a particular act. *While they are fine for the more experienced player, they are not recommended for players in the junior circuits.*

The value of flash signals is that they can be given quickly. By mixing them in with other movements, the coach can camouflage his signals. However, the player may miss the signals, since the coach has to give them quickly. He can give the flash sign in one quick motion. He may touch his face for a bunt, click a hand across his uniform chest for the take, or touch his leg for a hit-and-run. However, unless these signs are immediately preceded by the indicator signal, such as touching the belt buckle, the sign means nothing. Therefore, for the opposition to steal the signals, they would first have to determine what the indicator signal was.

Holding Signals

Holding signals are those which are held for several seconds and are ideal for younger players. The clenched fist, the bent elbow, or the hands on the knees are all examples of the holding type of signal. If the coach took off his cap for a few moments, he would be giving a holding sign.

The third base coach might assume a natural, relaxed position of his hands on the knees, which could be his bunt sign of the day. However, he had better give decoys before and after. He can make the hands-on-knees sign even more difficult to intercept by instructing his players to ignore the sign unless his thumbs are widely extended from the fingers.

The holding sign is the simplest for the player to get because it is held long enough for the message to sink in. A player can look more than once if he is in doubt about the signal.

The disadvantage of such a signal is that the sign is held for so long that the opposition may catch on to it. If the coach feels he is being closely watched by the opposition, he may have the player next to him send the signals to the players.

Block Signals

Signals that use different parts of the coach's body, or divide his body into blocks or sections, are called block signals. The coach can go from the head down to his shirt or arm. He can go clockwise, dividing his body into four parts. Or he can go up and down.

The bunt sign could be touching the face; hit-and-run, the letters of the shirt; the steal, the belt; and so on. Or the coach could give the hitting signs on one side of his body and the running signs on the other side.

Touching the cap, head, or face could be used for the first three hitters in the lineup, rubbing the shirt could be used for the next three hitters, while rubbing the pants could affect the last three.

The signal is sometimes determined by the number of rubs. For instance, the take sign could be one rub, and the bunt two rubs. If he rubs his shirt once or twice while the first three batters are up, this would mean nothing, since the shirt signals apply only to the fourth, fifth, and sixth hitters.

Regardless of the age level or the experience of the players, block signals are good to use.

This system does have a disadvantage in that, occasionally, the coach has trouble remembering the numerical position of the players in the lineup.

Combination Signals

A combination sign is two or more motions tied together to represent a single sign. Quite often, one of these motions or acts is the key sign. The key signal, for example, might be covering the belt buckle with the hand. This by itself means nothing. The steal sign which is touching the cap, also means nothing by itself. However when the cap is touched and the belt buckle is covered, the steal is on.

The coach could have a set of signs starting with the cap, face, shirt, and pants, which can be one, two, three, and four. He will tell his players: "I am going to give you a certain number of rubs, and any time I hit one of those spots, it counts."

Combination signals can also be used for the hit-and-run, bunt, and squeeze plays. Although a different sign is used for each, the same key sign can be used.

Rub-off Signals

A rub-off signal is a last-instant order used by the manager to cancel previous signs. Every team should have a rub-off sign that, when flashed, takes everything off. As an example, I have given the hit-and-run signal. However, I might reconsider because I feel a pitchout could be coming up. Changing my mind, I will give a rub-off signal, which takes the play off.

Removing the cap is commonly used as a rub-off signal, since it is easy for the players to catch.

Word Signals

Although word signals have some merit, they have a disadvantage in that the noise of the crowd will sometimes prevent the third base coach from hearing them distinctly. Word signals can be associated with the action desired. They are sometimes used for the base runner on third when the squeeze is on.

Main Signs Given to Hitters	
Take	Various bunts
Hit away	Fake bunt and steal
Run-and-hit	Fake bunt and slash
Hit-and-run	Bunt-and-run

Main Signs Given to Runners	
Steals on the pitch	Fake steal
Steals before the pitch	Fake bunt and steal
Delayed steals	Fake bunt and slash
Run-and-hit	Double steals
Hit-and-run	Green light ("You decide")

GIVING SIGNALS

Baseball signals are taken either directly from the head coach or from the manager on the bench, or are relayed to the coach on the coaching lines. Most major league managers prefer to stay in the dugout while their lieutenants handle the duties on the coaching lines.

Whatever arrangement is used, the system should not be awkward to the hitter at the plate. With the head coach in the dugout on the third base side, right-handed hitters will have to turn around constantly to look for the signs, unless they are relayed to a coach on the baselines.

If the team at bat is occupying the dugout on the first base side of the diamond and the head coach is on the bench, right-handed hitters might take their signals directly from him. The hitter can take an occasional glance at the coach as he approaches the batter's box or as he steps into the box. Left-handed batters can take their signs from the coach in the third base coaching box. The head coach should give this coach the signal in plenty of time so he can relay it to the hitter.

When the team occupies the third base dugout, left-handed batters get their signals directly from this coach, and right-handed batters from the first base coach.

Indicator System

Major league teams place considerable emphasis on the indicator system, using combination signs. In simpler terms, a specific key sign determines whether the signal is off or on. A coach may give any signal he wishes, but it does not mean a thing unless he has given an indicator sign first.

I like the indicator because it enables a lot of faking. If I do not give the indicator, nothing happens. If I give the indicator, the next thing I touch is usually the sign I want to give.

Let us assume the indicator is a clap of the hands. The coach can touch any part of his body, but he is not giving a signal. However, if he claps his hands and then adjusts the peak of his cap, the take sign is on.

The position of the coach in the coach's box may also be used as an indicator. If the coach is standing at the far end of the box the signs are off, but if he is standing at the end nearest the hitter the signs are on. This procedure can also be used in reverse, of course. There are various ways to convey the signs to the coaches, as well as for the coaches to relay them to the batters and base runners. Any signs are workable if they are disguised. This is particularly true concerning signals given from the coaching lines, since the coach is in open view and, therefore, a target for sign stealers on the opposing team. All signs are related to the coming pitch and are usually given after each pitch so that the coach may change his strategy to meet a different count on the batter, an advancement of a runner because of a wild pitch, or the failure of a batter to bunt the ball in fair territory. However, the sign may remain the same for the next pitch or for several pitches. In this case, the rubbing of the uniform in a certain manner is often used to cancel the sign. It may also be necessary to take the signal off if the opposing team anticipates a steal.

Signals from the Bench: Signals from the bench usually involve one hand, which simplifies the work of the coach. The following set of signs shows how the manager or coach may relay the various signals to the base coaches:

- Touching the letter on the cap—take
- Touching the face with the right hand—bunt
- Touching the letters on the uniform with the right hand—steal
- Touching the peak of the cap with the right hand—hit-and-run
- Touching the cap with two hands—squeeze play
- Folding the arms—delayed steal

Signals from the Coaching Lines: The previous set of signals could be used on the baseline, but the base coach will need to disguise his signals, since he is in open view and a target for sign stealers. There are innumerable gestures that can be used, but the simplest combination is the key series. The set of signals below shows this series:

- Touching the face with the right hand—key sign
- Right hand to cap—sacrifice
- Right hand to letters on uniform—steal
- Right hand on belt buckle—take
- Right hand on pants hit-and-run
- Right hand to letters on cap—squeeze play
- Both hands on letters of uniform—wipeoff

Receiving Signals

The correct execution of signals demands that the players look at the coach or manager at the right times. The proper times for the batter to look for the signals are when he is approaching the plate before entering the batter's box and just after each pitch thrown to him while he is at bat.

The hitter can take the signals either in the box or out of it. However, base runners should take the signals while standing on the base.

If the batter is doubtful about a sign, he should ask the umpire for time, step out of the batter's box, and take another look. I would rather have my hitter sure that he has not missed the sign. He can act as though he is tying his shoelaces. Then he can take another look at his coach, who will either give the sign again or give him the rub-off.

On the squeeze play, which is a surprise tactic, the coach might take the play off if he thinks the hitter has tipped the play.

POINTS TO REMEMBER AS BASE COACHES

The base coaches have a strong influence on the actions of the base runners, and they should keep in mind the following specific responsibilities that can help in this respect:

- *Do not allow the runner to take his lead until the ball is located.*

- Advise the runner of the number of outs and the game situation.

- Advise the runner to take his lead while the pitcher is getting his signs.

- Remind the runner of the pitcher's move to first base.

- Watch for predictable rhythm in the pitcher's motion and inform the runner if a cadence can be "counted."

- *Watch the first baseman when he is playing back of the runner.*

- Watch the second baseman in a sacrifice situation; he may sneak in behind the runner for a pickoff throw.

- Advise the runners what to do on fly balls and line drives.

- Alert the runner on second if a fielder sneaks behind him.

- Know the strengths and weaknesses of your opponent.

- *Inform the runner whether to take a chance or play it safe.*

- Remind the runner at second to make the ball go through on the left side of the infield before advancing if there are fewer than two outs.

- Remind the runner to go full speed if there is a chance he may be forced.

- Inform the runner as he rounds third if he should run hard or take his time.

- Concentrate on other base runners after the runner passes the third base coach.

- Alert the runner if there is a possible play on him as he takes his turn at third.

- Inform the runners if they should go on a ground ball or only on a ball through the infield.

- *Remind the runner at third to stay outside the baseline while taking his lead and be alert for passed balls.*

- *Inform the runner whether he should try to advance or bluff a break for the next base on foul fly balls.*

DUTIES OF BASE COACHES

The coaches at first and third bases can play an important role in the success of any team. *Essentially, their primary duties are giving signals and assisting base runners.* Therefore, they must be constantly alert and be the type of individuals who can remain calm and make the right decisions even when the action gets hectic.

The baseline coaches must be proficient at relaying signs from the bench coach to the hitters.

The First Base Coach

- Ask the runner the score. Correct him if he is wrong. He must know the score.

- Ask the runner the inning. *The inning of the game must be known. This, along with the score, will determine how he runs on certain play situations.*

- Ask the runner the number of outs. *A runner who doesn't know the number of outs is dangerous to himself and his team.* Knowing the number of outs is *so* important.

- Say, "You have to go on a grounder."

- Say, "Go way down on a deep fly" and "Go one third of the way on a short fly."

- If ahead by a few runs, say, "I want you on third base on a single." *He should be daring but sensible.*

- If there are two outs, yell, *"You have to go on anything hit."*

- The last thing to say before the pitch is, *"Break up the double play."* This is the last thing he hears before he runs.

If the count is three and two, with two outs, remind him that *he must go on the pitch, and to watch for a pickoff on all bases!*

Of course, the first base coach is also helping the first base runner get the sign. Both first base coach and first base runner must know the sign and the play coming up.

In a close ball game, the first base coach must be sure to remind the first base runner whether he represents the tying or the winning run. Always tell him that when he arrives at first base. This will determine how he runs from there on.

The first base coach can have a mechanical counter in his hand. With this he may keep the count—*and he must always remind the runner of the count after each pitch.*

A first base coach must always be alert for a pickoff from the catcher or pitcher. Yell very loudly, *"Get back"* or *"Dive"* on each pickoff try. Remind the runner not to be leaning toward the next base. *The first base coach also reminds the first base runner on which pitches the pickoff may be attempted.*

The first base coach must be always prodding the runner to get the maximum lead, small enough that the runner can get back safely, but if the ball is hit, long enough to get a good "break." *Each runner should know what his maximum lead is.* In high school baseball, it can be fourteen feet for extremely fast runners.

Always call a timeout if the runner and coach don't understand each other. Have a conference before resuming play. Go talk to the runner. Get it cleared up.

Very important: First base coach and runner—first find out who has the baseball!

The foregoing seems like a lot to do for each runner. But baseball is a slow game, and, believe it or not, each of those points mentioned can be rattled off and understood before the runner goes on the next hit. I have been doing this for over thirty years and have had no trouble at all, *if the runner was attentive.*

The minute the runner leaves first base and heads for second base, the only help you can give him on a hit ball is:

- Yell "Slide" if a grounder is hit to an infielder.

- Yell "Break up the double play" on a grounder.

- Yell "Get back, get back" if he foolishly goes on a fly and forgets the number of outs.

- *Be sure he comes back and tags first either on foul balls or after a fly is caught.* This is the responsibility of the first base coach.

When a double, triple, home run, or deep fly have been hit, and the runner is steaming around first base a mile a minute, your responsibility is to do these things:

- Yell "Take two, take two" if it is a sure double.

- Yell "Go for three, go for three" if it is a sure triple.

- If he hit a home run, yell "Don't loaf, hustle, get going."

- *Make sure he hits the base.* Watch his foot touch—in case of an appeal play at the bag.

Finally, once a player reaches second base and rounds that base headed for third, *he is no longer the first base coach's "property." The third base coach takes over there.*

The coach at first base gives encouragement to the hitter, and once the ball is hit he helps the batter-runner any way he can. If there is an error on the throw, the coach will instruct the runner to go to second or stop. If the ball is hit to the outfield, he will move to the front of the box and point toward second and yell "Make your turn!" or "Go for two!" He might wave his arm in a circle in addition to yelling for the runner to go to second. If he is sure the runner cannot advance, he should yell "Hold up!"

If the first baseman is playing behind the runner, the coach has to face the first baseman and let his runner know when to get back. He should warn the runner to be careful if the pitcher has a good move. A constant chatter will help the runner become more familiar with the coach's voice.

Most of the duties of the first base coach involve verbal communication. However, there are some exceptions. *When the batter unknowingly hits the ball foul and begins toward first, the first base coach holds both arms up so as to let him know that he should stop and return to home plate.* Also, on a hit to the outfield when the coach definitely feels that the runner should try for second or third, the first base coach, located near the baseline and as close to the outfield side of the coach's box as possible, waves his right arm in a large clockwise circle to indicate that the runner should go on to second. When a batter hits a grounder, he, of course, runs as fast as possible toward first and beyond as he tries to beat the ball to the first baseman. *However, when the fielder to whom the ball is hit lets the ball get by him, it becomes the duty of the first base coach to point the runner around the base.* That is, he indicates to the batter-runner that it is safe for him to round the base and to pick up the location of the ball from there.

With the ball having been hit to an infielder or outfielder and the runner coming down the line toward first, the first base coach will react in one of three ways. First, he may respond with an arm signal indicating that the runner should definitely continue to second base. Second, he may give an arm signal indicating that the runner should take a turn and pick up sight of the ball. In this situation, the runner is on his own to determine if he can take another base. Third, there may be no signal given at all, indicating that the runner should run through the base at his maximum speed.

There are special situations for which the runner must be his own coach and can't expect help from the first base coach:

- As mentioned earlier, on wild infield throws high and to the home plate side of first base, the decision of the runner to slide to avoid a tag must be his own.

- Following a hard bunt down the first base line in a sacrifice situation, the runner should slow down or even stop or back up to prevent a possible double play. In this way, more time is given to the advancing runner while the pitcher or first baseman tries to apply a tag on the batter-runner.

- On a bunt or topped ball fielded near the first base line, the batter must remember to observe the forty-five-foot line without the help of the coach.

- On what appears to be a first-baseman-to-pitcher ground out, the runner should remember that contact with the pitcher in the base path (before the pitcher has the ball) could result in an obstruction call benefiting the batter-runner. No hard contact is necessary, just a bump will do.

The Third Base Coach

The third base coach is not more important than the first base coach, for he doesn't get as many men over on third base to coach. But his duties are rather different from those of the first base coach. They are:

- Ask the runner quickly to review the score, inning, outs.

- *Make sure the runner tells him those three.*

- Remind the runner how to run the third base line—*on every pitch*. "Go down, foul. Come back, fair."

- Tell him *"Tag up* on a long fly—then *go* home."

- Tell him *"Tag up* on a medium fly—maybe *go."*

- Tell him "Stay on third base after a short fly."

- Tell him "Go home on a real slow grounder."

- Tell him "Stay at third base on a hard grounder."

- If bases are loaded yell "Gotta go on a grounder."

- If bases are loaded and the count is three and two, yell ''Gotta go on the pitch."

- Always remind "Watch passed ball;" or "Wild pitch."

- Always remind "Watch catcher pickoff. Get back!"

- Assist the third base runner on first base/third base trick plays. Step him off the base if he doesn't feel he's sure, and the two of you talk about it.

- Assist him with the suicide squeeze play. Tell him "Go!" after the pitcher has committed to the plate.

- Remind him of good outfielders' arms.

- Tell him "The hit has to go through"—before he goes home.

- Be sure to yell "Tag up"—then *"Now"* for his break—on all outfield fly balls hit.

- *Be sure the runner goes down the line toward home in foul territory and retreats back to third base in fair territory every time.*

Another important duty of the third base coach is to watch the shortstop and the second baseman to prevent a runner on second from being picked off the base. If both the shortstop and the second baseman play in their regular positions, the coach continually calls "All right." However, *if either of them moves toward the base, he yells "Get back."* The base runner at second should concentrate solely on the pitcher, while the coach watches both of the infielders.

On fly balls, the third base coach follows the same rules as the first base coach.

The coach at third base takes over the guiding of a base runner after he passes first base, particularly when the ball is behind the runner. Actually, the only guidance needed from the coach is on a ball hit down the right field line. If the ball is hit in front of him, the runner himself should make the decision.

When the ball is hit down the right field line, the ball is behind the runner, and we do not like our runners to turn around and look at that ball while running. Rather, he should look over to the third base coach to see whether he should come to third or stay at second. Some coaches instruct base runners to look at the coach when they are about twenty feet from second base.

If he wants the runner to round third base, the coach should move down the line toward home plate fifteen feet or more. If he wants to stop him at third, the coach has to be where the runner can see him. He can motion by signs: "Stay," "Hold up," or "Stay on the base."

If the runner is coming from second base and it is questionable whether or not he can score, the coach should go down the line where the runner can definitely see him. In this situation, we instruct our runners "You run until the coach stops you." Now, we would not have the coach down the line if we did not want the runner to round the bag. Therefore, it is necessary for the runner to keep running until he is stopped. This gives the coach a little more time to make up his mind whether this man can score or not. As he rounds third base, the runner can see the coach say either "Get back!" or "Come on!" although most of this is communicated by waving the hand or by arm motion, rather than by mouth.

The runner should not be reminded how the infield is playing, or to tag up on all fly balls. The coach might tell the runner to go home only if the ball goes through the infield, or to try to score on an infield ground ball.

On a ball hit behind the runner, help must be received from the third base coach. With about a third of the way still to go toward second, the runner picks up sight of the coach. The coach's arm signals will be the same as those used with a runner coming into third. Waving his arms in a circular motion indicates that he wants the runner to continue to third. Both arms held overhead indicates that the runner should round the bag and pick up sight of the ball, but should not attempt to advance beyond that point unless some miscue arises. One arm overhead and the other pointing at the bag differs only in that the runner should stop on the bag without rounding it. This is because it appears to the coach that a throw is about to be made to second by the outfielder handling the ball. *A pop-up slide is best used here to prevent the runner from overrunning the base.*

The coach will also be giving verbal directions. However, even when the coach has signaled the runner to advance to third, he may occasionally see reason to change his mind. For that reason, it's important that the runner pick up sight of the coach a second time, just after having rounded second.

The runner is on his own whenever the ball is hit in front of him. Just how daring he should be in this situation depends on a number of factors, most important of which are the number of outs, the importance of his run, and the hitter coming to the plate.

Another important set of signals given by the third base coach are those given to a runner approaching third base. When the coach wishes the runner to continue home, the usual signal consists of several large clockwise circles made with the right arm. With a close play, the coach will indicate that the runner slide by projecting both arms downward toward the base. If an advantage exists in sliding toward one side of the base or the other, the coach will definitely point his arms to that side of the base. If the coach wishes the runner to stop at third without a slide, he will raise both his arms toward the sky. The runner in this situation is allowed to take a short turn of the base, but is not to go any farther unless the play is muffed. Finally, if a throw is coming in to third, but the runner is sure to arrive before the throw, the coach will raise his right arm, but will point to the base with his left arm. This indicates that the runner is not only to stop at third, he is not to round the base at all.

HOW TO SCORE A RUN AHEAD OF THE LAST OUT OF AN INNING (A LESSON IN HUSTLE)

This is a true story about a very good coach and a very good team in the year 1958. The club was coached by Dick Bundy and was a "pony grad"-level team of all-star players in the city of San Bernardino, California. (Later that same summer, this team represented the state of California at the National Championship Playoffs in Springfield, Illinois. They took second place in the nation; in the final game, they were beaten by a team from Miami, Florida.)

The particular game that I am about to relate to you occurred in late July at the Perris Hill Ballpark in San Bernardino. I was the head coach at nearby Pacific High School, and I wanted to observe the play of my third baseman, Fred Pettengill, who was one of the leading hitters on the pony grad team. They were to begin the playoffs that evening for the right to go to the state playoffs.

I got to the ballpark during the second inning of a seven-inning scheduled game. San Bernardino batter hit a double down the left field line. It was a fair hit, and the man on second base hustled hard to third base, *but then, seeing that he had home made easily, he slowed down to a trot and turned back to the outfield as he headed toward home*. As he trotted the last half of the distance from third base to home plate, this is what was going on on the fields. The first base runner was on the move very fast after the base hit, and he rounded second and made it to third easily. The left fielder, seeing that, threw the ball very well to the second baseman. The man who hit the ball should have had a double, *the leftfielder's throw nailed him by half a step*. That was the third out, and the inning was over. The loafing runner who had started at second base on the hit was half a step from home plate when the sliding hitter was tagged at second base. His run did not count. His lack of hustle caused his team a run.

A few innings later, the same situation occurred. There were two outs again. Men were on first and third in this case. The coach gave the double delayed steal sign. While the pitcher was coming down to the set position in his stretch, the first base runner broke for second base, but he stopped halfway to the base to "get into a pickle." The pitcher stepped off the mound and threw to the second baseman. He started a rundown on the trapped runner with the first baseman. *They completely ignored the third base runner as he broke for home.*

Then he slowed down when he saw that they were going after the other runner. After two quick tosses, the second baseman tagged out the first base runner. *That was the third out, and the inning was over.* When the "last out tag" was made on that runner, again, the loafing runner was half a step from touching home plate. The umpire declared that the run did not score.

To make matters even worse, the other team won that gam 5-4, and the San Bernardino team had lost two sure runs because the lead runner failed to put all out and run hard all the way to home plate.

Baseball is a strange game. You may be about to step on home plate, but many odd things might be happening farther back on the base paths to other runners. These can affect your potential run greatly. The moral of this story is to *hustle at all times* in the game of baseball. (Also, lightning can strike twice in the same place.)

HOW TO RUN BASES ON A POP-UP TO THE DEEP SCREEN

This is the play that Pee Wee Reese tried in a World Series in the 1950s. Pee Wee was on first base, running for the Brooklyn Dodgers, Yogi Berra was the New York Yankee catcher.

The next Brooklyn batter lifted a high pop-up deep behind the plate. Yogi ripped off his mask and *turned his back to home plate.* He caught the ball inches from the screen in front of the press box. That was out number one. The screen was 120 feet from home plate, making a throw to second base for Yogi a total of 248 feet. Yogi turned toward second base and fired a perfect strike to the shortstop, who was covering second base. Pee Wee *had decided to try for second base after the pop-up was caught.* He was fast, so the race was almost a tie. But Yogi's throw out got there a split second before Pee Wee arrived. That was out number two. A nice way to execute a double play, eh?

The moral of the story is: Do not try this trick unless you are very fast, you have tagged up, the screen is major league distance (120 feet), and the catcher has a rather poor arm. *Don't try it from second base, because the catcher has a shorter throw to third base.*

OFFENSIVE APPEAL PLAYS

Appeal plays are requested by the offense only in the case of an error in the interpretation of rules-not on judgment calls.

If the umpire refuses to reverse a decision on the basis of your appeal and you are certain a rule has been misinterpreted, you may, at that point, announce to the umpire that you are playing the game "under protest." After the game is over, and you are the loser, you may appeal the call to the chief of umpires in the area or to the league officials. They will study the appeal request, and if you are allowed the decision, the game will be played over from that point of play. (If you win the game, go to the umpire after the game and declare that you are withdrawing the protest.)

THE "HIDDEN BALL TRICK"

The "hidden ball trick" is as old as the hills. In years past, it was a favorite trick to get a ball club out of a jam and cut an offensive rally short. Look for it when your club is having a big inning.

Some Little Leagues on up to high school leagues forbid the use of this play.

Here are runners' rules for coping with the "hidden ball trick":

- As soon as you hit a ball or are awarded first, have rounded the bag, and are now safely on the base—*the first thing you do is locate the ball*. Don't step off any base until you actually see the white of that baseball. Don't guess that the pitcher has it in his glove.

- If you don't see the ball, ask the first base coach, "Who has the ball?" If he says that a certain player has it in his glove, look for it there—fast.

- Remember—the pitcher does not have to have the ball in his *hand unless he is in "the immediate mound area."* He can be at the base of the mound, or he can be positioned as though he were ready to climb up to the rubber. Watch out!

- When will a team pull the "hidden ball trick"? Usually just as a rally is getting started, like bases loaded, no outs, two runs have scored quickly. The offensive team is having so much fun hitting it might let its guard down. Don't be careless!

- The defensive team will also pull the "hidden ball trick" when it is behind, the game is in the late innings, and they are desperate.

- This trick may be pulled on you at any time in any game. *Beware!*

- Don't forget—while you are looking around the diamond for the "missing baseball," *make sure you are standing on the base.*

Chapter 3

DEFENSIVE PLAYS AND SIGNS

This chapter was possibly as difficult to assemble as any in baseball literature. The author researched defenses in the game with the assistance of Coach Jim McGarry of the San Bernardino Unified School District in San Bernardino, California. Thanks to Jim we were able to assemble over fifty defensive plays and their signals for execution, giving each of these a double check for content and accuracy.

A big salute to Coach Jim McGarry for his knowledge and assistance.

DEFENSIVE BASEBALL SIGNS

The author has attempted to gather all the information possible on this topic and organize it in an informative and interesting manner. The majority of the defensive signs used in the higher levels of baseball are not obvious to the average fan. College and pro teams use many of them—many more than teams at the high school level and below.

In this chapter defensive signs are broken down into categories of the orthodox, or the "usual signs" that we know are used daily, and the very unorthodox, the real tricky defensive moves that are based on the element of surprise and are rarely tried during a game. (These last are the most fun of all—if you can make them work at the right moment.)

Everyone, I suppose, knows that the catcher gives the pitcher the sign for the next pitch. (Many people do not realize that it might be the pitcher who is actually giving the catcher the sign in some strange way.) Beyond that, the remainder of defensive communication becomes very complicated, and the general public knows little of it.

On the following pages each defensive play has been carefully explained by title, by who originates and who receives the sign or gesture, and by when this play is used and for what purpose.

It would certainly be an idealized statement to say that the author was able to dig out all of the tricks used in the history of the game, but it is his hope that the serious fan and the student of the game will enjoy this collection of defensive plays.

PLAY 1:   COACHES ON THE BENCH, CALLING THE PITCHES

Who gives the sign?

Coach from the bench, usually.

Who receives the sign?

Pitcher, or catcher, or both at the same time. Catcher relays it to pitcher with hand or finger signs, even if he has seen it, then catcher's signs are merely a decoy or a reenforcement.

What is the purpose of this play?

Either the coach does not trust the judgment of his catcher or may have a scouting report on each hitter in front of him.

When should this play be used?

Some coaches call every pitch of every game. At times some coaches allow the catchers to call some of the pitches.

Explanation of the timing of the play.

Coach decides, immediately, after the previous pitch, what the next pitch should be to that batter. He will touch a part of his body, signaling each type of pitch he wants. Another method used is that shortstop gets signs for each pitch and its location from the coach on the bench. This prevents either the pitcher or the catcher from having to stare in or turn around. Shortstop then relays them quickly to catcher, who then gives the usual set of signs to pitcher.

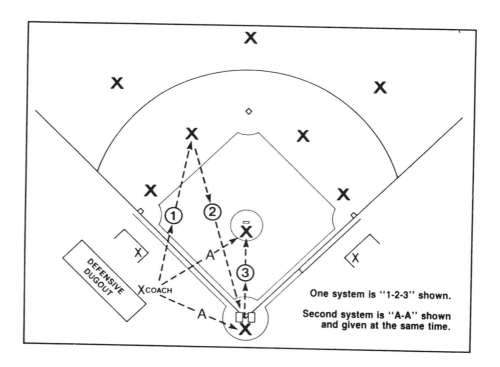

PLAY 2: CATCHER TO PITCHER, CALLING THE PITCHES

Who gives the sign?

Catcher gives the signs with fingers or hand, usually, while in the squat position, with legs closed somewhat to first base and third base coaches.

Who receives the sign?

Pitcher receives the sign before each pitch. He looks in, gets the sign, and pitches, or he looks in, gets the sign, and asks for a repeat sign, or he looks in, gets the sign, shakes it off, and asks for another.

What is the purpose of this play?

Pitcher-catcher communication only. They both know what will be pitched and are set for it. They will not cross each other up.

When should this play be used?

Whenever coach gives the catcher full responsibility for calling every pitch. Coach still might signal the catcher and throw in his sign for a pitch occasionally.

Explanation of the timing of the play.

Catcher squats into sign-giving position, gives sign, and makes certain pitcher understands it. If not, the catcher calls time out and goes out to the mound and gets the signals straightened out with the pitcher. Catcher gives sign again verifying what has been said. Pitcher gets the sign correctly, and he pitches.

Pitcher must have a shakeoff sign with the catcher. Pitcher must also have a decoy shakeoff sign, to cross up the batter's guessing of the next pitch.

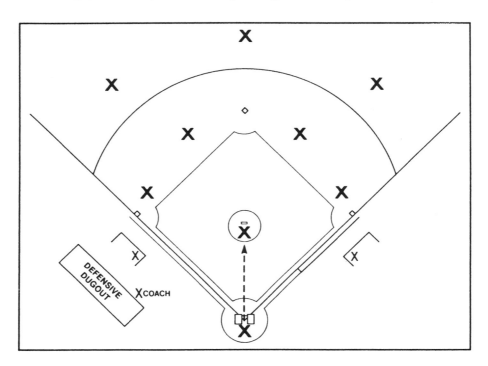

PLAY 3:   PITCHER TO CATCHER, CALLING THE PITCHES

Who gives the sign?

The previous situation is reversed. Now the pitcher is giving all of the signs. Catcher is receiving the signs by some signals.

Who receives the sign?

Only the catcher receives the pitcher's signs.

What is the purpose of this play?

This play is used to confuse the defense, which is really trying to steal the signs from coach, catcher, etc. This play also gives pitcher his choice of pitches, if he knows his batters well. Pitcher may be smarter than catcher.

When should this play be used?

Use this system when pitcher is poised, in charge, and confident that he knows his hitters. Use when the catcher is definitely an inferior one. Use if pitcher has scouted the hitters but catcher hasn't.

Explanation of the timing of the play.

Catcher squats in his regular sign-giving position. Pitcher touches part of his body with the glove or the ball, to indicate which pitch to the catcher. Catcher then squats down and takes the time to give some false finger or hand signs. Pitcher may nod "Yes" or shake it off, then catcher gives fake signs again. It's all decoy.

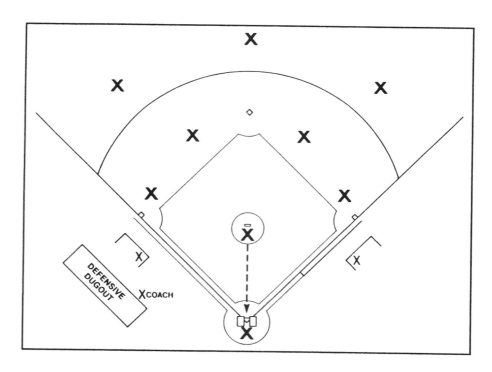

PLAY 4:   CATCHER TO INFIELDERS, RELAYING THE CALLED PITCH

Who gives the sign?

Catcher (or the pitcher) can give this sign to each of the four infielders watching the sign giver.

Who receives the sign?

It is only for the four infielders.

What is the purpose of this play?

To let each infielder know the type of pitch next being thrown to that hitter. This is a good indicator of how and where they can expect the ball to be hit.

When should this play be used?

On each and every pitch of the game. Why not? It's easy to give, easy to pick up. This set of signs gives the defense a tremendous advantage over the hitter and runners.

Explanation of the timing of the play.

Just after the catcher has given the sign to the pitcher. The catcher can use a glove or hand signal to the four infielders to indicate type of pitch. The pitcher may use his glove or the ball on his body to indicate type of pitch. Additional signs to the infielders can be given to indicate the location of the pitch as well.

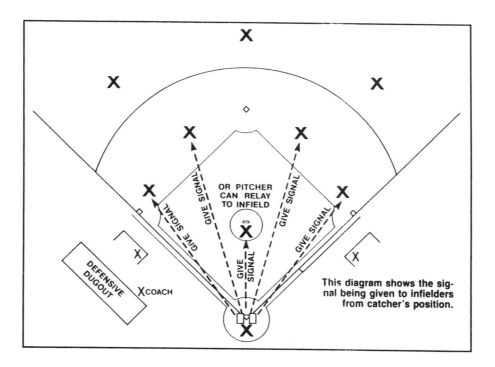

This diagram shows the signal being given to infielders from catcher's position.

PLAY 5:   INFIELD TO OUTFIELDERS, RELAYING THE CALLED PITCH

Who gives the sign?

Usually a designated infielder or one infielder on each side. Shortstop could relay easily to all three outfielders the pitch call catcher has just signaled to him.

Who receives the sign?

All three of the outfielders watch for the same sign from shortstop prior to the pitch. This allows them to adjust their positions to where the ball probably will be hit.

What is the purpose of this play?

To let the outfielders know what pitch is to be thrown, giving them time to adjust to the pitch.

When should this play be used?

On every pitch during the game: Why not?

Explanation of the timing of the play.

Catcher has already given sign to all the infielders. One or two of the infielders then use a quick, easy-to-see body, hand, or glove sign to the outfield. All see it and it still gives infield time to get set for the next hit ball. Now all nine defensive players know what pitch is coming. Think of the great advantage over the batting team.

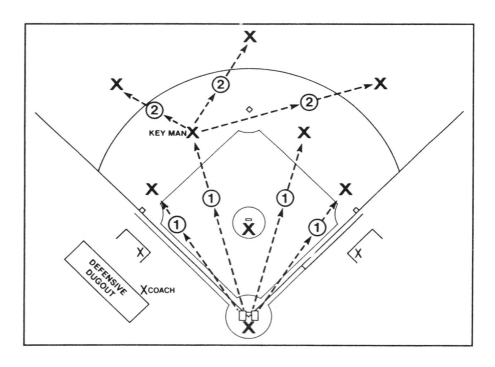

PLAY 6:   COACH'S SIGN FOR A PITCHOUT

Who gives the sign?
Coach gives the catcher the pitchout sign from the bench, particularly when the hitting team may be in a position to bunt, steal, or hit-and-run.

Who receives the sign?
Catcher and all other infielders must see this sign from the coach. If they do, the infielders will be able to cover their bases on a throw.

What is the purpose of this play?
To prevent the batter from hitting the ball at all. To prevent batter from assisting runner in any steal, bunting play, or the hit-and-run. It stops the squeeze or suicide squeeze play dead and gives the catcher a better throwdown.

When should this play be used?
Whenever the manager, coach, or catcher believes that a play is on in which catcher can throw out a runner going down. Also to prevent batter-runner combination plays. Whenever the squeeze plays are suspected.

Explanation of the timing of the play.
Catcher gets the pitchout sign. He squats to give the sign to the pitcher as he does on every pitch. Catcher steps away from the plate, on opposite side of the batter in the box, and receives the ball. He sees if runners are going on that pitch. If runners are going, catcher throws out one of the runners, usually the lead runner. If the runner is coming home, catcher drops down to block the plate and tags him, or he starts a rundown back toward third base if the runner is trapped.

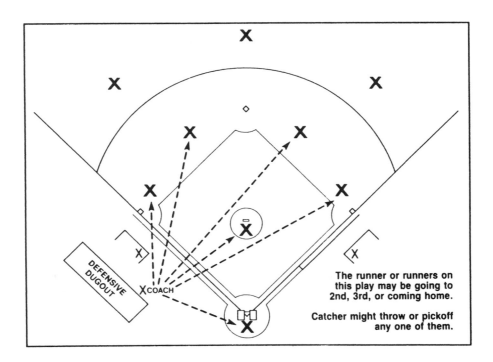

The runner or runners on this play may be going to 2nd, 3rd, or coming home.

Catcher might throw or pickoff any one of them.

PLAY 7:   INFIELDERS TO OUTFIELDERS, CALLING FLY BALLS

Who gives the sign?

On a fly ball to an infield-outfield combination, you want the outfielder to play the catch if possible. He is running into the diamond where he can see all of the base runners and has the whole infield in front of him.

Who receives the sign?

Outfielder yells "I got it, I got it." Infielder moves to the side, out of the outfielder's path, but he must keep his eye on the ball as it is caught, be alert to go after a dropped ball and make the next play quickly. Infielder yells "Take it, you take it."

What is the purpose of this play?

This play is practiced to prevent the fly ball from dropping untouched and to prevent serious injury to either player in case of collision. We want neither of these to happen.

When should this play be used?

This play is used any time that a high fly ball is too far beyond the infielder's normal range and would make it a difficult over-the shoulder throw for the infielder.

Explanation of the timing of the play.

The second the ball is hit, outfielder gets the quick jump on the ball. Infielder will not be able to break that quickly, so he may find the high fly ball hard to judge behind and to the side of him. If possible give the outfielder the catch as his momentum for throwing is toward the bases, he sees the diamond in front of him, and he can see all of the runners' positions.

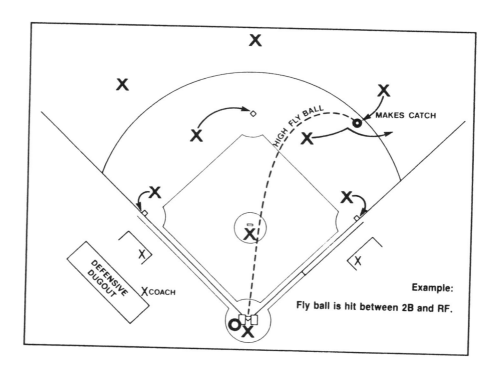

PLAY 8:   INFIELDERS TO INFIELDERS, CALLING FLY BALLS

Who gives the sign?

Infielder who is in the best position for the catch yells loudly, "I got it, I got it," waving arms outward away from the body to warn other fielders away from him.

Who receives the sign?

Other infielders who are in a position to catch the fly ball. They veer away from the one making the catch, yelling, "Take it, you take it."

What is the purpose of this play?

The play is practiced to prevent the fly ball from dropping untouched and to prevent serious injury to either player in case of collision.

When should this play be used?

The play is used any time a ball is hit so high and in such a position that several players feel they can make the play.

Explanation of the timing of the play.

The second the ball is hit, infielders get a quick jump toward the ball and the spot where the ball will drop. Who has the best position for a catch, without dropping the ball, calls for it. All other infielders run to cover all bases. (In any infield play, all bases must be covered in case of a necessary throw there.) The infielder closest to the man making the catch must be alert to field a dropped ball.

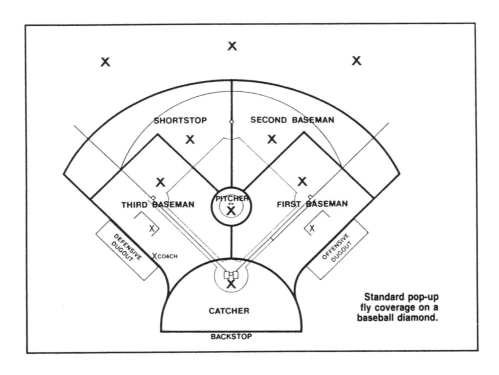

Standard pop-up
fly coverage on a
baseball diamond.

PLAY 9:   OUTFIELDERS TO OUTFIELDERS, CALLING FLY BALLS

Who gives the sign?

The outfielder who feels that he can catch the fly. A missed fly ball hit to the outfield can be most damaging to that team. If either of two outfielders can make the catch, the one with the greatest momentum toward the infield or the best arm calls for the fly.

Who receives the sign?

The outfielder who hears the other one yell, "I got it, I got it." He then yells loudly, "Take it, take it." If the fly is against the wall, the retreating man stays out in front to play a carom. Otherwise, he goes behind the man who catches the fly.

What is the purpose of this play?

To be certain that every fly ball is caught, if possible. To be sure someone backs up in case of an injury or missed fly or any kind of misplay. To keep the hitter from taking the extra base. To prevent serious injuries in the outfield from high-speed collisions.

When should this play be used?

Whenever a fairly deep fly is hit between positions in which outfielders had been set on the pitch. This routine must also be used whenever a long ball is hit that might go through to the wall. A quick retrieval is vital.

Explanation of the timing of the play.

Outfielders are taught to move back one step when the ball is hit if it is not certain how deep it will be. As the two fielders come toward each other, both with eyes on the ball, they do not see each other well. It is imperative that the player not making the catch move out of the way the earliest that he can. For this reason, the fielder who wants the fly must call early on the play. This gives the retreating fielder time to back up, and it will assure that there is not a collision.

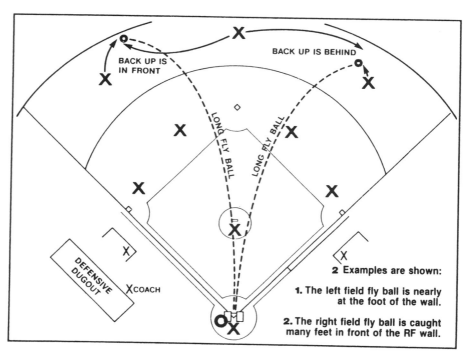

PLAY 10:   UNIVERSITY OF MIAMI'S FAMOUS "FAKE PITCHER PICKOFF PLAY" AT FIRST

Who gives the sign?

Coach in the dugout gives a very special oral or hand signal. The pitcher, shortstop, second baseman, and first baseman must all hear it or see it. Those on the bench must be alert, for they are in on this trick.

Who receives the sign?

Pitcher, catcher, first baseman, second baseman, and shortstop pick this sign up at the same time. All people not involved in the play directly must raise a real ruckus, lots of noise and distraction.

What is the purpose of this play?

To fool the first base coach and the first base runner. To make the first base runner dive into first, get up, dash to second. As the runner dives, he takes his eye off the ball, which is in the hands of the pitcher.

When should this play be used?

Not too often. It is based entirely on the element of surprise, good when the first base runner is a fast-reacting speed demon with quick reflexes. Can also be used when the defense is desperate to get an out.

Explanation of the timing of the play.

This is a very sneaky play based on a fake throw. Pitcher quick-fakes a pickoff throw to first baseman. First baseman quickly dashes out into foul territory, away from the base toward the stands. He looks as if he were chasing a wild pickoff throw. The second baseman and right fielder run out to that spot and converge. During all of this flurry of yelling and chasing, the pitcher has the ball hidden in his glove. Pitcher looks angry, stomping his foot as if he had made a wild throw to first base. As the alert first base runner gets up and dashes toward second, the first base coach may be yelling at him to get back. Too late. He cannot hear the coach. When runner gets within forty feet of second base, pitcher throws to shortstop at second base, and he tags runner coming in.

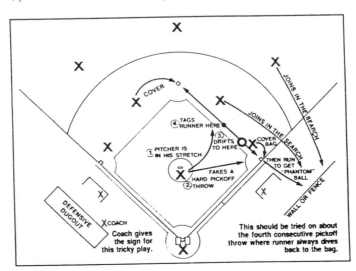

PLAY 11:   RIGHT-HANDED PITCHER, PICKOFF AT FIRST

Who gives the sign?

First baseman gives the sign. Pitcher acknowledges the sign, goes into his stretch, then looks at second base. First baseman breaks for the bag. Pitcher turns and throws.

Who receives the sign?

Pitcher will receive the sign if first baseman gives it. If the catcher or coach gives the sign, then the pitcher and first baseman get it and acknowledge it.

What is the timing of this play?

With the first baseman holding the runner on base, the pitcher *throws from one of three positions*: stretch, preset, or set. With the first baseman back in position, the pitcher, looking out of the corner of his eye, wheels and throws as first baseman breaks for the bag.

When should this play be used?

First baseman can be creeping in on a bunt play, suddenly break back to first base, and take pitcher's pickoff throw, as runner is way too far off. To hold first base runner to set up a double play on a grounder. On any fast runner who is a steal threat. Excellent time is two outs, full count on batter, and position runner must go. With runners at first and second.

Explanation of the timing of the play.

Catcher can give the sign to both the pitcher and first baseman, or first baseman can give it to the pitcher. Whether first baseman is playing on or off the bag, timing is such as to chase the runner back to first base. It is vital that first base runner not steal or get to second base on a hit ground ball. Must be constantly rehearsed between pitcher and catcher; all throws should be knee-high at the corner of the bag nearest the runner.

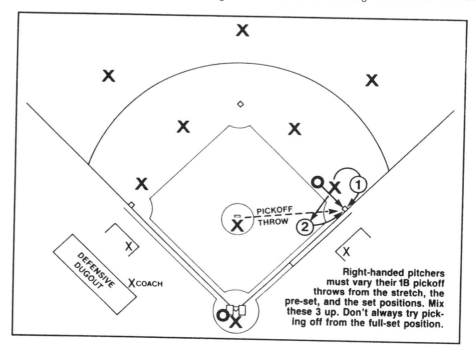

PICKOFF THROW

Right-handed pitchers must vary their 1B pickoff throws from the stretch, the pre-set, and the set positions. Mix these 3 up. Don't always try picking off from the full-set position.

DEFENSIVE DUGOUT   X COACH

PLAY 12: LEFT-HANDED PITCHER, PICKOFF AT FIRST

Who gives the sign?

First baseman can give the sign. Pitcher can acknowledge that sign. Left-hander goes into full set position, then uses the deceptive leg kick, eye, or head movement as runner leads off.

Who receives the sign?

Pitcher will receive the sign if first baseman gives it. If the catcher gives the sign, first baseman and pitcher both get it and acknowledge it.

What is the timing of this play?

With the first baseman holding the runner on first, pitcher throws from the full set position, which is the best position for the left-hander. From this he can use his deceptive moves. With the first baseman playing back of the bag, the pitcher, looking at second base out of the corner of his eye, sees the first baseman break for the bag. He then steps and throws.

When should this play be used?

To hold the first base runner, to set up the double play on a grounder, on any runner who is a steal threat. We don't want him in scoring position. Excellent time is two outs, full count on the batter, runner starting to go on the pitch. This is very effective in any bunting situation.

Explanation of the timing of the play.

Catcher can give a sign to both the pitcher and first baseman, or the first baseman can give it to the pitcher. Whether the first baseman is playing on or off the bag, the timing is such as to chase the runner back to the first base. It is vital that first base runner not steal or get to second base on a ground ball. Timing on this play must be rehearsed between pitchers and first basemen. All throws should be knee-high at the corner of the bag nearest the runner.

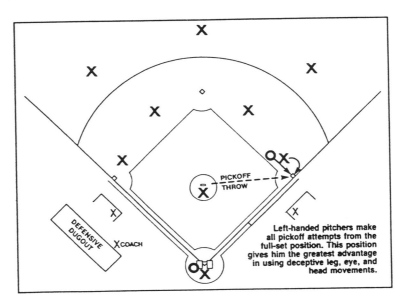

Left-handed pitchers make all pickoff attempts from the full-set position. This position gives him the greatest advantage in using deceptive leg, eye, and head movements.

PLAY 13:   RIGHT- OR LEFT-HANDED PITCHER, PICKOFF AT SECOND

Who gives the sign?

Depending upon the type of play, either the shortstop or second baseman gives the sign.

Who receives the sign?

Coach signals to the pitcher, shortstop, and second baseman.

What is the purpose of this play?

To get another out on the team at bat. To eliminate a runner who is already in scoring position. To hold second base runner close to the base, even if he isn't picked off.

When should this play be used?

Whenever the second base runner takes too long a lead or is too daring. Can be used by a desperate defense. The ideal time to use it is with bases loaded, two outs, and a full count on the batter.

Explanation of the timing of the play.

Individual play breakdowns follow.

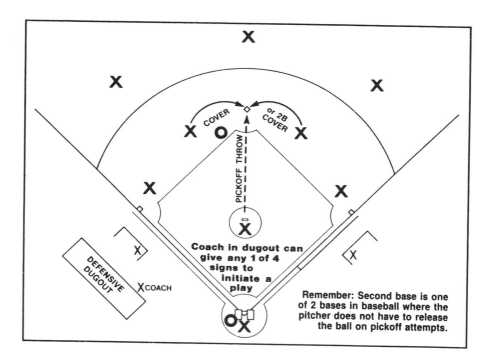

PLAY 14:   RIGHT- OR LEFT-HANDED PITCHER, PICKOFF AT THIRD

Who gives the sign?

Coach on the bench, or the catcher, can flash this sign to the pitcher and third baseman. They both acknowledge it. Pitcher can also be given the sign by the third baseman. It is imperative that third baseman be sure of the sign, as a throwing or fielding error at this base gives up a run.

Who receives the sign?

Third baseman and pitcher will receive coach's sign or pitcher can get sign from the third baseman.

What is the purpose of this play?

This play can cut off an important run or the winning run. This play prevents a squeeze play or safe squeeze play. This play prevents the sacrifice fly, or a passed ball from scoring. This play can cut off a runner who may try to steal home.

When should this play be used?

In the stretch: runners on first and third. Whenever a possible squeeze or suicide squeeze is suspected. From a windup stance, but the foot is not on the rubber. Careful to not be on the rubber here.

Explanation of the timing of the play.

Third baseman walks over to third base to shade runner back to base. Then he walks toward his normal position, breaks fast to third base. Pitcher times the throw with the arrival of third baseman at third base. This play is such a risk play, used so seldom, runner is never ready for it. This tactic should not be used often. Save it for the right moment. Pitchers and third basemen must rehearse this often. Get the timing down carefully, be careful of low throws here; pickoff throws should be knee-high at the corner of the bag nearest the runner.

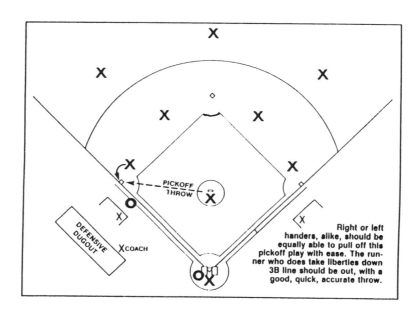

PLAY 15:   SPECIAL PICKOFF SITUATION, RUNNERS ON FIRST AND THIRD
(OR SECOND AND THIRD)

Who gives the sign?

Coach gives this sign from the dugout. This is one of several tactics against a team that is known to run several options of double steal plays.

Who receives the sign?

Pitcher, first baseman, and third baseman.

What is the purpose of this play?

To catch the first base runner asleep. Or he may be thinking about his assignment on a double steal play. (Run this tactic to let offense know you have this play in your book and are not afraid to use it.)

When should this play be used?

Bunt, steal, hit-and-run, and, squeeze situations.

Explanation of the timing of the play.

Pitcher is in his stretch. He does not look at first base. He looks at third base. Pitcher lifts the front foot, then pivots toward third base, then pump-fakes to third base. The first baseman then breaks to first base. Pitcher wheels and throws to first base if runner is off too far. If runner is not off, pitcher does not have to throw, as he is not on the rubber, but is several steps away. (He may fake a throw to first base then.) With runners at second and third, pitcher fakes to third base, then throws or fakes to second base.

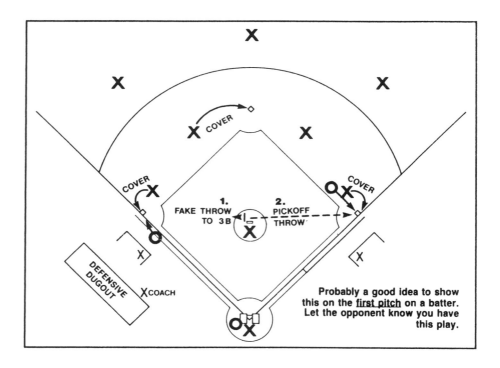

PLAY 16:   SPECIAL PICKOFFS

Who gives the sign?

Shortstop usually gives this sign, such as wiggling the glove in a certain manner.

Who receives the sign?

Pitcher and second baseman receive the sign at the same time from the shortstop. Both the pitcher and second baseman acknowledge with an easy, quick sign.

What is the purpose of this play?

To get another out on the team at bat. To eliminate a runner in scoring position. To hold the second base runner close to the base, even if he is not picked off.

When should this play be used?

Whenever the second base runner takes too long a lead, is too daring. Can be used by a defense when it is desperate. Ideal time to use it is two outs, bases loaded, full count on the batter. Another good time is right after hitter has gotten a two-base hit; he is thinking about his good hit.

Explanation of the timing of the play.

Pitcher goes into his stretch. Shortstop darts behind second base runner. Runner will shade back toward second base some. As shortstop darts back toward his position in front of the runner, so he can see him, second baseman darts straight toward second base. Runner shades back again toward second. Now the second base runner leads off a third time, leaning somewhat toward third base. Shortstop again breaks to second base in time to get the pickoff throw from pitcher. This 1-2-3 sequence gets the runner's rhythm off and should catch him off base.

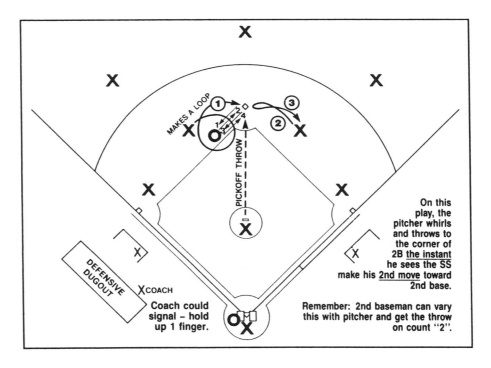

PLAY 17:   SPECIAL PICKOFFS

Who gives the sign?

Shortstop initiates this play placing some daylight between himself and the second base runner. That is the only signal. Second baseman is not in on this play at all.

Who receives the sign?

Pitcher receives the sign, which is merely seeing daylight between the shortstop and the runner, while he is in his stretch position.

What is the purpose of this play?

To get another out on the team at bat. To eliminate a runner in scoring position. To hold the second base runner close to the base, even if he is not picked off.

When should this play be used?

Whenever the second base runner takes too long a lead, is too daring. Can be used by a team when they are desperate. Ideal time to use it is two outs, bases loaded, full count on the batter, runners probably going. Use this after hitter has gotten a double. He is thinking about his hit.

Explanation of the timing of the play.

Pitcher uses his own judgment. The time to whirl and throw is when pitcher sees daylight between shortstop and the runner. Pitcher throws the ball to the corner of the bag nearest the runner, knee-high. Shortstop drops his glove to lower corner of the bag and takes the throw, making the instant tag.

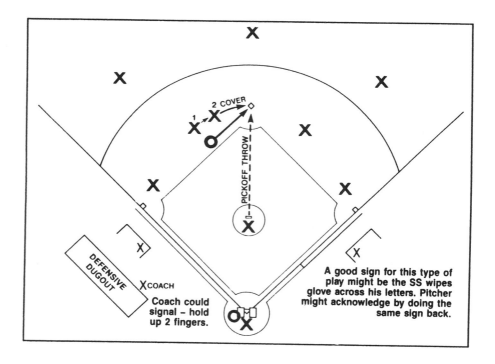

PLAY 18:   SPECIAL PICKOFFS

Who gives the sign?

This play is signaled by the second baseman. It is a fine play when the shortstop must play too far over in the hole on a pull hitter to be of help on second base pickoff plays.

Who receives the sign?

Pitcher receives the sign from the second baseman and gives a simple acknowledgment sign.

What is the purpose of this play?

To get another out on the team at bat. To eliminate a runner in scoring position. To hold the second base runner close, even if he isn't picked off.

When should this play be used?

Whenever a wild or reckless runner is on second base and the shortstop is too deep in the hole to run the play with the second baseman. On a pull hitter, infield will be rotated such that second baseman will be closer to his bag anyway.

Explanation of the timing of the play.

The play is nothing but a footrace between the second baseman and the second base runner. The defense can get runner off too far and make a good, quick throw to get him diving back. Pitcher comes to the set position. Counts "1-2-3-4." Second baseman starts his count at the pitcher's set position, but he breaks for the base on the "2" count. He should be there ahead of the runner and just as the throw reaches second base.

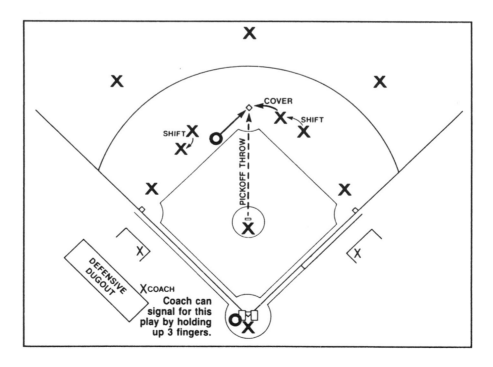

PLAY 19:   SPECIAL PICKOFFS

Who gives the sign?

The shortstop starts this option. He gives the sign to the pitcher. The second baseman is not in on this play.

Who receives the sign?

Pitcher receives his sign from the shortstop while he is in his set position, looking back. The pitcher then looks toward the batter, then whirls and throws to second base.

What is the purpose of this play?

To get another out on the team at bat. To eliminate a runner who is in scoring position. To hold the second base runner close to second base, even if he isn't picked off.

When should this play be used?

When the runner at second base is daring and takes an extra-long lead, and the shortstop is playing in normal position and depth.

Explanation of the timing of the play.

While the pitcher is looking back at the runner, shortstop flashes the sign. He breaks fast to second base as pitcher turns once more to face the batter. As the pitcher turns toward the plate, he counts "1,2." He turns and throws on the count of "3." Shortstop starts his break to the bag on the count of "2."

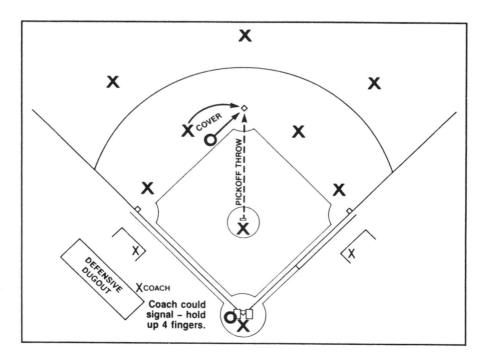

PLAY 20:   CATCHER PICKOFF TO FIRST

Who gives the sign?

Catcher can use a signal to tip off the pitcher and all infielders that a pickoff attempt is coming. Wiping hands across chest protector is a typical sign. This next pitch can be run as a true pitchout, or the pitch may be a wide slider pitchout.

Who receives the sign?

All infielders receive the sign, but all infielders near the bases where the runners are must be alert to cover their bags. They can acknowledge catcher with a simple sign.

What is the purpose of this play?

To get another out on the team at bat. To eliminate one of the runners and a possible run. To hold the runners close to their bases, even if they are not picked off. To reduce the length of secondary leads.

When should this play be used?

Catcher pickoffs occur automatically whenever a broken play has occurred, such as a bunt, steal, or hit-and-run. This is not done on sign, however. Used whenever a runner takes too much lead on any pitch. Used by a defense that is desperate.

Explanation of the timing of the play.

Catcher gives all of the infielders his sign that he will try to pick off a runner after the pitch. He receives the pitch, slightly turns toward first base, and can throw from standing, half kneeling, or full kneeling position. Kneeling position is the fastest throw, but catcher must have a very strong arm, for he is getting no body into the throw. This is most effective with a left-handed batter, for the first base runner is then screened from the play.

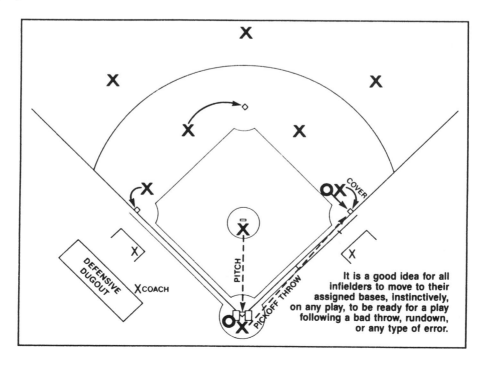

It is a good idea for all infielders to move to their assigned bases, instinctively, on any play, to be ready for a play following a bad throw, rundown, or any type of error.

PLAY 21:   CATCHER PICKOFF TO SECOND

Who gives the sign?

Catcher can use a signal to tip off the pitcher and all infielders that a pickoff attempt is coming. The wiping of a hand across the chest protector is a typical sign. Next pitch can be a true pitchout or a wide slider pitchout.

Who receives the sign?

All infielders receive the sign, but all the infielders near the bases where the runners are must be alert to cover their bags. They can acknowledge the catcher with a simple sign.

What is the purpose of this play?

To get another out on the team at bat. To eliminate one of the runners and a possible run. To hold the runners close to their bases, even if they are not picked off. To reduce the length of secondary leads.

When should this play be used?

Catcher pickoffs can occur automatically when a broken play has occurred, such as a bunt, steal, or hit-and-run. This is not done on the sign, however. Used whenever a runner takes too much lead on any pitch. Used by a defense that is desperate.

Explanation of the timing of the play.

Catcher gives all of the infielders a sign that he will try to pick the runner off of second base after the pitch. He then receives the pitch, firing it instantly toward second base. He can throw from a full standing, half kneeling, or full kneeling position (few catchers can throw down to second base from a full kneeling position). Kneeling is the fastest throw, but catcher must have a very strong arm, for he is getting no body into the throw. This play is equally effective with either a right- or left-handed hitter.

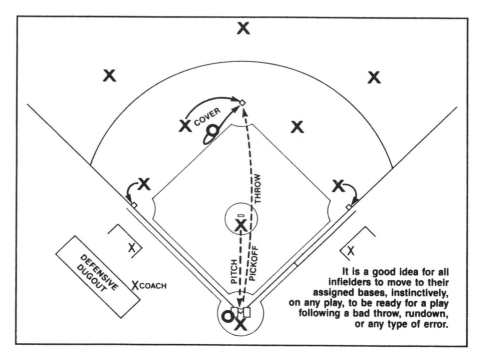

It is a good idea for all infielders to move to their assigned bases, instinctively, on any play, to be ready for a play following a bad throw, rundown, or any type of error.

PLAY 22:   CATCHER PICKOFF TO THIRD

Who gives the sign?

Catcher can use a signal to tip off the pitcher and all the infielders that a pickoff attempt is coming. Wiping a hand across the chest protector is a typical sign. The next pitch can be a true pitchout or a wide slider pitchout. The catcher can call for the pitch to be up and in on a right-handed batter rather than a wide slider. The effect of this is that the batter goes down and gives the catcher a clear path to third base. He now does not have to worry about throwing around the standing batter.

When should this play be used?

Catcher pickoffs can occur automatically when a broken play has occurred, such as a bunt, steal, squeeze, or hit-and-run. This is not done on a sign, however. Used whenever a runner takes too much lead on any pitch. Used by a defense that is desperate.

Explanation of the timing of the play.

Catcher gives all of the infielders the sign that he will try to pick the runner off third base. He receives the pitch, turns slightly toward third base, and can throw from a kneeling, half kneeling, or full kneeling position. Kneeling is the fastest throw, but catcher must have a very strong arm, for he can get no body into the throw. This play is most effective with a right-handed batter, as the third base runner will be screened out from the play.

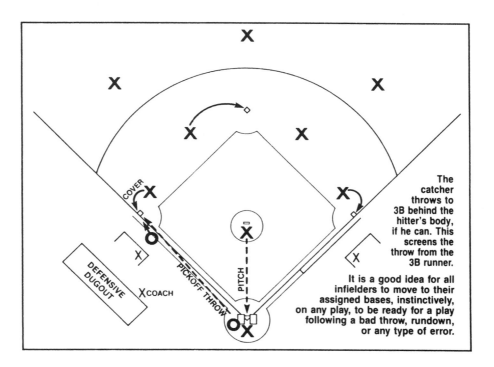

The catcher throws to 3B behind the hitter's body, if he can. This screens the throw from the 3B runner.

It is a good idea for all infielders to move to their assigned bases, instinctively, on any play, to be ready for a play following a bad throw, rundown, or any type of error.

PLAY 23:   COVERING SECOND ON CATCHER'S THROWDOWN

Who gives the sign?

Second baseman and shortstop give the same sign to each other. These signs are given so that runners cannot see them, only the two infielders.

Who receives the sign?

They give the sign to each other before the pitch.

What is the purpose of this play?

To be certain that both shortstop and second base know who will take the catcher's throwdown on a steal attempt by the first base runner. Can be used at any time there might be any question as to which of the two covers second base.

When should this play be used?

Any time it is expected that a catcher's throw is coming to second

Explanation of the timing of the play.

Shortstop and second baseman both kneel down in their fielding positions ready for the next pitch to be hit. They shield their faces with their gloves so that only they can see each other's mouths. The fielder who wants to cover second base will open his mouth wide enough for the other to see plainly. The other infielder acknowledges by keeping his mouth closed.

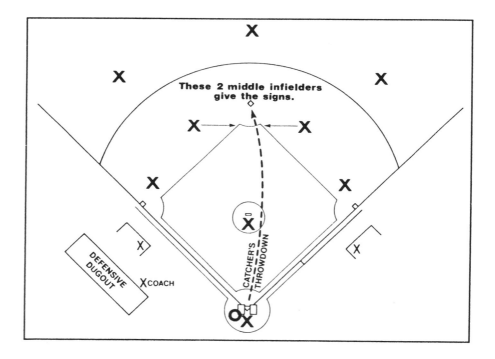

PLAY 24:   COACHES' SIGNS FOR MOVING INFIELDERS

Who gives the sign?

Coach on the bench or in the dugout signals his infielders to move into certain positions. He does this with hand or arm movements. These are signs that are not obvious to all.

Who receives the sign?

One or several infielders who need to be moved into a new·position.

What is the purpose of this play?

As the new hitter comes to bat, or the outs, count on the batter, etc. changes, coach may feel the ball will be hit to a different spot in the infield. Perhaps the type of pitch to be thrown will change this. Infielders are moved to counter these changes.

Explanation of the timing of the play.

Quite a while before the next pitch, coach moves hands in toward him, signaling to move in. Or hands are pushed out away from him, signaling to move back. One or two hands can be used in parallel fashion, motioning to the right or to the left, signaling the infielders to move in that direction.

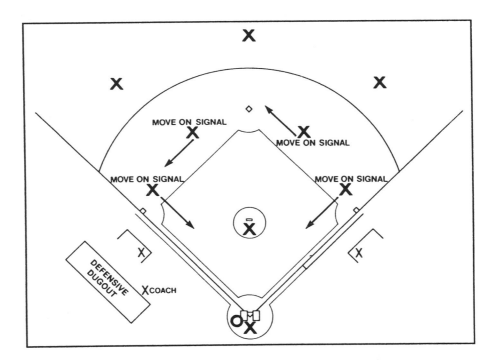

PLAY 25:   COACHES' SIGNS FOR MOVING OUTFIELDERS

Who gives the sign?

Manager or coaches on the bench. Use Walter Alston's old method of moving the outfielders by waving a towel. Outfielders are so far away that they may not be able to see hand signals, especially from that part of the diamond.

Who receives the sign?

One outfielder, or two, or all three outfielders.

What is the purpose of this play?

To move an outfielder to that spot where it is anticipated the ball will be hit on the next pitch.

When should this play be used?

When the coaches have better knowledge than the outfielders do concerning where the batter will hit the ball.

Explanation of the timing of the play.

Coach and outfielders can work out signals before the game. The manner in which a white towel is waved indicates to the outfielder to move in, move back, or move left or right. Occasionally, especially if it is a key play in the game or to prevent the winning run from scoring, coaches may have outfielders switch position. This tactic gives the defense, perhaps, the faster fly chaser, the surer fielder, or the stronger arm for throws home or to the next base.

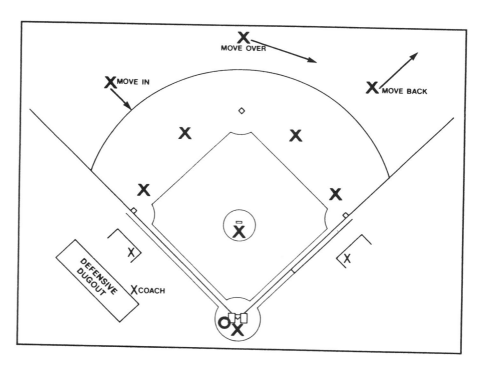

PLAY 26:   COACHES' SIGNS FOR BUNT COVERAGE

Who gives the sign?

Coach signals infielders to rotate clockwise for the best bunt coverage. It is imperative that second base is covered by shortstop and that first base is covered by the second baseman.

Who receives the sign?

All six infielders must receive the same sign, so that they may move as a unit.

What is the purpose of this play?

To be certain that all bases are covered on throws when the bunt is fielded. To be sure that defense gets at least one out on every play, perhaps a double play on a pop-up or a grounder.

When should this play be used?

When there are none on base. When there is a man only at first base. When there are men on first base and second base only.

Explanation of the timing of the play.

As the bunter squares around to bunt the pitcher, third baseman, first baseman, and catcher are alert to field the bunted grounder or fly quickly. If the bunt is a hard one, any fielder fires a quick throw to second base for the force-out, perhaps on to a double play throw. This gives at least the lead runner out. If the bunt is soft and slow, any fielder makes the throw to first base for the out there. If the ball is popped up, any fielder who catches the fly will throw to any base where the sure double play can be gotten.

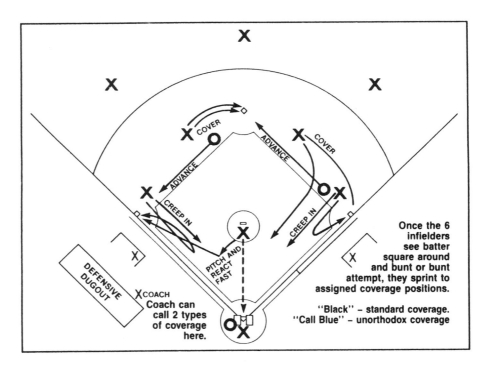

PLAY 27:   COACHES' SIGNS FOR BUNT COVERAGE

Who gives the sign?

Coach on the bench signals for correct moves for bunt coverage. He moves his two arms in front of him, up and out to the sides, to indicate "Peel away" to the outside. Shortstop covers third base, second base covers first base. Leave the middle open.

Who receives the sign?

All six of the infielders must receive the same sign, and they move as a unit. First baseman and third baseman may creep in a step or two prematurely before the two middle infielders break.

What is the purpose of this play?

To be certain that all bases where runners can be thrown out are covered. To be sure to get one out on a play, perhaps two.

When should this play be used?

Man on third base only. Men on second base and third base only. Bases loaded. (Only these three situations does the infield "peel away," leaving the middle open.)

Explanation of the timing of the play.

As the bunter squares away to bunt, not before (for example, with men on second base and third base), the pitcher, third baseman, and first baseman are alert to field the bunt quickly. Perhaps the catcher will field a slow one close to the plate. If the bunt is missed, catcher fires a quick pickoff throw to shortstop covering third base. If the bunt is successful, but hard enough, toss to catcher for tag. If it is a very good bunt and there's no play at the plate, then one of the three fielders makes the good throw to second base covering first base for the sure out.

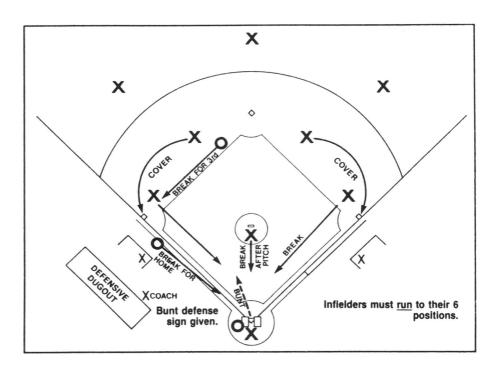

PLAY 28:   COACHES' SIGNS FOR BUNT COVERAGE

Who gives the sign?

Coach on the bench signals for correct moves for bunt coverage in this particular (and very special) situation. He signals with one or two hands, a clockwise rotation, the third baseman creeping in quickly.

Who receives the sign?

All six of the infielders must receive the same sign, so that they move as a unit.

What is the purpose of this play?

The pitcher, third baseman, and first baseman must toss home if they field a bunt and feel that they can throw him out on a tag play. If bunt is good, make throw to first base to get the sure out.

When should this play be used?

With opposing runners on first and third bases only.

Explanation of the timing of the play.

Pitcher always covers third base if the third baseman fields the bunt, for there is a runner rounding second base. As the hitter squares around to bunt, not before, the pitcher, third baseman, and first baseman are alert to field the bunt quickly and throw home for a tag play to cut off the run. If it is not a good bunt, and the third base runner holds up or goes back to third base, bluff him back to third and make the sure out with a throw to the second baseman covering first base.

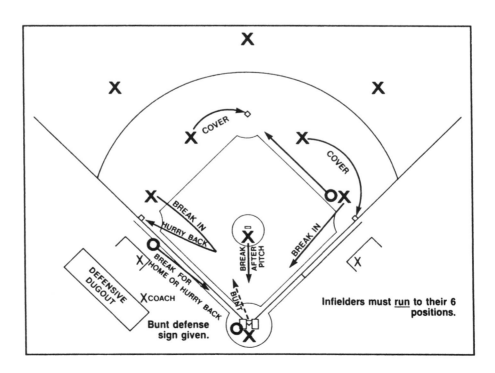

PLAY 29:   COACHES' SIGNS FOR BUNT COVERAGE

Who gives the sign?

Coach on the bench signals for correct moves for bunt coverage in this particular situation. He signals with one or two hands, a clockwise rotation, the third baseman creeping in quickly.

Who receives the sign?

All six of the infielders must receive the same sign, as they must all move as a unit.

What is the purpose of this play?

To hold the second base runner on so he cannot advance on a bunt or base hit. Be certain that first base is covered on the throw. Third baseman has a tough play here. He must come in quick to field a real bunt, but not so far that he cannot hustle back to his bag to take a catcher's throw on the possible steal.

When should this play be used?

When opponents have a man on second base *only;* it is an important run, and it looks as though they will bunt.

Explanation of the timing of the play.

As the hitter squares around to bunt, not before, the pitcher, first baseman, and third baseman, possibly the catcher, are all alert to field the bunt quickly and throw to third base for a tag play, if it is a hard bunt and the second base runner does not get a good jump on the pitch. If the bunt is successful and second base runner has a good jump, one of the three infielders fields the bunt and throws to first base for the sure out.

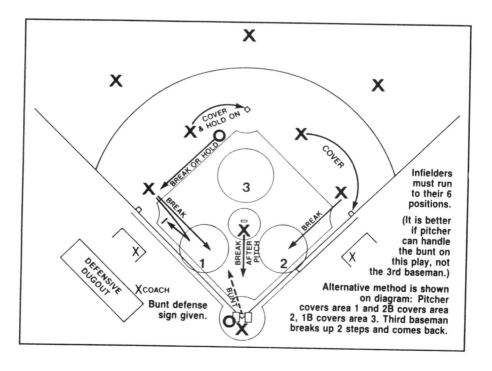

PLAY 30:   COACHES' SIGNS FOR BUNT COVERAGE

Who gives the sign?
Coach gives a very special verbal sign, "Crash," well ahead of the play or the pitch, since this is a bunt coverage *decoy* to set up a pickoff play.

Who receives the sign?
All six infielders must receive the same sign at the same time to make this work. Since it is a special play, call a time-out and confer with coach if signal is misunderstood.

What is the purpose of this play?
To deceive the offensive team into thinking your infield is shifting around a lot to be sure of good bunt coverage. The movement of the first baseman and third baseman very early indicates that infield is defending a sacrifice bunt. Actually they are setting up to pick off the second base runner.

When should this play be used?
Only with runners at first base and second base, and when it is dead certain that opponents are about to attempt a sacrifice bunt to move the runners over.

Explanation of the timing of the play.
A standard bunting situation, men on first base and second base. Run this play the first time in a game that they try a sacrifice bunt. On the coaches' yell, "Crash," *nothing happens. No one moves.* The runner at second base is off his base quite a way, not being held on very closely. Just as pitcher comes down in the middle of his stretch and is about to set for a fairly long count, pitcher yells loudly "Go." All four infielders break to their assigned spots in a sprint. Shortstop sprints to second base. Instead of pitching, the pitcher picks off the runner at second base. We get an out on them and also never give them a chance to bunt.

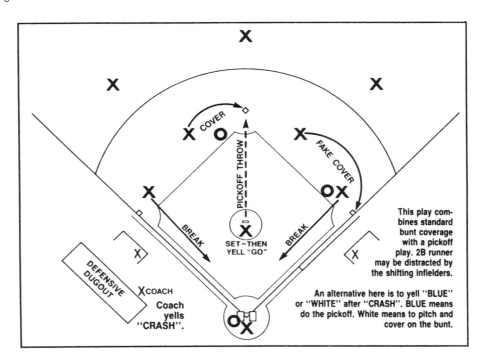

This play combines standard bunt coverage with a pickoff play. 2B runner may be distracted by the shifting infielders.

An alternative here is to yell "BLUE" or "WHITE" after "CRASH". BLUE means do the pickoff. White means to pitch and cover on the bunt.

PLAY 31:   COACHES' SIGNS FOR BUNT COVERAGE

Who gives the sign?

Coach gives a very special verbal sign, "Kill," well ahead of the pitch or the play. This is not a pickoff play, but one designed to cause a hurried or bad bunt.

Who receives the sign?

All six infielders must receive the same sign at the same time to make this work. The first baseman *must* get this sign, for he is the key man.

What is the purpose of this play?

To get a pop-up and a double play off it. To get a hard bad bunt and to get a double play off it. Mainly, to foul up the bunter, and to be "right in his face."

When should this play be used?

With men on first base and second base *only*, when it is obvious that a bunt has been called for by the opposing coach. (This is an excellent play to use alternately with the "Crash" play.)

Explanation of the timing of the play.

Coach yells "Kill" loudly. All of the infield hears it, but only the first baseman charges up *full speed to within fifteen feet of the batter*, right in front of him. Pitcher goes into his stretch, then the other men move in their clockwise rotation, breaking to their spots. The first baseman can yell at the batter to distract him, but he better be prepared to duck in case the batter swings instead of bunting. Third baseman breaks in, then back fast, to third base to cover. Pitcher and first base must cover all bunts and pop-ups on this play. Throw to third base on a hard grounder. Throw to second base on a pop-up.

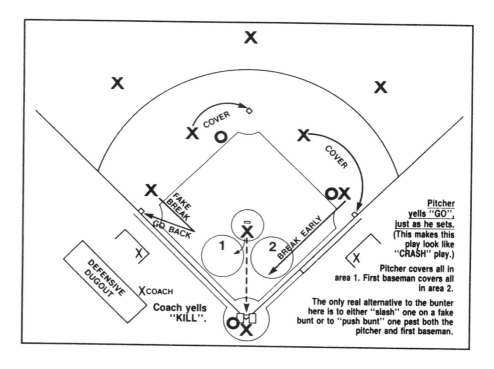

PLAY 32:   SPECIAL CRISSCROSS PLAY

Who gives the sign?

Coach John Herbold used this play at Long Beach in a situation where men were on first and second and a sacrifice bunt was almost certain.

Who receives the sign?

All six infielders must get this sign and be ready to break together.

What is the purpose of this play?

Pitcher holds runners on base with the first baseman and shortstop holding them close. The purpose of this unusual defensive tactic against the bunt is that all the sprinting around and unorthodox positioning of defense will confuse the second base runner.

When should this play be used?

Only with men on first and second bases.

Explanation of the timing of the play.

Coach yells his sign, such as "Cross" or "Circus." Pitcher looks from set position at second base. If shortstop can work a daylight pickoff, do that first. If not, then second baseman is coming over to pick off second base runner. Try that. Then the shortstop and second baseman keep streaking for first base and third base positions to cover those bases. Shortstop covers first base and second base. Leave second base uncovered on this play (or you can have shortstop go halfway to first base and be able to cover first base on a grounder throw or go back to second base to cover on a throw after a pop-up). Pitcher delivers after a long set. Pitcher, first baseman, and third baseman are all in close to field either the pop-up or the grounder.

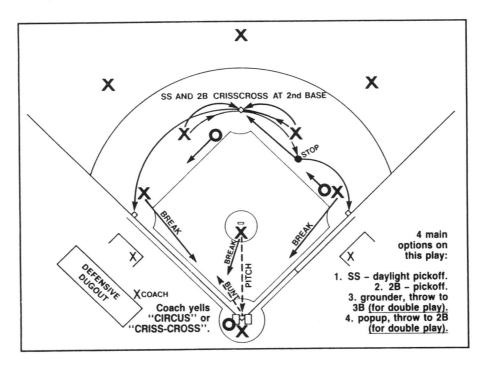

PLAY 33:   COACHES' SIGN FOR TAKING CATCHER'S THROWS

Who gives the sign?

Coach on the bench gives four oral signals or he may give hand signals.

Who receives the sign?

All six infielders must hear or see this sign, for any one or pair of them may end up executing the play.

What is the purpose of this play?

First, to throw out a runner trying to steal second base without allowing the third base runner to steal home on the play. It is possible to get a double play on this, first at second base, then at home. Second, to fake-throw to second base, then turn and pick off the third base runner.

When should this play be used?

When opponent has runners on first base and third base.

Explanation of the timing of the play.

Signal is called well before each pitch. Give infielders plenty of time to see or hear it. Coach calls last name of pitcher, then pitcher cuts off throw and fires to third base, or runs at trapped third base runner. Coach calls last name of second baseman, who cuts off the throw or throws to third base or home, or runs at the trapped runner. Coach calls the last name of the catcher, who fakes a step and throws to second base, then steps back and picks off the diving third base runner. Coach yells the last name of the shortstop, who takes the throw going through to second base, then fires home fast for the double play. Shortstop tags sliding runner, then throws home.

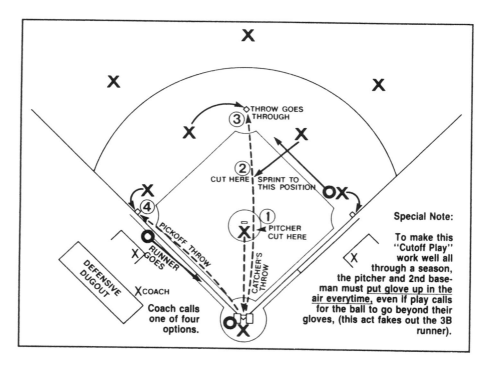

PLAY 34:   DEFENSIVE APPEAL PLAY NUMBER 1

Who gives the sign?

The infielder nearest the play, or who actually observes a runner missing base. He yells the fact to his coach and the pitcher.

Who receives the sign?

Coach hears the sign first. The nearest infielder yells, "Runner missed second base." Coach then tells his pitcher and catcher to run the appeal play properly.

What is the purpose of this play?

To get one more out in the offense. To give them one less base runner who might score later.

When should this play be used?

Any time that any defensive man even suspects that a runner has failed to touch a base. The umpire might have seen it, but he only calls the play if you appeal.

Explanation of the timing of the play.

The pitcher receives the ball, goes into his stretch position on the mound. *He then steps off the rubber*, turns, and throws to that base which the runner missed. That infielder must hold the ball and personally say, "Umpire, is he safe or out?" The umpire must be asked as infielder stands on the base in question, holding the ball. Umpire will then signal safe or out.

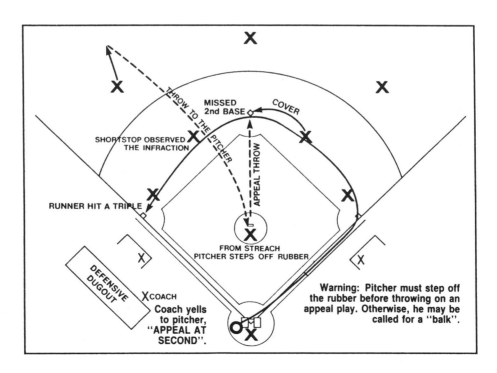

PLAY 35:   DEFENSIVE APPEAL PLAY NUMBER 2

Who gives the sign?

The infielder nearest the runner who leaves his base too soon after a caught fly ball. He notifies the coach and the pitcher after the infraction.

Who receives the sign?

The coach hears the nearest infielder yell, "Runner left too soon at third." The coach then tells the pitcher and catcher to run the appeal play. Third baseman would hear this sign.

What is the purpose of this play?

To get one more out on the offense. To give them one less base runner who might score later.

When should this play be used?

Any time that any defensive man even suspects that any base runner has failed to tag up after a fair or foul ball has been caught. Will only call it on appeal.

Explanation of the timing of the play.

The pitcher receives the ball, goes into his stretch position on the mound. He then steps off the rubber, turns, and throws to the base the runner left too soon. The infielder stands on the base in question. The infielder must hold the ball, while touching that base, and say, "Umpire, is he safe or out?" The umpire must be asked as infielder stands on the base, holding the ball. The umpire will then signal safe or out.

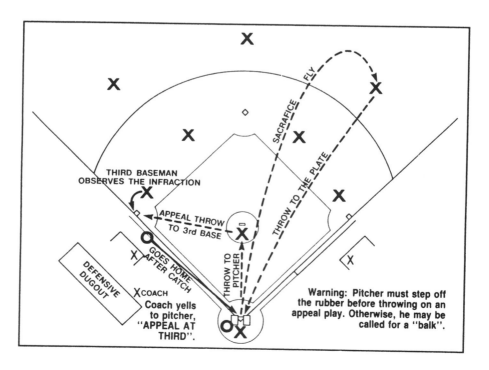

PLAY 36: DEFENSIVE APPEAL PLAY NUMBER 3

Who gives the sign?

The coach on the bench, the scorekeeper, the catcher, or anyone who immediately observes that the batter has batted out of turn. (Let us assume that that batter reached a base safely.)

Who receives the sign?

It is the coach who wants to know first. Either the coach, catcher, or pitcher is likely to draw attention to the fact.

What is the purpose of this play?

To get one more out on the offense. To take away a base runner, if the batter was safely on base. To negate a run, if the batter hit a home run.

When should this play be used?

Any time anyone on the defensive team even suspects that an opposing batter batted out of turn. It may be an honest error, or it may have been intentional. Teams sometimes change the order of batters to bring up the good hitter with men on base, to keep a rally going.

Explanation of the timing of the play.

Anyone appealing this infraction must do so before the first pitch is thrown to the following batter. If the appeal is not made by then, nothing will be done to correct the error. If batter hits and gets on safely, defensive coach calls a time-out, asks the plate umpire to bring the two scorekeepers together to look at the lineup. Plate umpire then determines whether the batter hit out of turn. If he did, the umpire yells, "The batter is out," and he removes that batter from his base gained. He also removes all scoring or base runners advancing as a result of that hit. The next batter then comes up in correct order. Runners return to their bases.

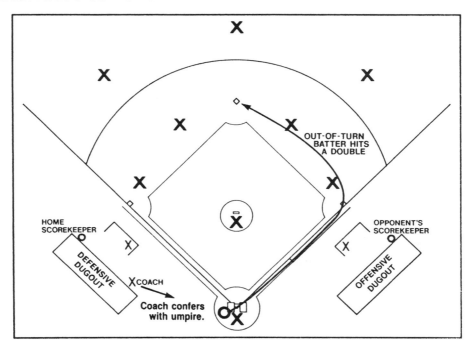

OUT-OF-TURN BATTER HITS A DOUBLE

HOME SCOREKEEPER

OPPONENT'S SCOREKEEPER

DEFENSIVE DUGOUT

OFFENSIVE DUGOUT

X COACH

Coach confers with umpire.

PLAY 37:   DEFENSIVE APPEAL PLAY NUMBER 4

Who gives the sign?

The infielder who is watching a runner touch a base, reverse direction, and go back over the base he touched. He must watch for the retouching of each base in order.

Who receives the sign?

Coach on the bench hears nearest infielder yell, "The runner did not retouch second base." (In this case the base runner had advanced from first base to third base on a play that was called back for some reason.)

What is the purpose of this play?

To get one more out on the offense. To remove one base runner who might score later.

When should this play be used?

Any time a runner is stealing on the pitch and advances beyond the next base, perhaps on a deep fly caught, or in any situation where he must retrace his steps back two bases.

Explanation of the timing of the play.

A deep fly is hit while a runner is stealing. The runner thinks it will not be caught, but it is. He has passed one base and is on his way to the next. He reverses and retouches two bases, but he misses the middle one. Or he may just cut across the diamond. (Runners have tried that.) The throw comes in to a base from the outfield, then it goes to the pitcher. The coach yells to the pitcher to run the appeal play from his stretch. Pitcher throws to the base in question. The baseman covering holds the ball, asks the umpire, "Is he out or safe?" The umpire will then make his decision. He will not call the play unless asked by the infielder.

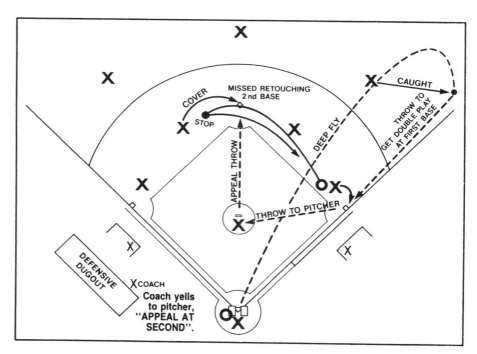

PLAY 38:   DEFENSIVE APPEAL PLAY NUMBER 5

Who gives the sign?

The catcher, who sees the runner who has scored safely but fails to touch the plate, either sliding or standing up.

Who receives the sign?

The catcher yells to the coach on the bench, "Runner did not touch home plate," then catcher springs into action and tags runner or touches the plate.

What is the purpose of this play?

To prevent the run from scoring. To get one more out on the opponent. To end an inning and a rally.

When should this play be used?

Any time a runner scores on a close play, or on a sliding or standing play that is not close, catcher watches carefully to see if the runner touched the plate.

Explanation of the timing of the play.

Just to be safe, catcher tags runner after he crosses the plate if he even suspects that the plate was missed. The umpire will be watching and waiting for an appeal to be made. Or, catcher may hold the ball in his hand and touch home plate if the runner makes no attempt to come back to the plate. The sequence of events is this: Touch home plate while catcher is holding the ball, go over and touch runner as he either is diving back or walking back to touch home plate, then, after doing both of these, say to the umpire, "Umpire, runner did not touch home plate. Is he out or safe?" You must request the appeal. Umpire will call out or safe only if you ask for the decision.

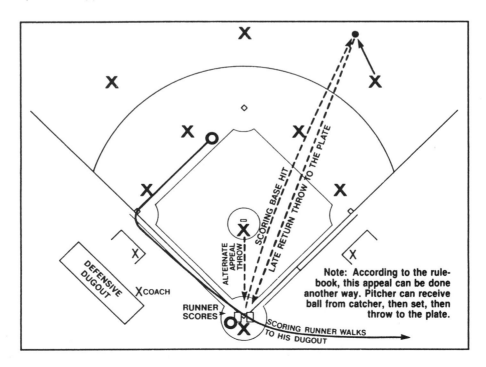

PLAY 39:   DEFENSIVE APPEAL PLAY NUMBER 6

Who gives the sign?

The catcher, who is watching the runner scoring and also may be watching the action at another part of the diamond. The umpire should be doing this same thing, watching both places, if there are two outs at the time.

Who receives the sign?

The catcher tells his coach and the plate umpire that the runner scored after the third out was made at another base.

What is the purpose of the play?

To prevent the run from scoring. To get one more out on the opponent. In this case, to end a rally and the inning.

When should this play be used?

Any time a throw is made to another base except home plate, or while an out is being made anywhere else on the diamond from any other type of action—any of this occurring at the same time that a runner is coming in to score.

Explanation of the timing of the play.

Example: With a runner in scoring position, the batter hits the ball. Batter may be thrown out trying to stretch the hit an extra base, or he may be tagged out in a rundown that ensues while the defense is ignoring the scoring runner. Only upon appeal by the catcher or the defensive coach will the plate umpire yell, "Yes, run scores" or "No, run does not count" and "the inning is over." Either catcher or coach must say, specifically, to the plate umpire, "Umpire, the third out was made before the run scored. Does the run count or not?"

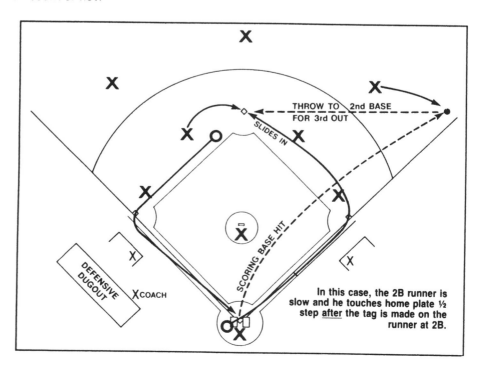

THROW TO 2nd BASE FOR 3rd OUT

SLIDES IN

SCORING BASE HIT

DEFENSIVE DUGOUT

X COACH

In this case, the 2B runner is slow and he touches home plate ½ step after the tag is made on the runner at 2B.

PLAY 40:   PLATE UMPIRE ASKING BASE UMPIRE FOR ASSISTANCE

Who gives the sign?

Catcher or any infielder or the coach can ask the plate umpire to call for assistance from a base umpire on the batter's swing. However, plate umpire does not have to grant the request if he thinks he judged it correctly himself. The familiar cry from the defense is "How about it, Blue?"

Who receives the sign?

Plate umpire gets the first request. First base or third base umpire gets the second request from plate umpire. Plate umpire will request by pointing to one or the other base umpires (depending upon whether the hitter is a right- or left-handed batter).

What is the purpose of this play?

To get another strike on the hitter.

When should this play be used?

Any time the catcher, coach, or plate umpire cannot determine whether the swing was more or less than a half swing.

Explanation of the timing of the play.

Batter swings. Catcher or coach on the bench must request the plate umpire, unless umpire already called it a strike. After plate umpire points to the base umpire, the base umpire will signal "Safe" or "Out" with the usual hand signs. His out sign means it was a strike. The safe sign means it was a ball.

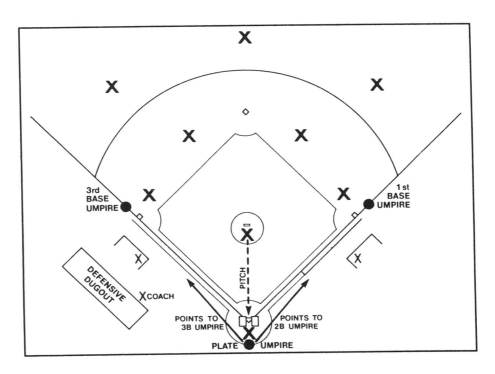

PLAY 41: "WHIP PLAY" NUMBER 1

Who gives the sign?

Coach can yell "Whip" or other prearranged sign. The catcher (who has run down behind first base deep) and the first baseman shortstop, and second baseman all hear this loud sign. Five players are involved, including an outfielder.

Who receives the sign?

Outfielder, catcher, first baseman, second baseman, and shortstop.

What is the purpose of this play?

To surprise the hitter who rounds first base too far and is thinking about the good hit he got. To get him to taking too wide a turn at first base and leaning too far toward second base.

When should this play be used?

Any time there is no one on base, any number of outs (and especially with two outs, in order to end an inning and prevent a rally).

Explanation of the timing of the play.

As soon as the ball is hit to the outfield, the outfielder picks up the ball and quickly throws to the cutoff man, who normally would toss it to the man covering second base, or run in and throw to the pitcher. Instead, he immediately fires a surprise hard throw to the first baseman, covering first base. The catcher stays back on this play, to get a bad throw, in case. This should catch the runner off first base, and he will be tagged diving back to first base, or a rundown will ensue.

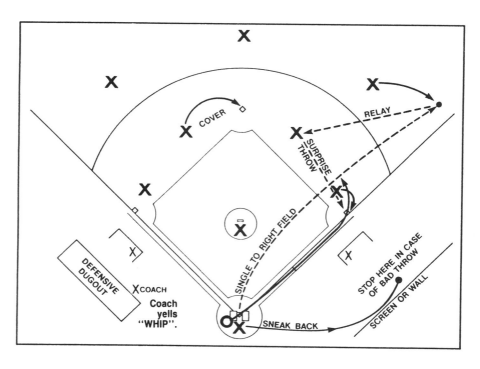

PLAY 42: "WHIP PLAY" NUMBER 2

Who gives the sign?
Coach yells loudly, "Whip," to remind all of the infielders, including catcher, what to do.

Who receives the sign?
All six infielders must hear the sign so that they can plan ahead on the play.

What is the purpose of this play?
To get a double play quickly off of what looked like a successful sacrifice bunt play. To leave the opponent with no one on base and two outs.

When should this play be used?
Anytime there is a man on first base or men on first and second bases, and a sacrifice bunt has been laid down successfully and played to the person covering first base.

Explanation of the timing of the play.
The ball has been bunted well. One of the infielders picks it up and throws to first base, second baseman covering. The first base runner is in to second, maybe sliding and maybe standing and rounding the bag too much. He may take a wide turn and lean toward third base too much. The man covering second base will fire a quick throw to shortstop, covering second base, and will pick the runner off diving back, or a rundown may ensue.

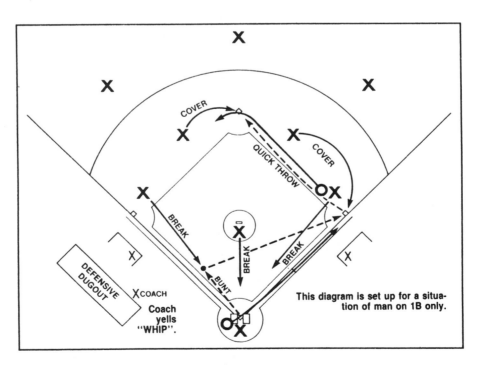

PLAY 43:   "WHIP PLAY" NUMBER 3

Who gives the sign?

Coach can yell "Whip" or other prearranged sign. The catcher (who has run down behind first base deep) and the first baseman, second baseman, and shortstop all hear this loud sign. Five players are involved, including an outfielder.

Who receives the sign?

Outfielder, catcher, first baseman, second baseman, and shortstop.

What is the purpose of this play?

To surprise the hitter who rounds first base too far and is thinking about the good hit he got. Get him to taking too wide a turn at first base and leaning too far toward second base.

When should this play be used?

Any time there is no one on base, any number of outs (and especially with two outs, in order to end an inning and prevent a rally from starting).

Explanation of the timing the play

As soon as the ball is hit to the outfield, the outfielder picks up the ball and quickly throws to the cutoff man, who normally would casually toss it to the man covering second base, or run in and throw to the pitcher. Instead, he immediately fires a surprise hard throw to the catcher or first baseman covering first base. If the catcher sneaks up and covers first base, the first baseman plays way out toward second base (to lure the base runner off the bag). This should catch the runner off first base, and he will be tagged diving back to first base, or a rundown will ensue.

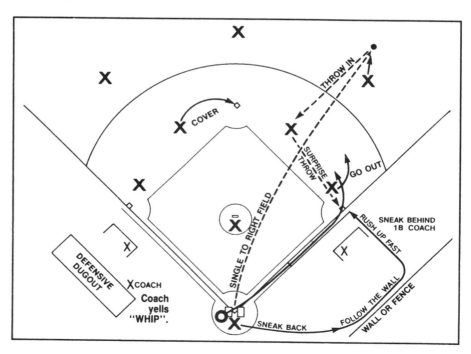

PLAY 44: "WHIP PLAY" NUMBER 4

Who gives the sign?

Coach can yell "Whip" or other prearranged sign. The catcher (who has run down behind first base deep) and the first baseman, shortstop, and second baseman all hear this loud sign. Five players are involved, including an outfielder.

Explanation of the timing of the play.

As soon as the ball is hit to the outfield, the outfielder picks up the ball and quickly throws to the cutoff man, who normally would toss it to the man covering second base, or run in and throw it to the pitcher. Instead, he *intentionally throws a bad relay to first* base. The ball bounces in front of the first baseman, he makes a *fake swipe* at it, it bounces right into the catcher's mitt on one hop. Catcher has backed up first base for this purpose. The runner takes off for second base, *seeing the bad throw*. Catcher then either throws to second base for the tag play, or first base, if runner dives back.

Another option of this play is for the outfielder's throw to go to the man covering second base (instead of the cutoff man, who then relays it to the man covering second base). This tactic gives the hitter more of a wide turn at first base, drawing him off the base for the next tactic, the fake bad throw past the first baseman. As the man covering second base receives the ball, it is he who intentionally makes a bad throw over the first baseman's head or in the dirt, so that the catcher backing up can play the ball, then fire the ball to the man covering the base where the runner is headed.

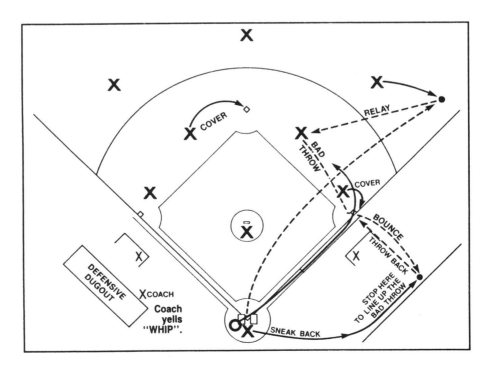

PLAY 45:   INFIELD SIGNS, GESTURES, AND MANNERISMS

Indicating Number of Outs

After one is out, hold up the index finger to each other. After two are out, hold up the index and little fingers only. If there are none out, form a big zero with thumb and index finger.

All the infielders give these signs to each other to remind each other of the number of outs. Any defensive man who forgets the number of outs can really hurt his team.

Spit in Glove

An infielder will spit in his glove. This is not just a nervous habit. All he is trying to do is to provide a little moisture in the pocket of his mitt so as to provide for friction. This reduces the chance of having a ball slide or jump out of his mitt when he catches it.

Checking the Wind

Infielders can pick up strands of grass and throw them into the air or look at the flag on the flagpole. Some players wet their index finger, then hold it in the air. The three methods listed will tell the player the wind strength and direction.

Using Sunglasses

Some fielders wear flip-down-type sunglasses. When the high pop-up into the sun occurs, the player flips down the sunshades, enabling him to pick up the ball's flight, even in the sunlight.

Glove Taps

Infielders can sign to each other with glove taps. The number of times an infielder taps the glove on bent knee or body can have a definite meaning to the other infielders.

First Baseman Holding Runner On

Sometimes the first baseman will cross his arms while in his standing position. This indicates to the pitcher and catcher that he is playing behind the runner and is not holding the runner on.

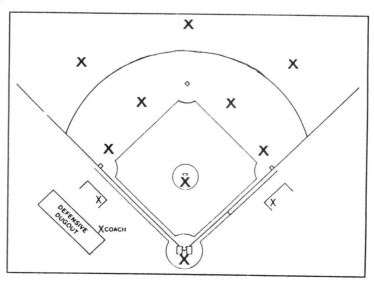

PLAY 46:   OUTFIELD SIGNS, GESTURES, AND MANNERISMS

Indicating Number of Outs

After one is out, hold up the index finger to each other. After two are out, hold up the little and index fingers only. If there are none out, form a big zero with the thumb and index finger.

All of the outfielders give these signs to each other to remind each other of the number of outs. Defensive men who forget the number of outs can really hurt the team, especially way out in the outfield.

Spit in Glove

An outfielder will spit in his glove. This is not just a nervous habit. All he is trying to do is to provide a little moisture in the pocket of his mitt so as to provide for friction. This reduces the chance that a ground ball or fly ball will pop out of the mitt after the catch.

Checking the Wind

Outfielders will pick up strands of grass and throw them into the air or look at the flag on the flagpole. Some players wet their index fingers, then hold them up in the air. The three methods listed will tell the player the wind strength and direction.

Using Sunglasses

Some fielders wear flip-down-type sunglasses. When the high pop-up or fly occurs, the player flips down the sunshades, enabling him to pick up the ball's flight, even in the bright sun.

Glove Taps

Outfielders can signal to each other with glove taps on the knee, body, etc. for communicating signs to each other.

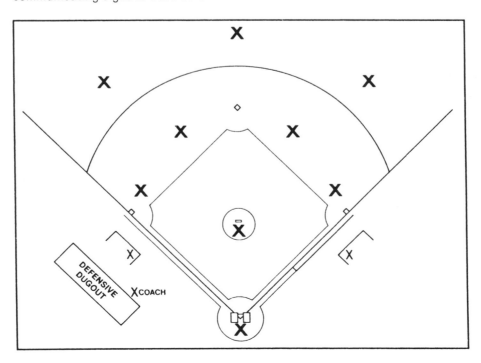

PLAY 47:   HITTERS' SIGNS AND GESTURES

Who gives the sign?

Hitter gives the signs to the plate umpire, the pitcher, and the catcher, mainly.

Who receives the sign?

Pitcher, catcher, other defensemen, and plate umpire and base umpires.

What is the purpose of this play?

To call time in, when the batter is ready for the pitch. To call a timeout, if the batter is not ready for the pitch or in case of a sudden emergency.

When should this play be used?

These can be used by all batters every time at bat. These are his two main signals to everyone in the game.

Explanation of the timing of the play.

Batter moves at least one of his feet out of the batter's box and puts one hand up in the air as he steps out for a timeout indication. Batter steps into the batter's box so that both feet are inside it and drops his upraised hand to signal time in, or he merely places the upraised hand and places it on the bat to start his practice swings.

(But it is the umpire how will signal "Time in" and "Time out" in accordance with the batter's signals.) Batter can ask for a timeout verbally (so he does not get quick-pitched). It is the umpire's discretion as to whether to call "No pitch" or to count the pitch, calling "Ball" or "Strike."

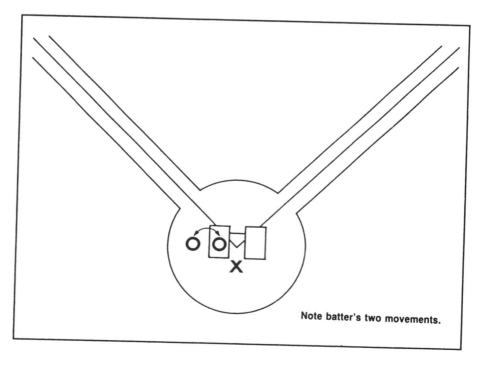

Note batter's two movements.

PLAY 48:   SPECIAL INSTRUCTIONS TO CATCHERS

Who gives the sign?

Coach yells to the catcher, loudly, "Hold the ball, run at him." Of course, the coach has had catchers practice this maneuver in practice and in "skull sessions." Catcher should be instantly ready to react correctly.

Who receives the sign?

Catcher is the key man here. He receives the ball on the pitch, if it has not been hit. Assume he now has it in his hand.

What is the purpose of this play?

To discourage opponents from running delayed steal plays, depending on the catcher throwing to the wrong bases, or throwing the ball at all. To discourage "trick plays" based on catcher's wrong moves.

When should this play be used?

Any time a runner purposely leads off a base far too much. This is especially true if it looks intentional on the part of the runner.

Explanation of the timing of the play.

This is a definite ritual, rehearsed. Catcher receives the pitch. He holds the ball in his hand up near his ear, where all can see it, yells to pitcher or first baseman to cover home plate and fast. Catcher runs out on the diamond with the ball. He cuts off the runner so he cannot return to his last base. He walks the runners into each other. While they both occupy one base, he tags each of them and maybe gets a double play, if the other runner leaves the base. If a lead runner breaks for home plate from third, he can fire a throw to the man covering home. This same play can be executed as described, but catcher hands the ball to the first baseman, and he runs the runners into each other. In this case, the catcher will quickly return to cover home plate.

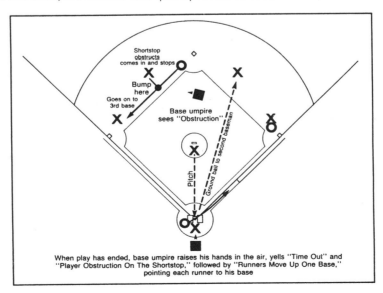

Shortstop obstructs comes in and stops

Bump here

Goes on to 3rd base

Base umpire sees "Obstruction"

Ground ball to second baseman

Pitch

When play has ended, base umpire raises his hands in the air, yells "Time Out" and "Player Obstruction On The Shortstop," followed by "Runners Move Up One Base," pointing each runner to his base

PLAY 49:   THE RIGHT-FIELD-TO-FIRST-BASE-OUT

Who gives the sign?

Right fielder and first baseman must practice this play often to make it an automatic reaction in a game. The two could have a prearranged verbal sign they yell. There is no actual sign given for this play.

Who receives the sign?

Right fielder, when the ball is hit hard and on one fast hop to him, and he is playing up close to first base.

What is the timing of this play?

Hitter, left- or right-handed, tees off on a one-bounce hit to the drawn-in right fielder, who charges in as soon as the ball is hit, fires to the first baseman instantly, beating the runner. He might be able to do it on a two- or three-hop hit, but fielder's momentum must be fast as he charges in.

When should this play be used?

Look for this whenever you face a hard-hitting batter who drills one-hoppers to right fielder. Also be aware of this possibility when you suspect they have a hit-and-run play on.

Explanation of the timing of this play.

Hitter hits a very quick, hard ball directly to the right fielder as he is coming in. The hitter will slow down some, knowing it is a base hit. If he doesn't hustle, he finds himself out at first base, for the quick return throw from the right fielder has been rehearsed. He is simply beaten to the bag by the throw.

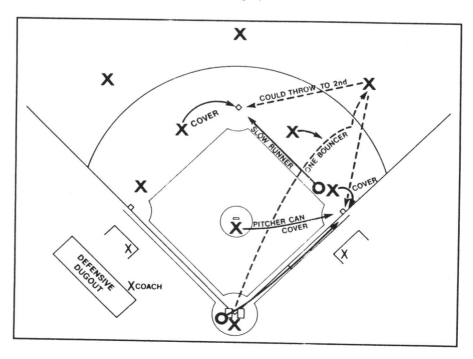

PLAY 50: COACHES' SIGNAL FOR THE INTENTIONAL WALK

Who gives the sign?

Coach on the bench gives the sign to the pitcher or catcher, or both. Catcher then calls for four straight outside balls to be thrown by the pitcher.

Who receives the sign?

Usually the catcher gets it first, then relays it to the pitcher.

When should this play be used?

Man on third base (walk the next two hitters). Man on second base (walk the next batter). Man on second base and third base (walk the next batter). Men on first base and third base (walk the next batter). Or any time the winning run is sitting on second base or third base.

What is the purpose of this play?

To fill an empty base and prevent a good hitter from being able to hit the ball. This tactic may set up a double play at any base, or it may set up a force-out at any base.

Explanation of the timing of the play.

Coach signals to the catcher that he wants the next batter walked. He usually points to first base or just holds up four fingers. The catcher signals the pitcher by closing his fist and pointing that arm straight out to his side, pointing to away outside. The pitcher pitches outside the batter's box to the catcher's outstretched hand. Caution: Be sure pitcher throws the ball far enough away from the hitter that he can't reach it at all.

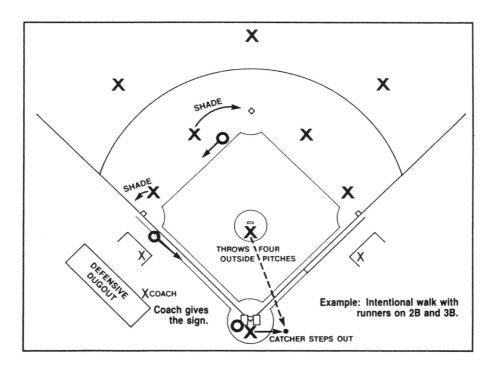

PLAY 51:   MANAGER OR COACH, TRIPS TO THE MOUND

Who gives the sign?

The coach or the manager will go to the mound to encourage, assist, advise, or change pitchers at that point in the game. After the conversation, or before conversing, coach may signal the bullpen which pitcher to bring in or he may make no change then.

Who receives the sign?

Bullpen coach and pitchers warming up in the bullpen.

What is the purpose of this play?

So that everyone in the ballpark knows who the pitcher's replacement will be. To speed up the game and the new pitcher's arrival into the game.

When should this play be used?

Whenever a pitching change is deemed necessary by the coach.

Explanation of the timing of the play.

In most leagues, head coach or pitching coach may go to the mound once to talk to pitcher without removal from the game. Pitcher must be removed on the second trip to the mound. Coach signaling bullpen touches left arm to signify the left-hander warming up is the one to come in the game. He will touch his right arm to signify the right-handed pitcher is to come in.

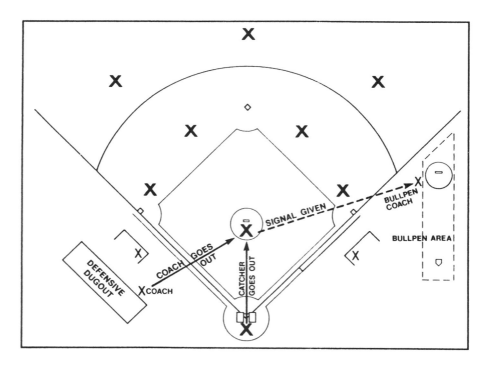

PLAY 52: "THE OLD HIDDEN BALL TRICK"

Who gives the sign?

Coach on the bench, or any infielder who feels that the base runner nearest his base may forget and lose track of where the ball is.

Who receives the sign?

All six infielders are involved. Any one of them may have the "hidden ball" after a huddle.

What is the purpose of this play?

More than two men huddle at the mound, to hold a discussion or to encourage one another or to straighten out a signal given. Or it can begin by an infielder holding on to a ball at the conclusion of a play.

When should this play be used?

Excellent time: two outs, three and two count, runners going. Also excellent: bases loaded (gives three men to pick off).

Explanation of the timing of the play.

Runner or runners lose sight of the ball on a play or after a play. Pitcher stays in the grass area near the mound and acts as though he has the ball and is getting ready to go up on the mound. He can't be on the dirt, though, while the hidden ball trick is under way. Defensive men may assume usual positions, as if ready for the batter to hit. Infielder with the ball can throw to a man covering another base, or he can just move slowly toward a runner off base, then tag him. A rundown play may ensue if runner sees the ball too early.

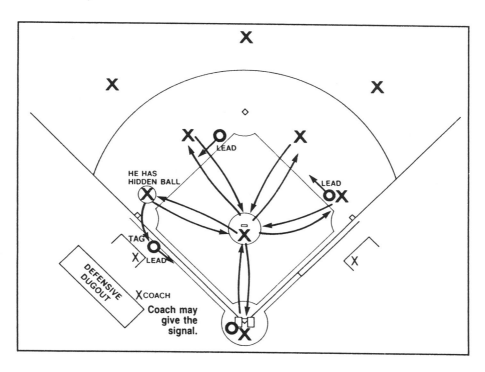

Conclusions

Baseball is a unique sport in the very nature of its defense. In baseball—unlike football, basketball, hockey, and soccer—the defense cannot turn instantly into offense and score. In this respect it is much like the game of volleyball. Your team must be up at bat to put runs on the scoreboard. So the obvious anxiety of all baseball defenses is "to get to bat as soon as possible." How can we get those three necessary outs as quickly as possible before the offense can score even one run? It boils down to the dual objective of *getting outs* and *preventing runs.*

Of course the prime weapon in this game of defense is the pitcher. Certainly, pitching is 80 percent of the defensive game, but what can we do about the other 20 percent? Many of the finest pitchers have been losers with a poor defense behind them. Some quite frequently.

We are often told, in team sports, that the "best offense is a good defense." This is not always entirely true. Let's qualify that famous baseball adage by rewording it to "A great defense merely means that your offense needs fewer runs to win." The Los Angeles Dodgers have been proving this point since their move to Chavez Ravine. Back to that 20 percent of the defense *not in the hands of the pitcher.* Baseball teams had better be spending their time practicing this phase of the game. Hitting isn't everything.

How many coaches have come up short in the runs department at the end of a game? Their typical comment is, "We left thirteen men on base and scored only two runs." What psychological frustration occurs in baseball when the offense realizes that the defense is well coached, always in the correct positions for the next pitch, makes the big play many times, is cutting them off with force-outs and double plays, and is countering their offensive plays with counter-defensive skill? The defense may be coupling just good solid ball with the "element of surprise" in many instances. The team at bat can become a picture of discouragement.

In summarizing this chapter the reader can see that he has learned a great deal about baseball defenses. There are actually more defensive tricks or plays in the game than there are offensive ones. From the author's research into both offense and defense during the past eight years, he has found this to be true.

With the increased emphasis on offense in all sports, the love of playing the defensive part of the game, and the time spent on perfecting it, seems to diminish in many of our team sports. What is even more frustrating to the coach and player than the 0-0 tie in football is the losing of a game of baseball 13-12. It may delight the fans, but the defense has failed.

Chapter 4

UMPIRES' CALLS AND SIGNS

Baseball umpiring is a most difficult task. The umpire, in this complicated game of strategies, must know the rules "cold" (and there are many), must maintain control, and is required to make both usual and unusual calls. His decisions are based on observing the play and may depend on a hundredth of a second or a fraction of an inch.

Certainly the motions, gyrations, and words of these men are integral parts of this game. Although the umpire is not a player and is impartial to either offense or defense, he has as many signs to communicate as does any player or coach on either team. This chapter will discuss and illustrate the calls that must be made by the umpire in the course of a game. Some are silently given, some are indicated in a loud voice, and others are given vocally and with body gestures as well.

The players, coaches, and fans all look to the umpire instantly for his call on any play. We will look at those calls in three categories: calls at home plate, calls on the bases or in the field, and some little known language that the umpires use among themselves. To further facilitate an understanding of these calls, each situation is described fully for the reader's ease in defining each play called.

The fan of our national pastime will, undoubtedly, be surprised to know that there are so many situations in which a baseball umpire must be ready to make a call in an instant. But all who are interested in baseball will widen their knowledge of the game's plays and strategies greatly by reading through this chapter.

Finally, this chapter will also indicate the placement of umpires on the diamond during a baseball game, whether one man is required to work alone or with one, two, or three other umpires. These placements of the umpiring stations depend upon the number of outs in the inning and the number of umpires available for that game.

For reasons of long association and umpiring skills, the author has consulted Charlie Lewis, the premier high school and college baseball umpire in the San Bernardino area, in the writing of this chapter on umpires' calls and language. As always, it has been fun and a learning experience working with this fine athlete-coach-umpire. The author has also employed umpire Gene Cestaro, of San Bernardino High School, and NCAA college umpire

Phil Meyer, from Yorba Linda, California, to assist in this section of the book. The combined efforts of these men should give the reader the best treatise on umpires' calls and signs in baseball literature.

UMPIRES' CALLS AND SIGNS AT HOME PLATE

PLAY 1:   CALLING THE RUNNER OUT OR SAFE

Jerk the mask off fast. Have it in the left hand. This can be a tag play or a close force play. The umpire must move around into position to see this close play. He gets into position where the ball coming in will neither hit him nor interfere with his concentration on the call.

If runner is out, the umpire makes a sweeping movement down toward the ground with one arm, or he can jerk one hand upward as he yells loudly "Yer out."

If runner is safe, the umpire makes a sweeping movement with both arms outward from the body and yells loudly "Safe."

Special Instructions and Notations

The out sign can be a closed fist and forearm jerked up into the air over the umpire's head, or it can be the entire right arm swung down in a vertical arc toward the ground. *Umpire at the plate takes off his mask quickly,* then lines himself up on the extension of the third base line, very close to the catcher and incoming ball and runner. Umpire is standing up, one foot ahead, leaning forward into the play area.

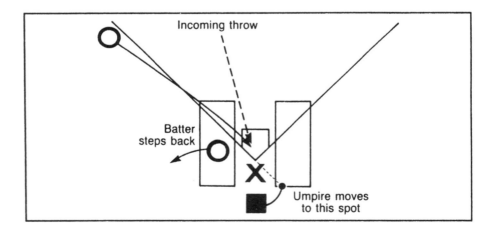

PLAY 2:   CALLING THE FAIR BALL ON THE BATTER

As soon as the ball is hit on the chalk line or near the line, and fair, the umpire points with one arm to the inside of the diamond.

The umpire must be careful not to yell anything at this time, for to yell "Fair ball" can be easily confused with "Foul ball."

Special Instructions and Notations

If the ball is hit slowly just a few feet from the plate, umpire leaves his spot and follows the catcher and the ball up the line to be right on top of the play. Umpire, however, straddles the foul line to be able to see if the ball rolls out and in, or in and out, and to see who plays the ball and where it is played, finally.

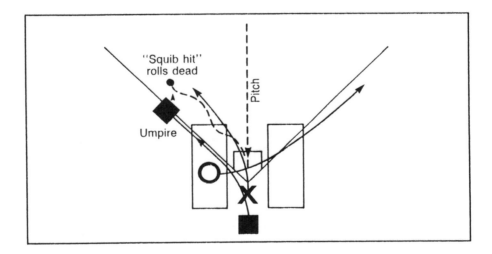

PLAY 3:   CALLING THE FOUL BALL ON THE BATTER

Any time the ball is hit near the foul line, the plate umpire must move over slightly to be able to see the foul line in respect to the ball hit. This helps him judge those balls hit beyond the base or those rolling foul before getting to the base.

Plate umpire waits to see if the ball was hit beyond the base, then makes the call. The base umpire can make the same call if he is near or on the line.

Plate umpire calls balls hit to the base. Base umpire calls balls hit beyond the base.

As soon as the plate umpire, sighting the ball and its rolling path, and where it was picked up for play, determines the ball to be foul he turns outward to the foul area and declares loudly, several times "Foul ball, foul ball," so everyone on the diamond and in the dugout can hear it.

Special Instructions and Notations

If the ball is hit slowly down the line, but might roll all the way over the base, and has that much momentum, the umpire leaves his spot and follows the catcher and the ball up the line to be right on top of the movement and location of the ball. The umpire, however stays on the foul line, straddling it, to see if the ball rolls out and in, or in and out, and to see who plays the ball, and where it is finally played.

It is important for the umpire who has just called the foul ball loudly to remember to raise his hands above his head quickly, indicating "time out," for he "kills the ball" in this manner. All foul balls are determined to be "dead balls" until returned to play.

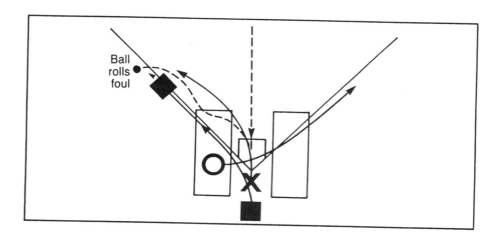

PLAY 4:   FOUL LINE CALLS BEFORE OR AFTER THE BALL PASSES FIRST OR THIRD BASE

The umpire must be alert for various kinds of foul balls *before reaching first or third base.* If the ball is hit straight down at batter's feet, then goes fair, umpire immediately yells "Foul ball" several times. If the ball is hit down on home plate, then goes fair, the umpire immediately points Fair *but remains silent.* If the ball is a slow roller down the line, it may curve fair or foul. If no one touches the ball, umpire makes his decision after the ball is at rest.

Special Instructions and Notations

If the ball is hit slowly down the line, but might roll all the way over the base, and has that much momentum, the umpire leaves his spot and follows the catcher and the ball up the line to be right on top of the movement and location of the ball. The umpire, however, stays on the foul line, straddling it, to see if the ball rolls out and in, in and out, and to see who plays the ball, and where it is finally played.

It is important for the umpire who has just called the foul ball loudly to remember to raise his hands above his head quickly, indicating "Time out," for he "kills the ball" in this manner. All foul balls are determined to be "dead balls" until returned to play.

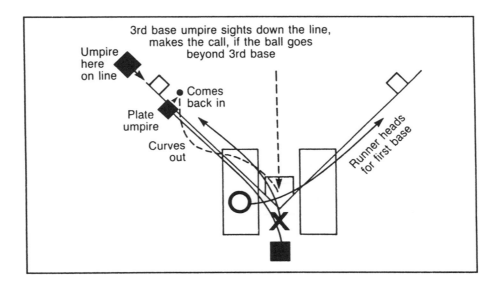

PLAY 5:   GIVING THE COUNT ON THE BATTER

Some umpires do this on every pitch to remind themselves. The right-hand fingers pointing into the air signify the number of strikes. The left-hand fingers signify the number of balls. Most umpires give these finger counts every two or three pitches.

If the coach in the dugout or on the base coaching areas asks for a count, umpire gives it to him. If a runner or the batter needs to know the count, the umpire will give it to him.

Some umpires have the habit of holding up the number of right and left fingers for balls and strikes after every pitch. This would be ideal for everyone concerned, and it would assist the plate umpire in not forgetting the count. Most umpires will give the count on every other pitch or on every pitch after the third pitch. Some umpires will yell "Eleven," meaning a one-and-one count, or "Twenty-two," meaning a two-and-two count, and so on.

Special Instructions and Notations

It is a very good idea for all base umpires, as well as the plate umpire, to hold a plastic or metal counter, a device upon which the correct count is kept. The counter requires that something be held in the hand at all times, but it certainly prevents the embarrassing situation of any umpire forgetting the count or calling out the wrong count, which error could drastically change a ball game's outcome.

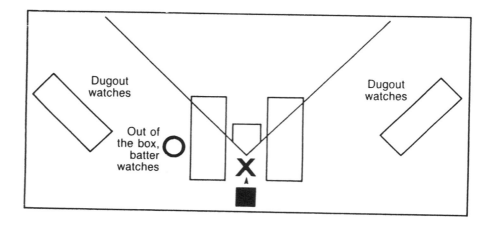

PLAY 6:   CALLING A TIME-OUT AT HOME PLATE

A time-out might be requested at any time by anyone on the field for many reasons. It may be requested by players in the dugout, but it must be for a good reason. However, the umpire may not necessarily award it, for any number of good reasons.

It is best to wait for the umpire's hands to shoot straight up in the air above his head before *assuming* that it has been granted. The umpire will usually yell loudly "Time" or "Time out" as he raises his arms over his head. If this sign is given before the pitch, it tells the pitcher that the ball is dead, and he is not to pitch. (The "Pitcher, don't throw" sign is actually the hand opposite of the batter's position at the plate extended out, palm forward, resembling a policeman stopping traffic. When this sign is used, there is no verbal signal that accompanies the outstretched palm of the hand.)

Special Instructions and Notations

Players and managers should not become irritated if time is not called when requested. There may be a good reason at that instant for not granting it. After the play or the pitch has been delivered, however, the coach and/or player has the right to ask that umpire why he did not grant the timeout.

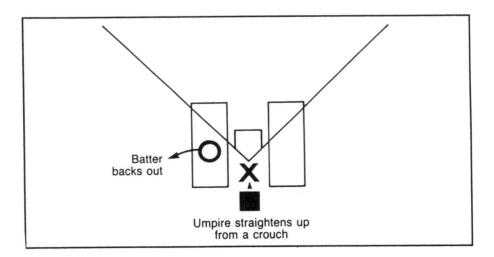

PLAY 7:   PUTTING THE BALL BACK INTO PLAY

When time is called for any reason on the diamond, or when the ball is dead or declared dead, the progress of the game stops. When it has been decided by the plate umpire that play should resume, some plate umpires will use the sign of pointing directly at the pitcher. Since game action begins with the pitch to the batter, that is an appropriate sign: The umpire can use either hand, depending upon the position of the batter. He may also yell "Play ball."

Special Instructions and Notations

When the call "Play" or "Play ball" is heard throughout the ballpark, that is the signal for the batter to be in the batter's box, ready for the pitch, for the pitcher to begin his signal and pitch, for the defense to be down and ready for the ground ball, and for all runners to step off their bases to take their leads.

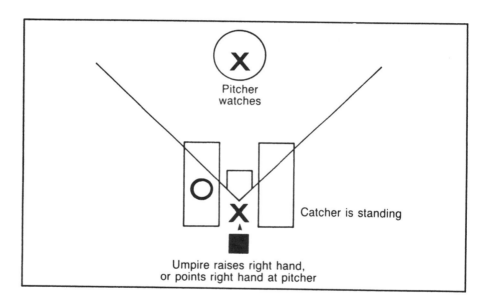

PLAY 8:   ADVANCING THE RUNNERS OR THE BATTER BY ONE OR MORE BASES

There may be several types of plays in which runner or batter may be called back to their original positions. Also, there are as many plays in which runner or batter may be advanced one or more bases. To do this, some umpire on the diamond has called "Time out." When it has been determined to which bases the runners advance, the umpire will use his left hand and point to each runner, yelling "Runner, take third base." He is giving orders to runners. He uses the left hand to point to the base each runner is to take.

If a balk has been called, to advance base runners along one base, the call is "Balk" or "That's a balk."

All other oral signs will be the umpire pointing with the left hand, directing each individual base runner to his next base, saying, for example, "First base runner, take second," etc.

If a balk has been called, umpire lets all action stop if the pitch was thrown before balk was called. Then he awards the runners their bases.

Special Instructions and Notations

Runners must be alert that they do not assume certain bases have been awarded and advance on their own. They could be quickly tagged out. Runner goes to next base *only* after he hears the umpire direct him to it.

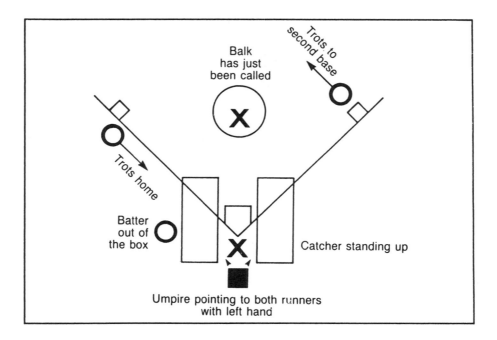

PLAY 9:   BATTER INTERFERENCE WITH THE POSSIBLE DOUBLE PLAY

The umpire sees the batter interfere with the catcher or in any way impede a throw to a base on a steal. The umpire then calls the batter out for interference, if the runner is safe.

If the ball was hit while interference occurred, and runners advanced, the umpire will call runners back to the bases they occupied before the interference. The batter is out and the lead runner is out, and all other runners will be sent back to the bases last occupied.

The umpire stands up, yells "Time out" followed by "Batter interference" and "Batter is out." He points to the lead runner who was stealing on the interference play. He yells, "Runner is out, batter interference."

Special Instructions and Notations

This play could also occur when the batter swung at a third strike, missed, and the runner was going on the pitch. If the batter stepped in front of the catcher or interfered in any way after striking out, then the umpire calls the stealing runner out, completing the double play.

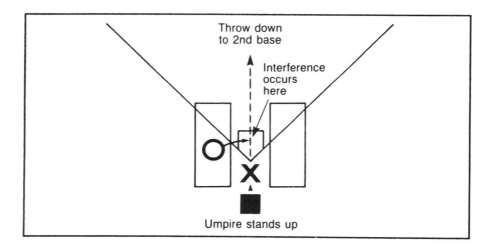

PLAY 10:   CATCHER INTERFERENCE AT HOME PLATE

The umpire sees the catcher interfere with the batter's swing, or with a bunt attempt. The umpire will then yell "That's obstruction" and point his right hand out 90 degrees from his body, showing the signal for a delayed dead ball. The umpire waits for all action to stop before awarding the batter first base. Other base runners advance only one base, and only if they are forced by the umpire's awarding the batter first base.

If the batter hits safely, the interference call is then waived.

The first oral call made by the umpire is yelling "That's obstruction" to the catcher as soon as he sees it. The second oral call made would be the umpire pointing to first base in awarding that base to the batter with the call "Batter, take first base, catcher interference" and directing any other base runners to move up one base.

Special Instructions and Notations

A common spot for this to occur is in cases where the catcher stands up too close to the plate and the batter. One of two things can happen when this occurs: the catcher will touch the bat as hitter draws back to bunt; or the batter may be deep in the batter's box, and as he may swing late, his bat will nick the edge of the catcher's glove.

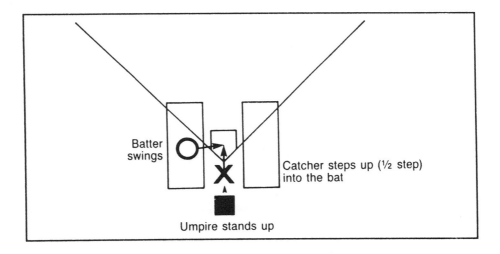

PLAY 11:   PLAYER OBSTRUCTION AROUND HOME PLATE

Obstruction occurs when a defensive player, in this case the catcher, not making a play, impedes, slows down, or touches a base runner. When this occurs, after action stops, the umpire yells to the catcher "That is obstruction." The umpire then imposes the proper penalties. The batter is advanced by the umpire to that base which he feels would have been gained had there been no obstruction.

The umpire will first throw his hands above his head and yell "Time out" followed by "That's player obstruction," then point to and name the player doing the obstructing. The umpire then imposes the penalties for obstructing. The batter is advanced only to those bases which he feels the batter would have made had there been no obstruction. Any other runners on base will be moved to other bases only if forced by the batter-runner.

Special Instructions and Notations

This is an unusual play at the plate, but several men on the defensive team could become guilty of this. The first baseman, the catcher, and the pitcher could obstruct a batter or bunter in some way or another.

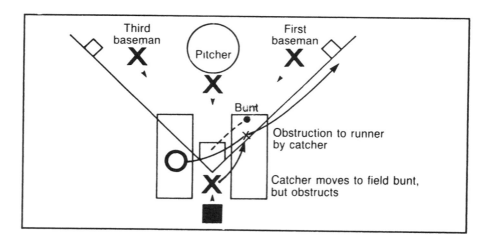

PLAY 12: CALLING FOR ASSISTANCE FROM A BASE UMPIRE ON A BATTER'S CHECKED SWING

Only the defensive team will be asking for assistance by the base umpire. On the batter's checked swing, the plate umpire may point to a field umpire to ask him for a second opinion, *but only* if he is uncertain. The field umpire will give the "Swung" or "Did not swing" sign when asked.

The plate umpire does not have to ask for assistance when it is requested by the defense.

The plate umpire will often yell down to the base umpire, while also pointing to him, saying, "Did he go?"

The first signal, the plate umpire pointing to the umpire on the first base line, if the batter is a right-hander, is a silent one. The plate umpire merely points directly at the umpire on the right field line. If the batter is a left-hander, plate umpire will point to the umpire near the third base line, asking his opinion.

Either umpire called upon to express his opinion will then raise the fist quickly to signify 'Strike" or lower both arms parallel to the ground to signify "Ball" or "No, he did not go around far enough for it to be called a strike."

While giving these arm signals, those umpires may or may not add various verbal signals, such as yelling "Strike" or "Ball"or "Yes" or "No."

Special Instructions and Notations

At the levels of college baseball and below, *the catcher must ask the plate umpire to point to a base umpire for assistance.* The base umpire will render a quick decision *only when asked to do so by the plate umpire.* In professional baseball, you will see the catcher often doing the pointing to the base umpire for the opinion. *But it should* still *go to the plate umpire* for he is in charge of the game.

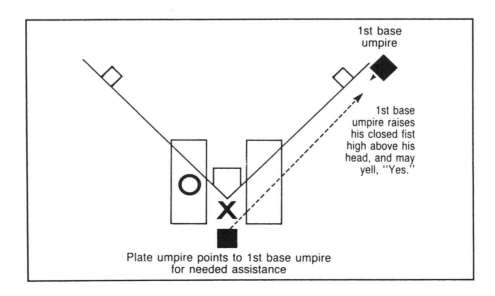

1st base
umpire

1st base
umpire raises
his closed fist
high above his
head, and may
yell, "Yes."

Plate umpire points to 1st base umpire
for needed assistance

PLAY 13:   CALLING THE INFIELD FLY, IF FAIR

When the right index finger is held high by any of the umpires on the field, it signifies that the pop-up just hit is properly ruled an infield fly. This means that the batter is immediately out, and really need not run. This rule is primarily to govern the action of the base runners, for they proceed, after the catch or the "muff," *at their own peril.*

This infield fly situation occurs with men on second and first only, or with bases loaded, and there must be less than two outs.

The batter is ruled out as the umpire raises his right fist, not the index finger (which is used by umpires to remind each other of this situation before the ball is hit).

The "infield fly rule" prevents the infield from dropping an infield pop-up intentionally and executing a double play.

If the infield fly is hit close to either the right field line or the left field line, *only the plate umpire* will yell loudly "Infield fly, if fair."

Special Instructions and Notations

Another signal that is given on this play will be by the base umpires, who will raise their right fists into the air and declare, "The batter is out, infield fly."

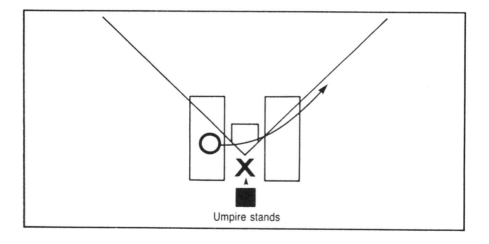

Umpire stands

PLAY 14:   CALLING THE DEAD BALL AND DELAYED DEAD BALL

When an umpire shoves his fist to the right of his body and holds it out in that position, it signifies a delayed dead ball. If an infraction has been committed and the offended player actually gained an advantage on the play, the infraction might be ignored.

A good example of this call would be an umpire calling a balk on a pitcher after he had delivered. If the batting team gains more than the infraction would have given them, the umpire will waive the penalty.

In the case of a balk, the pitch might have been pitched and the ball hit before the pitcher or defense heard the call. In this case, the only verbal signal would be "Balk" yelled, loudly followed by the "Delayed dead ball" arm signal called after action has stopped.

In the case of obstruction on a runner not being played on, the umpire would yell "Obstruction" loudly, followed by the "Delayed dead ball" arm signal called after action has stopped.

Special Instructions and Notations

Usually the left arm is thrust out at a right angle to the body to signify "Delayed dead ball," although some umpires use either arm. The reason for the left fist and arm going out 90 degrees to the body is that the right arm is used to call strikes.

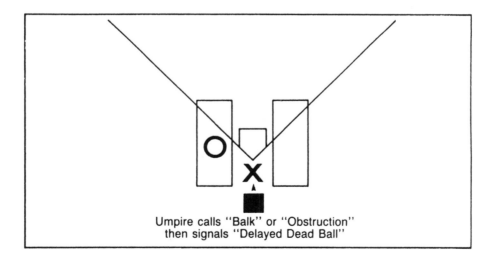

Umpire calls "Balk" or "Obstruction"
then signals "Delayed Dead Ball"

PLAY 15:   CALLING BOTH TEAMS TO RESUME PLAY

To resume action, and to get the pitcher to deliver to the batter, the umpire's signal is a motion with the arm at head level, one of "beckoning." A variation of this umpire's signal would be a direct pointing at the pitcher with the index finger of the right hand. As the umpire points to the pitcher to deliver the ball, and with that hand makes a beckoning motion, he may also cry out loudly "Play ball."

Special Instructions and Notations

In all dead ball situations, the umpire at the plate will indicate "Resume play" by both hand and vocal sign.

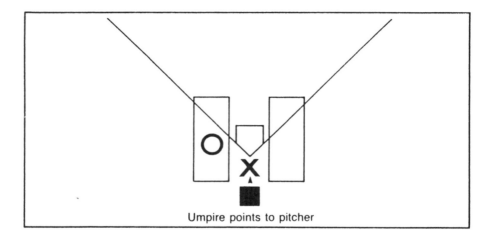
Umpire points to pitcher

PLAY 16:   CALLING THE EJECTION OF A PLAYER, COACH, OR MANAGER

An umpire, upon finally deciding that a player or a coach should be ejected from a ball game, will yell "Yer out of the ball game" and point toward the dugout and out of the stadium using the right hand.

Special Instructions and Notations

Play will not resume until the umpire has seen to it that the player or coach is off the playing field and not sitting on the bench or in the dugout. Should that person refuse to leave the game and the premises, *the umpire will warn him of the danger of forfeit of the game against his team. Finally, a forfeit is declared.*

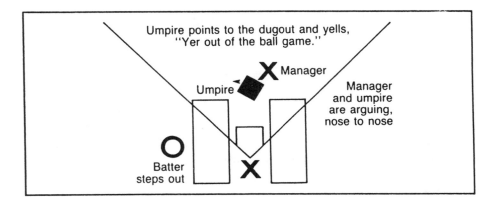

PLAY 17: CALLING THE THIRD STRIKE, THE BATTER IS OUT

On either a called or a swinging third strike, the umpire points out to the right of his body with the right hand in a short jabbing motion. This indicates the "Strike" call. *The umpire will yell loudly "Strike three."* Since it is the third strike, the umpire will follow the "Strike three" call with the umpire's usual gesture for an out, raising the right fist in the air in a jabbing motion.

There is a warning here—the umpire never says "The batter is out" unless it is a dropped or trapped third strike. Then the catcher must tag the runner or throw down to first base to complete that out.

Special Instructions and Notations

There are two good reasons why the umpire does not follow his "Strike three" call with the call "Batter is out."

First, this adds insult to injury. On a close call, it might add to causing the batter to have a confrontation with the plate umpire.

Second, if the ball is dropped on the third strike, called or swinging, or trapped on that strike, the catcher must tag the runner or fire a throw down to first base to retire that batter. For this reason, the batter would not actually be out until one of those two acts was performed. The plate umpire saves this call for only that situation.

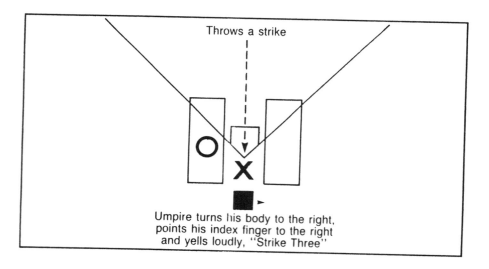

Throws a strike

Umpire turns his body to the right,
points his index finger to the right
and yells loudly, "Strike Three"

PLAY 18:   CALLING "BALL FOUR" AND "TAKE YOUR BASE"

On the fourth called ball the pitcher delivers, the umpire calls out "Ball four." He does not usually call "Ball one," "Ball two," "Ball three," but he will loudly declare "Ball four."

The umpire usually does not yell "Batter, take your base," but he points to first base with his left index finger.

Special Instructions and Notations

Base coaches, coaches in the dugout, runners, the batter, the catcher—all who might be involved in a possible play called by the offense—must be aware that they must watch and listen to the plate umpire carefully on a possible "Ball four" call. If it were a questionable call, strike or ball, and not heard or not called, the offense and/or defense could be crossed up.

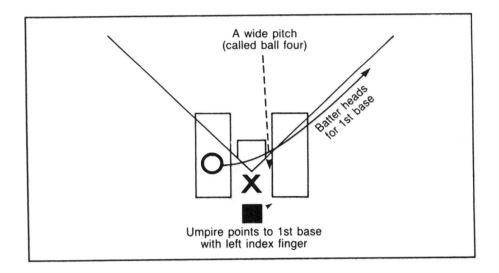

PLAY 19:   CALLING THE HIT BATSMAN AND "TAKE YOUR BASE"

Where it has been determined that the batter was hit by a pitch (and made a reasonable attempt to avoid being hit) the umpire will hold up his arms and declare "Dead ball" followed by "Time out." Umpire will then point to first base with his left hand or left index finger. Some umpires will follow all of this with the oral signal "Batter hit by the pitch. Take your base."

Special Instructions and Notations

Some umpires will use no verbal signs at all. The batter and catcher will look to the plate umpire to see if he has determined it a "hit by the pitch." The umpire will simply say nothing and point to first base once or twice with the left arm.

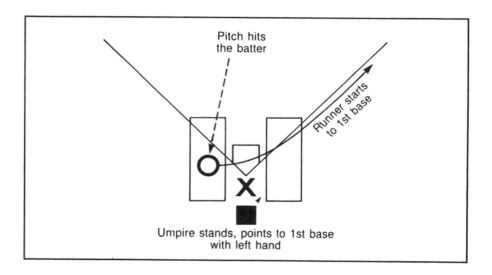

Pitch hits
the batter

Runner starts
to 1st base

Umpire stands, points to 1st base
with left hand

PLAY 20:   CALLING THE BATTER STEPPING ON HOME PLATE OR OUT OF THE BATTER'S BOX

If the lines of the batter's box are not obliterated so as to make a decision difficult to judge, if the batter steps out of the batter's box or on home plate, any part of it, he should be called out. Umpire will call "Time out" after action of the hit ball is finished then make the call. Some umpires will warn a batter if they see that this is a habit or tendency. Usually one warning will suffice.

Being called out only occurs if the batter contacts the ball, fair or foul. If he misses hitting the ball or lets the ball go by, he is not determined to be out by the umpire.

If he is thrown out on a ground ball play or on a caught fly, his out nullifies the out call by the plate umpire. The plate umpire could tell the batter that he would have been called out if he had not been put out by the defense.

After all action has stopped on a ball hit fair or foul, the plate umpire will declare "Time out," will yell "The batter is out, he stepped on home plate [or out of the batter's box]." He will nullify all bases that the batter gained on that hit ball, and he will direct all base runners back to their original bases.

Special Instructions and Notations

Umpires should be careful in making this drastic call, being certain that they know where the drawn lines of that batter's box are (or were). Of course, if the lead foot steps down on enough of the plate to make it an obvious infraction of the rule, then "Out" is called. However, if it is a borderline (stepping on the black edge or a portion of the black), the umpire should use sound judgment and not be too quick to call it. *A warning here might be in order, but only the first time the umpire sees the batter step in this manner.*

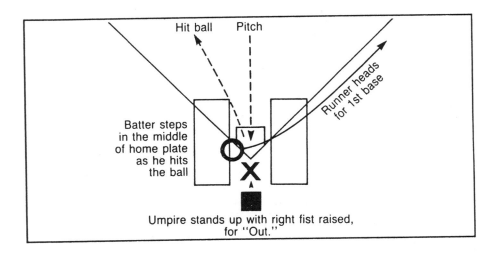

PLAY 21:   CALLING THE TOPPED BALL HIT BY THE BATTER

A ball hit down on home plate is a fair ball. A ball hit down on the batter's foot or leg is a foul ball. Knowing these two facts makes topped ball calls fairly simple. If the ball is topped out anywhere other than home plate or the batter's leg or foot, this may then require some immediate perception on the part of the plate umpire, for he must see quickly whether the ball first hit foul or fair dirt. After he determines "Fair," the umpire must quickly move to an extension of the foul line the ball was topped near, sighting down that line, and watching the ball until it rolls foul or is played by an infielder.

If the ball is determined to be foul, umpire turns away toward foul ground, yelling loudly "Foul ball, foul ball."

If the ball is determined to be fair, umpire turns in toward fair ground; simply pointing several times, saying nothing.

Again, the umpire wants to let the ball roll as far as it will, before going foul or being picked up or touched by an infielder, before he determines foul or fair and makes a call.

Special Instructions and Notations

Moving over to sight down the foul line, the umpire must not watch the fielder who makes a play on the ball or the fielder's feet. He should watch where the ball is when it is picked up. It is easy to become distracted.

A player could be in a foul area, but play a fair ball. A player could be in a fair area, but play a foul ball.

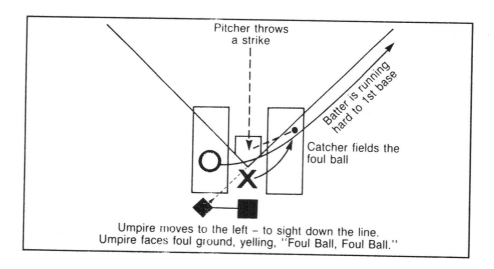

PLAY 22:   CALLING BATTER'S ILLEGAL EQUIPMENT

This is usually a plate umpire's call. The umpire may suspect a bat which has too much pine tar on it, or which has been "doctored" in any way. The umpire will raise his arms, call "Time," and inspect the bat or any other illegal equipment.

After inspection the umpire may ask the hitter to replace the bat with a legal one, or he may have to ask a runner or batter to remove illegal equipment.

If the batter hits the ball safely, he is out, and all runners return to their original bases.

Special Instructions and Notations

All statistics for the batter are removed from the records if he hits safely with an illegal bat. Your umpire should direct the scorekeepers of this. Batter is out, with no statistics recorded except a time at bat resulting in an out.

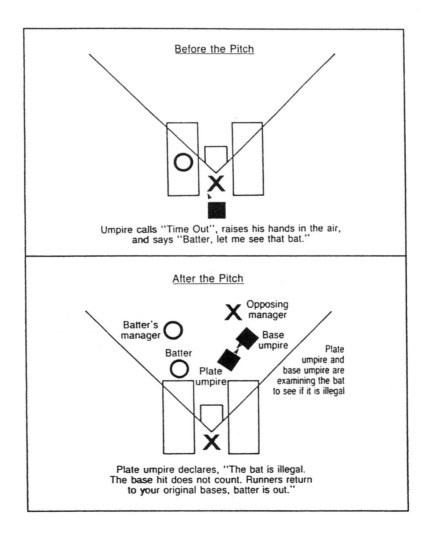

PLAY 23: CALLING THE BATTER OUT FOR BATTING OUT OF ORDER

An umpire must get an appeal from a member of the defensive team before the first pitch is thrown to the following batter. If the defensive team realizes that the wrong batter is hitting, they may not make the appeal while the wrong batter is hitting. If they do, the umpire will ignore it until the batter has had his turn at bat.

Upon an appeal *at the proper time,* the umpire throws his arms in the air and calls "Time out." He then looks at his line-up card, using it to make his decision to grant or refuse the defensive team's claim of a batter hitting out of order. If the lineup card is not proof, he asks for the home scorebook. He may ask to look at and compare both scorebooks.

If the appeal is correct, the batter who hit out of turn is declared out. The runners are then returned to their original bases. Teams and umpires then make certain the lineup is correct from that point on.

Special Instructions and Notations

It is a wise thing for umpires to check with the batting team quickly to see that the succeeding batters are in order and that the disorder has been cleared up to prevent this from occurring again with the next batter.

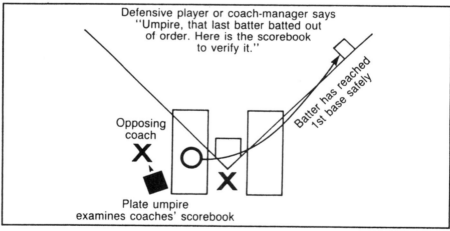

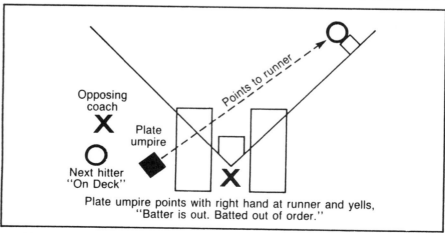

PLAY 24:   CALLING A FOUL TIP, NOT HELD

If the foul tip is held on the third strike, umpire will indicate that the batter is out by yelling "Yer out." Umpire must indicate to everyone when a batter hits a foul tip. When a batter barely touches a ball with the bat, it might appear that he missed the ball, appearing that the catcher missed it, too. To indicate to all that it was actually tipped, the umpire immediately slides the palms of his hands together like the cymbal player in an orchestra. Runners are returned and batter is not out.

When a foul tip is not held, is dropped by the catcher, or goes past the catcher, the umpire will indicate "Strike" with his usual right-hand signal, but he will raise his hands over his head and slide the palm of one against the palm of the other. He should yell "Foul ball. "

This "cymbal" signal tells everyone concerned that the ball was definitely a foul tip, not held, and it is not a passed ball and a missed strike.

A foul tip on the third strike, not held, is not a strike, and the batter is not out. If it is held, it is a strike and batter is out.

Special Instructions and Notations

Runners, especially, must be very alert to this signal, for they may not know that they can advance and try a steal on some foul tips, and they must return to their original bases on other foul tips.

They must know the rules and the signals of the plate umpire.

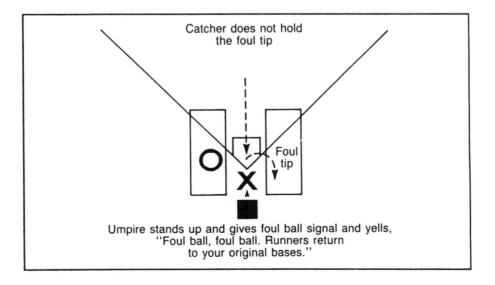

Catcher does not hold
the foul tip

Foul
tip

Umpire stands up and gives foul ball signal and yells,
"Foul ball, foul ball. Runners return
to your original bases."

PLAY 25:   CALLING A FOUL TIP, HELD

If the foul tip is held on the third strike, then the batter is out and the umpire will indicate that. He will call "Strike three" but will merely signal the batter is out with the jerking up of the right fist into the air.

If the foul tip is held on the first or second strike. It is treated as any strike, as if it were never foul.   •

In other words, a foul tip held on any strike allows any runner to advance to the next base at his own peril, of course, without having to return to his original base before beginning the steal of the next one.

Special Instructions and Notations

Another very interesting point for offense, defense, and base umpires to consider on foul tips held is that the catcher may throw down to a base for a pickoff after the pitch.

Since runners do not have to return to their original bases, as they do in foul tips not held, this makes them easy prey for catcher pickoffs at any base. If the runners do know the rules, and do not return after the tip is held by the catcher, then they are even more vulnerable to this catcher's ploy.

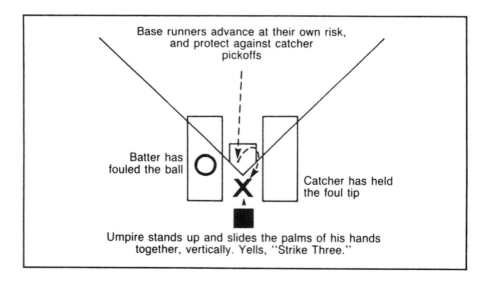

PLAY 26:   CALLING A WARNING TO THE PITCHER FOR THROWING AT THE HITTER

Usually, the pitcher is allowed one warning when he is suspected of throwing at a batter. If the pitcher throws again, and it is very close or hits the batter, the umpire must judge whether it was "intentional." If he judges it to be, the umpire will eject the pitcher from the game.

In some baseball leagues, the manager or coach is also ejected with the pitcher, for the manager is deemed to be as responsible as the pitcher, and the warning actually was given to him, too.

A new pitcher must be brought in, and an assistant coach is assigned by the ejected head coach to run the ball club until the end of the game.

Warning signal: "This is a warning, Pitcher, for intentionally throwing at the hitter."

Ejection signal: "Pitcher, you are out of the ball game for intentionally throwing at the batter." The umpire will turn and give the sign to the manager or coach as well.

Special Instructions and Notations

For both the warning and ejection signals, the umpire calls "Time out," then takes off his mask, walks about halfway to the plate, and gives the proper warning or ejection sign orally.

On each of these signs to the pitcher and manager or coach, that umpire should also warn the opposing team with these words: "No retaliation."

As the umpire is either warning or ejecting after the close pitches, he will point to the pitcher with the right index finger as he is talking.

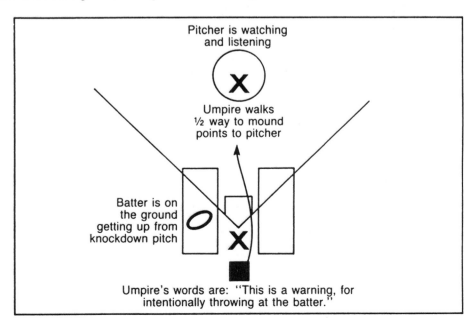

Pitcher is watching
and listening

Umpire walks
½ way to mound
points to pitcher

Batter is on
the ground
getting up from
knockdown pitch

Umpire's words are: "This is a warning, for
intentionally throwing at the batter."

PLAY 27:   CALLING THE BALK ON THE PITCHER

If the plate umpire sees the pitcher balk during any part of his stretch or delivery, he yells "Balk" immediately. If the umpire calls " Balk" after the pitch is released, he must wait for the action to stop on that play before assessing the penalty, moving the runners up one base. If the batter got a hit, or reached first base safely, the balk call is ignored. If the batter swung at the pitch and missed, or was thrown out on a grounder, or was out on a fly ball, the action of that play would be cancelled and the balk would be enforced.

The oral signal is simple. Umpire simply yells "Balk." This could be before or after the pitch. The umpire will throw his hands up over his head, as in calling "Time out."

After the action has stopped, the second oral signal given will be the umpire yelling to each base runner to advance to the next base, while pointing and directing with his left hand.

Special Instructions and Notations

The umpire must be certain to inform the pitcher and his manager the reason the balk was called.

All runners will be advanced one base on the balk call. A third base runner scores a run on the call.

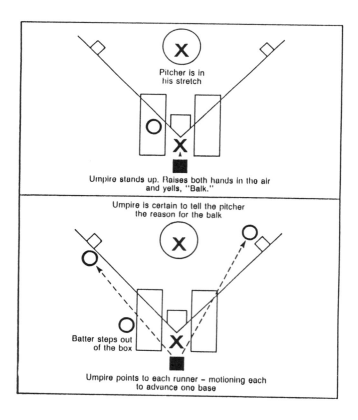

PLAY 28:   SEARCHING THE PITCHER AND HIS EQUIPMENT FOR AN ILLEGAL SUBSTANCE ON THE BALL

When an umpire goes to the mound reminiscent of a police officer frisking a suspect, he is doing exactly that. If it appears that the pitches have been "juiced up" with any kind of foreign substance, the umpire will do his best to find it.

The umpire will throw his arms up and yell "Time out," then he goes to the mound, inspects the ball or glove, or searches the pitcher's uniform, cap, etc.

The pitcher will be removed from the game if anything illegal is found.

After examining the body and equipment of the pitcher, if nothing is found, the umpire will return to his position behind the catcher and give the "Play ball" sign. Nothing else need be said.

However, if an illegal substance (or anything used to deface or rough up the baseball) is found, the umpire will yell loudly, to both pitcher and his manager, "Illegal substance on the baseball. The pitcher is ejected from the game."

Special Instructions and Notations

The umpire has the right to "frisk" any pitcher and examine his external layer of clothing, cap, glove, belt, hands, etc. He can also examine the baseball the pitcher is holding at the moment, looking for evidence of defacing.

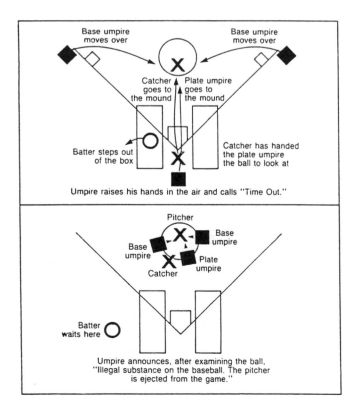

PLAY 29:   CALLING THE PITCHER'S DELAY OF THE GAME

After the designated number of seconds allowed a pitcher to make his delivery to the hitter (twenty seconds), if the pitcher does not then pitch to the batter, the plate umpire can start counting out loud, every twenty seconds, "Ball one," "Ball two," "Ball three," etc. until the batter receives four balls, then is awarded the walk.

If the pitcher refuses to pitch at all, the plate umpire will give ample warning to the team coach and the pitcher that he is delaying the game.

The first oral signal is to the pitcher, telling him to speed up his deliveries, he has only twenty seconds to deliver. The umpire walks out about thirty feet toward the mound to inform him.

Second calls would be "Ball one," "Ball two," "Ball three," until that batter walks.

Third calls would be the plate umpire informing the manager that the pitcher is delaying the game. Manager must now move the pitcher to speed it up.

Final call would be warning to pitcher and manager that the refusal to continue the game, to deliver the ball within proper time, could be grounds for forfeit of the game to the opponent.

Special Instructions and Notations

This is a favorite tactic for a team that has fallen behind when rain or darkness could cause the ball game to be called. If that inning is not finished, the score reverts back to the complete previous inning in which the "stalling" team could have been tied or even ahead. Therefore, teams may stall on every pitch, hoping for the game to be called, to be replayed at a later date with play starting from the end of the previous inning.

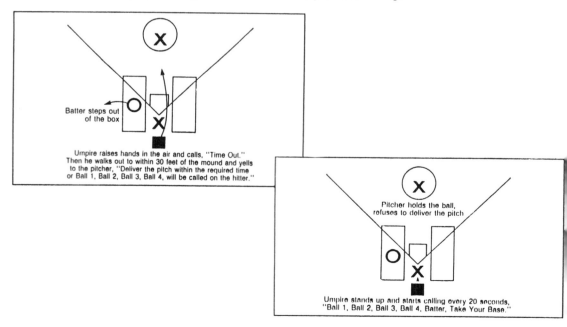

Batter steps out of the box

Umpire raises hands in the air and calls, "Time Out." Then he walks out to within 30 feet of the mound and yells to the pitcher, "Deliver the pitch within the required time or Ball 1, Ball 2, Ball 3, Ball 4, will be called on the hitter."

Pitcher holds the ball, refuses to deliver the pitch

Umpire stands up and starts calling every 20 seconds, "Ball 1, Ball 2, Ball 3, Ball 4, Batter, Take Your Base."

PLAY 30:   CALLING A PITCHER'S QUICK PITCH

The quick pitch is not allowed in any level of baseball. When the pitcher commits this infraction of the rules, the umpire will raise his hands, after the pitch, and will call "Balk" if runners are on base. The umpire then announces to the pitcher, the team, coaches, opponents, and the team scorekeeper that the quick pitch shall be counted as an "automatic ball" if no runners are on bases.

If runners are on base, umpire will use his left hand, directing each runner up one base, because of the balk rule.

If there are no runners on base, "Ball" is called loudly; plate umpire makes sure that his other umpires hear the call and know the count. He verbally informs both teams and scorekeeper of his call.

Since this a very dangerous pitch, the last thing the umpire says to the pitcher is in the form of a stern warning: "Pitcher, throw no more quick pitches."

Special Instructions and Notations

Assuming that the pitcher and catcher have rehearsed this pitch before, and have a signal for it: the batter may be looking away for signs and doesn't see the ball; the umpire could be looking away, not in position yet, mask not on, chest protector not on.

It is obvious that either batter or umpire could receive serious injury from this "sneaky" pitch, so it is outlawed.

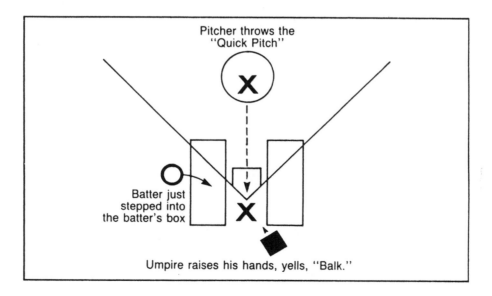

PLAY 31:   CALLING THE OFFENSIVE APPEAL PLAY AT THE PLATE

This play is the "trapped third strike with two outs." In this case, if batter swings or lets a breaking pitch go by for the third strike, the umpire will not award the batter first base unless the offense appeals the play. This could cost the defense as many as four runs. If the third strike is "trapped" by the catcher, he must tag the batter or throw down to first base for the final out.

The important thing to remember in this play is that it is an appeal play—the plate umpire will not call it unless the batting team appeals the defensive mental lapses.

With the third swing on and missed, the plate umpire does not yell "Batter is out." He does, however, yell "Strike three."

If an appeal is made to the plate umpire immediately, and the umpire observed that the catcher "trapped" the third strike, or dropped it, the umpire will then yell, "Appeal is granted. The inning is not over. All runners advance at their own peril. Batter is safe at first. Defense, stay on the field." *You see, the inning cannot be over since the third out was never made.*

Special Instructions and Notations

There is a common practice among catchers to "trap" a downward breaking curve or drop ball that is swung on and missed. This is not a "caught ball," just as it isn't a caught ball for an outfielder. Many catchers don't know this rule, and, with two outs, will assume that the third out has been recorded by the swing, the miss, and the trap. So catchers will commonly roll the ball out on the mound and hurry in to the dugout. Then his team sees this, and they follow him in. This is where the trouble begins, for all base runners, include the batter who just struck out on the third strike, are free to advance as far as they wish at their own peril. This play comes up quite often. Most often, however, the defense doesn't see this.

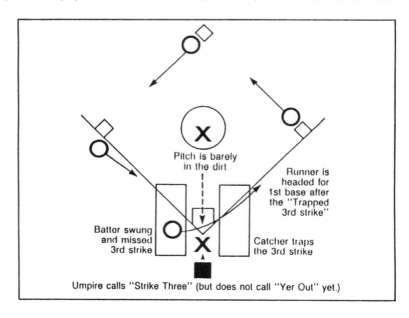

Pitch is barely
in the dirt

Runner is
headed for
1st base after
the "Trapped
3rd strike"

Batter swung
and missed
3rd strike

Catcher traps
the 3rd strike

Umpire calls "Strike Three" (but does not call "Yer Out" yet.)

PLAY 32: CALLING DEFENSIVE APPEAL PLAYS

Usually this will be the case of the runner who misses home plate and attempts to return to touch the plate. Or he may run to the dugout. The umpire will not call that runner out on a missed tag, but the run scores if no appeal is made. The umpire here must make no out or safe call. He makes his decision only after an appeal has been made by the defense.

The umpire, upon an appeal, must be sure the catcher touches the plate with the ball held by him. Or the catcher can tag the runner who is coming back to tag the plate. Or the catcher can chase the runner clear to the dugout, if he wishes to. In any case, either the plate or the runner must be tagged with the ball in possession.

As is true in all appeal plays in baseball, the umpire will not call it, just as if he never saw it occur, unless the opposing team appeals the infraction. Therefore, there is no oral signal indicating that an infraction has occurred until the appeal has been granted or denied.

When the appeal has been made, and the catcher either tags home plate while holding the ball, or tags the runner who is diving back to touch home plate too late (realizing he did miss it when he came home), or the catcher tags the runner headed for the dugout, the umpire either grants the appeal or denies it (perhaps he didn't see the runner miss home plate on his slide).

If he grants the appeal, he calls the runner out and no run scores. If not, he says "No, the run scored."

Special Instructions and Notations

On either a force play or a tag play at home plate, this situation can occur. Catchers should know that all they have to do is stand on home plate with the ball in their possession as they are appealing the play to the plate umpire. If ever there is a doubt in a catcher's mind that the sliding or standing runner missed home plate as he came home, whether the errant runner tries to dive back to the plate or not, *catcher should always appeal.* The umpire can always deny it.

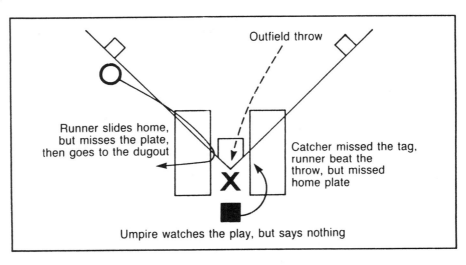

Umpire watches the play, but says nothing

PLAY 33:   CALLING THE SQUEEZE PLAYS AT HOME PLATE

First things first. The umpire must be certain that he has called the pitch correctly then he moves to judge the tag play at home. In fact, he has little time to move at all.

After the umpire has determined the pitch to be a ball or strike, and sees the third base runner breaking for the plate, he wants to get a framed view of the runner's body, the catcher's tag on the body, and if the tag beats the runner to the plate. Then he must determine whether the body touched the plate before the tag to the body. (Actually fairly simple to do.)

The umpire's call should not be made too quickly, for he must look for a dropped ball by the catcher, also for any batter interference on the play.

After he has judged the play where the runner is sliding in home, the umpire waits, then loudly proclaims his "Yer out" or "Safe," using the appropriate arm signal for his decision.

Special Instructions and Notations

To prepare for this surprise squeeze play in baseball, the umpire must have good peripheral vision. Any time a runner is on third base, and especially one who takes a long lead down the line on each pitch, out of the corner of his eye he must be instantly ready for this call at the plate. This is one of baseball's closest plays.

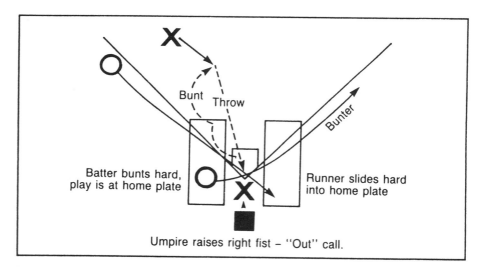

Bunt Throw

Bunter

Batter bunts hard,
play is at home plate

Runner slides hard
into home plate

Umpire raises right fist – "Out" call.

PLAY 34:   CALLING THE RUNNER'S ATTEMPT TO STEAL HOME

The umpire has no time to move. He calls the pitch first, then crouches in his position and frames the runner's body, the catcher's tag, and whether the tag beats the body part to the plate.

After seeing if the ball is dropped, and if batter was in any way interfering with the catcher's tag of the sliding runner, the plate umpire makes a very deliberate decision, never called hastily.

After he has judged the play, the plate umpire loudly proclaims his "Yer out" or "Safe," using the appropriate arm signal for his decision.

The umpire must first call the pitch before calling the tag play at the plate.

Special Instructions and Notations

To prepare for this surprise "steal home" play, certainly the premier running play, the umpire must have good peripheral vision.

Any time a runner is on third base, and especially one who takes a long lead down the line on each pitch, out of the corner of his eye he must be instantly ready for this most rare play at the plate. Of course, this is one of baseball's closest plays.

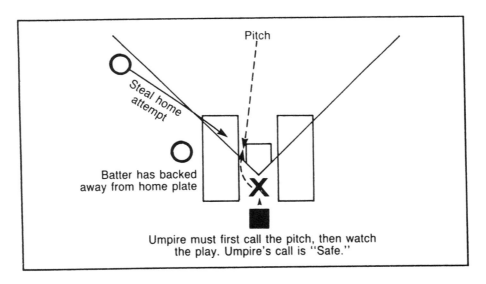

Umpire must first call the pitch, then watch the play. Umpire's call is "Safe."

PLAY 35:   CALLING A STRIKE ON THE BATTER

There are several variations umpires have developed to show a strike on the batter. The accepted and official way is for the plate umpire to raise his right fist above his shoulder in a short jabbing motion. Another sign is the right arm shoved straight out from the body and held there slightly.

Whatever signal is used, plate umpires always use the right fist or arm for strikes, never the left arm.

Umpires at the plate can either call "Strike" as they indicate with the arm, or they can indicate which strike it is, as in "Strike two."

Umpires only call called strikes as they pump with their right fist or arm. They never yell out on swinging strikes.

"Strike three" is called on the third strike, called or swinging, even though the catcher may drop that strike, or it may be a passed ball, and the runner reaches first base safely. So "Strike three" is not always "Out" in baseball.

Special Instructions and Notations

The strike zone varies on each individual batter, so the plate umpire must learn, through experience, what is the correct strike zone for each type of hitter, from very short to very tall.

Other than the variable strike zone on hitters, an umpire's calls should be consistent throughout the game and the season. Umpires usually develop their own peculiarities in judging pitches of each type. Consistency is one of the most difficult skills to develop behind the plate.

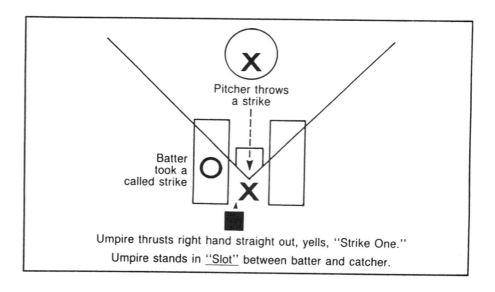

Umpire thrusts right hand straight out, yells, "Strike One."
Umpire stands in "Slot" between batter and catcher.

PLAY 36:   CALLING A BALL ON THE BATTER

A ball is defined as any pitch that does not cross that batter's strike zone, which varies with different batters.

Umpires will call "Ball" on any pitch that is not a strike.

Umpires do not indicate balls with a left arm signal as they do strikes with a right arm signal. When a ball is pitched, they simply stand there and do nothing. By showing no hand or arm signal, everyone knows that the last pitch was a ball. He says "Ball," but not loudly.

When the fourth ball has been thrown, the umpire will call "Ball four" and either say "Batter, take your base" or indicate so, pointing to first base with the left arm.

Special Instructions and Notations

There are some very special situations in which an umpire at the plate will call an "automatic ball" on the pitch, even though it may have passed through the strike zone. Two such examples are: The quick pitch and delay of game by pitcher, in which the plate umpire will call "Ball" even though a pitch has not been delivered.

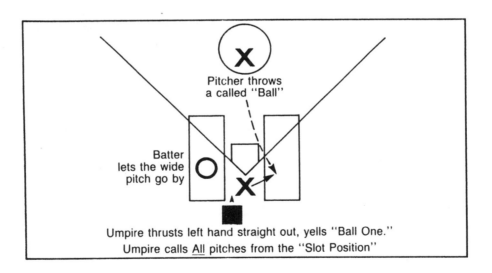

UMPIRES' CALLS AND SIGNS ON THE BASES

PLAY 37:   CALLING THE RUNNER OUT AT A BASE

The umpire gets himself into proper position to make the call on a tag play or a close force play. As soon as the umpire has determined that the fielder has tagged the runner (with either the ball or the glove holding the ball), the umpire comes around in a sweeping downward motion, using only the right arm. The umpire also yells loudly "Yer out" or "Runner's out."

On a force play, the umpire simply makes sure that the baseman's foot is touching the base involved while the baseman clearly has full possession of the ball, either held in his glove or in one or two hands. The ball must be in full possession, not juggled, not bobbled or handled loosely.

Special Instructions and Notations

In this call, the umpire may use either of two signals for "Yer out." He may raise his right fist in a short jab, or he may swing the right arm downward toward the ground in a sweeping motion. Both signals are used by various umpires.

It is vital, on, all out or safe calls at bases, that the umpire anticipate the play, be, in the best possible position, and have the best possible angle from which to make a correct call.

The umpire's actual body position will usually be a crouch on one knee to get the head and eyes down as low as possible and as close to the "ball versus runner" play as he can position himself without interfering.

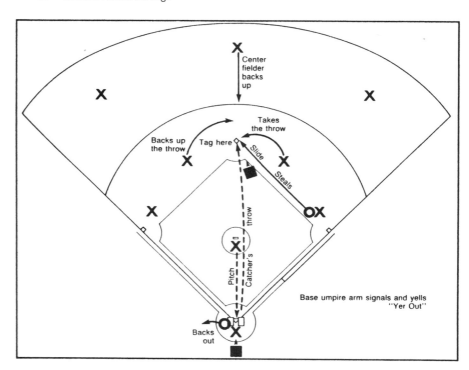

PLAY 38:   CALLING THE RUNNER SAFE AT A BASE

If the runner is safe on a tag play or a close force play at any bag, the umpire makes a series of several sweeping motions parallel to the ground with both arms moved outward from his body. He also yells loudly "Yer safe" or maybe "Runner's safe."

On a force play the umpire simply makes sure that the baseman's foot is touching the base involved after the base runner's foot has touched the base, or while the baseman does not have full possession of the ball. The runner is safe if the ball is juggled, bobbled, or handled loosely so as not to constitute full possession before the runner's foot touches that base.

Special Instructions and Notations

As soon as the base umpire decides that the base runner is safe, that umpire will crouch down somewhat and spread his arms out parallel to the ground once or twice with a sweeping motion.

It is vital, on all out or safe calls at bases, that the umpire anticipate the play, be in the best possible position, and have the best possible angle from which to make a correct call.

The umpire's best body position will usually be a crouch on one knee to get the head and eyes down as low as possible and as close to the "ball versus runner" play as he can position himself without interfering.

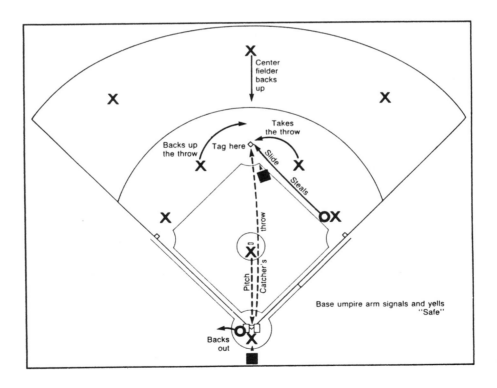

PLAY 39:   CALLING THE FAIR BALL HIT CLOSE TO THE FOUL LINE

When a ball is hit fair close to the foul line, the base umpire will turn his body and point with one hand toward fair territory. Umpire will not yell anything at that play. If he yelled "Fair ball" it might sound very much like "Foul ball" and confuse the runners, the batter, and the defensive men.

Special Instructions and Notations

The third base umpire's normal position is just outside the third base line, so he is in an excellent position to peer over a few feet to see whether the ball was barely foul, whether it hit any part of the white foul line (which, in baseball, is judged fair), or whether it clearly was barely inside the foul line in fair territory.

At this position outside the foul line, the base umpire must be ready to instantly turn inside or outside with his body to show "Fair" or "Foul" to everyone in the ballpark. The movement must be fast.

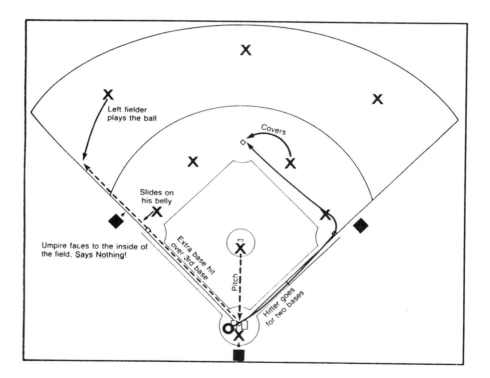

PLAY 40:   CALLING THE FOUL BALL HIT CLOSE TO THE FOUL LINE

When a ball is hit close to a foul line, if foul, the base umpire will turn his body and point the right hand in the direction of foul territory.

If it is clearly foul, the umpire will also yell loudly "Foul ball" several times so that batter, runners, and defensive men can hear it easily. He makes the call instantly.

It is important on this umpire's decision that there be a loud call of "Foul ball, foul ball" *instantly* after it is determined that the ball did pass the first or third base line as a foul ball.

Special Instructions and Notations

The third base umpire's normal position is just outside the third base line, so he is in excellent position to peer over a few feet to see whether the ball was barely foul, whether it hit any part of the white foul line (which in baseball, is judged fair), or whether it clearly was barely inside or outside the foul line, enough to make an easy instant call.

At this position outside the foul line, the base umpire must instantly react to turn inside or outside with his body to show "Fair" or "Foul" to everyone in the ballpark. The movement must be fast.

It is important for the umpire who has just called the foul ball loudly to remember to raise his hands above his head quickly, indicating "Time out," for he "kills the ball" in this manner. All foul balls are determined to be "dead balls" until returned to play.

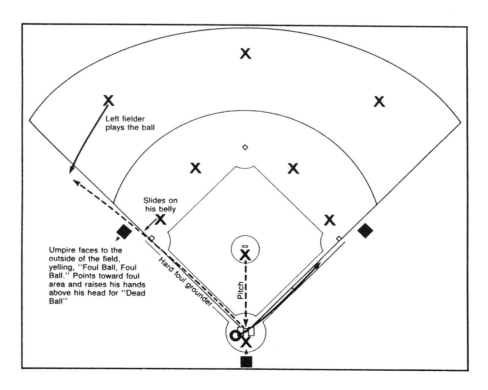

PLAY 41:   FOUL LINE CALLS BEFORE AND AFTER BALL PASSES FIRST OR THIRD BASE

If the base umpire is on the foul line behind third or first base, he may assist the umpire-in-chief with difficult decisions on balls hit sharply along the foul lines. If foul, he will raise both arms and signal into foul territory and will yell "Foul ball" several times. If it is a fair ball, umpire will point into fair territory *but will say nothing.*

The plate umpire has a better view if sighting down either foul line, but the field umpire who is near the play should be on top of the play. However, he should give the " Foul ball, foul ball" signal or fair ball pointing signal *only* if asked for assistance by the plate umpire.

Special Instructions and Notations

Although the plate umpire has the call if the ball is played or goes foul before it reaches a base, he may still have close calls, such as the ball curving foul just before reaching the base or a ball that curves in and out or out and in several times before coming to rest. If that ball is allowed to roll almost to the bag, then the base umpire's assistance might be needed.

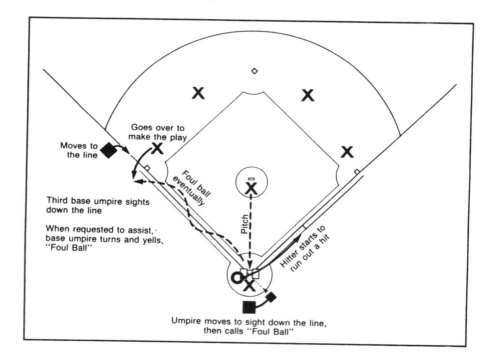

PLAY 42:   ASSISTING THE PLATE UMPIRE ON THE BATTER'S CHECKED SWING

When asked to do so (and if he is not certain if the batter's swing should be a called strike) the plate umpire points to either first base umpire (if it is a right-handed batter) or third base umpire (if it is a left-handed batter). The assisting field umpire will then make a "Safe" or "Out" call. The "Out" sign means that it was judged a full strike.

Remember: The plate umpire does not have to grant the request for assistance on strike calls.

Special Instructions and Notations

At the baseball levels of college and below, the catcher must ask the plate umpire to do the pointing to a base umpire for assistance. However, the base umpire will render a quick decision *only* when asked to do so by the plate umpire. In professional baseball, you will see the catcher often doing the initial pointing to the base umpire for assistance. But the pointing still should be done by the plate umpire, for it is he who is in charge of the game.

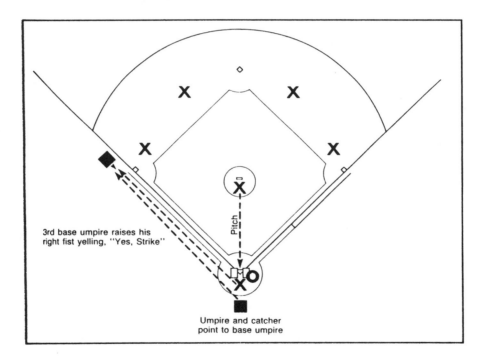

3rd base umpire raises his right fist yelling, "Yes, Strike"

Pitch

Umpire and catcher point to base umpire

PLAY 43: CALLING THE CAUGHT FLY BALL

The nearest base umpire to the line of flight of a fly ball runs out onto the outfield area. He must get as close as possible before the catch. Umpire should be able to stop and be motionless at the time he must make the call. If the umpire sees the ball cleanly "caught and held" for the required amount of time, he raises one arm upward as if to signal "Out." He yells at the time that he signals the out with the one arm, "Ball is caught" or "That's a catch."

Special Instructions and Notations

The umpire covering the play starts his run to the vantage spot as early as he can, then must stop and become motionless at the instant of the catch or no-catch, in order not to be moving as he makes the call. He must see the ball cleanly "caught and held" for the required amount of time. The ball can be dropped only if it was caught and held the required time in the judgment of the umpire.

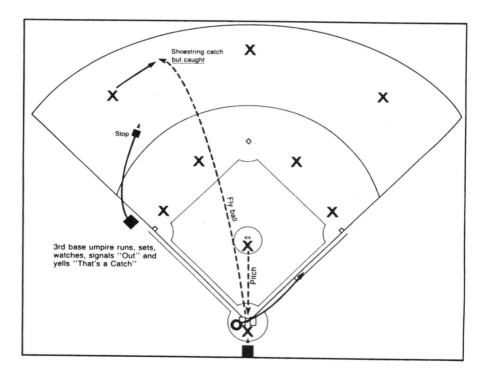

PLAY 44: CALLING THE TRAPPED FLY BALL, NOT CAUGHT

The nearest base umpire to the line of flight of the ball runs out on the outfield area and as close as he can get before the catch. If he sees the outfielder clearly trap the ball (glove it as it hits the ground under the glove) he swings both arms out away from the body parallel to the ground. This "Safe" sign tells everyone that the ball was not caught for an out. He can vocally indicate the ball was trapped by also yelling "Batter's safe, trapped ball." Another set of words easy to hear from that umpire is "Catch" or "No catch."

Special Instructions and Notations

The umpire covering the play starts his run to the vantage spot as early as he can, then must stop and become motionless at the instant of the catch or no-catch in order to not be moving as he makes the call. That umpire must see the ball clearly touch the ground between the grass and the glove. A good clue that it is trapped is the fact that the glove appears to be on top of the ball at the ground and the ball cannot be seen. If there is a question in the umpire's mind as to "Catch" or "No catch," and it is that difficult to judge, the umpire's call will usually be that a catch was made.

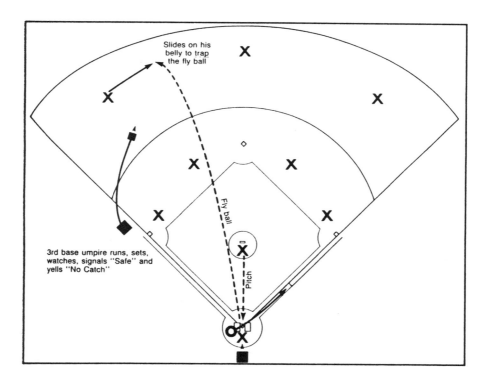

PLAY 45:　CALLING THE INFIELD FLY RULE, A REMINDER

When the infield fly rule situation presents itself, even before waiting to see what the batter will do with the pitch, the umpiring crew will almost always remind each other of this impending situation. This is done by tapping the top of the cap, which means "Attention," then raising the right arm up into the sky. This reminds the umpires that the required runners are on the bases with less than two outs. (Base umpires are reminded that this special situation occurs only with less than two outs and runners at first and second bases or bases loaded.)

The base umpire *does not* yell the special oral signal, "Infield fly, if fair." This signal is called out only by the plate umpire.

(An alternate reminder sign can be for the umpires to rub their hands on their bellies. Some umpires will place an index finger on the cap brim to signify one out at the time. A closed fist on the brim shows there are no outs.)

Special Instructions and Notations

After the base umpires have yelled for all to hear, "Infield fly, the batter is out," they are then alert to watch the base runners in their area of the diamond. These runners may stay on their bases or advance at their own peril, especially if the infielder should drop the ball—intentionally or unintentionally. Base umpires must be alert for possible tag plays at the next bases or rundown plays.

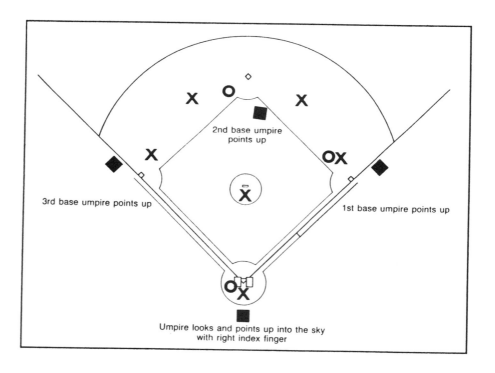

2nd base umpire points up

3rd base umpire points up

1st base umpire points up

Umpire looks and points up into the sky with right index finger

PLAY 46: CALLING PLAYER INTERFERENCE ON THE BASES

Player interference is an act of the offensive player in any way impeding the defensive man from making his usual play, *whether intentional or unintentional.* The umpire sees the infraction of the rules occur. When the play has ended, the umpire throws his hands into the air and yells "Time out," and he then yells "Player interference."

That umpire calls that interfering runner out, he puts the batter on first base, and he moves all other base runners back to the last base they occupied before the interference occurred. If the awarding of first base to the batter creates a force situation, all runners forced will move up one base.

Play must end before the base umpire having jurisdiction over the play yells loudly "Time out" followed by "Player interference." Next, that umpire will, with the left hand pointing, direct all runners to their correct bases, also yelling "You, move to second base," etc.

Special Instructions and Notations

Base runners and batter-runners must remember that at no time during their running from base to base may they make contact with a defensive man during his execution of a fielding play. This does not apply, of course, to a runner sliding into a base where the baseman is making a tag or force play on him. In the breaking up of the double play at second base, some contact is allowed, depending upon the level of baseball played.

If a defensive man is blocking the plate or a base to which the runner is going, runner may slide into him or "take him out" from standing position, as this would be defensive interference or obstruction. This is not considered offensive interference.

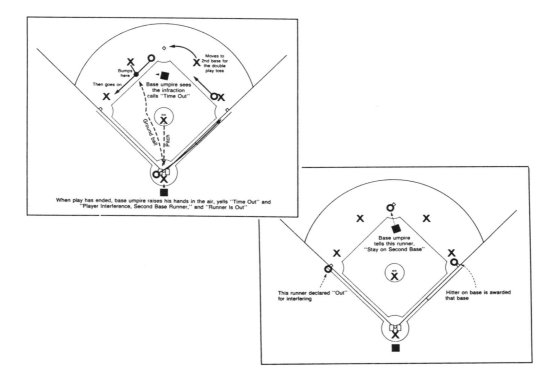

PLAY 47:   CALLING SPECTATOR INTERFERENCE

Spectator interference is called by the umpire immediately after the action stops on that play. On this play, the ball is dead when a spectator reaches into the playing field or comes out on the diamond and touches a live ball.

Upon seeing this gross infraction of the rules, the nearest umpire will throw both hands up into the air, grabbing the wrist of one hand with the other hand, and yell loudly "Time out, spectator interference." Umpire must also determine the correct bases for batter and each runner to take.

Special Instructions and Notations

Umpires must remember that this special play covers two situations. One, a fly ball lands in the area of the interfering spectator, and could have been caught for an out by the outfielder, who was there in time and easily able to make the catch. In this case the umpire would follow his usual interference sign with a right fist in the air for "Batter's out."

Or two, a bounding ground ball has been hit beyond the reach of a fielder and takes a bounce into a spectator who does interfere preventing a fielder who might have retrieved the ball while it bounded toward or into the stands. In this case, the umpire would follow his usual interference sign with the oral signal "Ground rule double" and move all runners to bases.

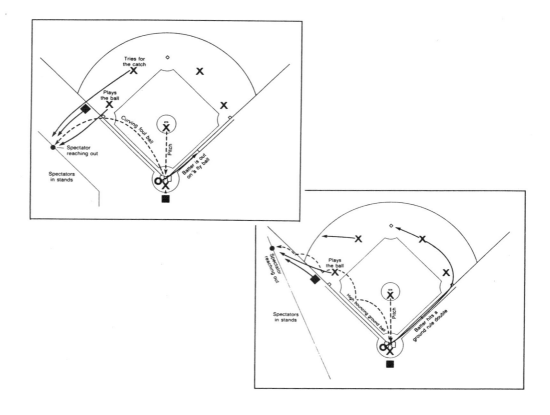

PLAY 48:   CALLING PLAYER OBSTRUCTION

Obstruction occurs when a defensive player, usually away from the ball and the play, touches, holds back, or impedes a base runner. When this occurs, after action stops, the umpire yells to the defensive player who committed the infraction, "That is obstruction," then points to or names the offending player, then tells him the reason for the call.

The umpire then imposes the proper penalties. The obstructed player *only* is advanced to the next base; this call does not affect other runners or the batter-runner. However, the umpire should award, to *all* runners on bases at the time of obstruction, those bases which the umpire feels would have been safely gained had there been no obstruction.

As the umpire yells "That's obstruction" he will also give the "Delayed dead ball sign," which is the right arm held out away from the body and parallel to the ground.

Obstruction is a "delayed dead ball" call.

Special Instructions and Notations

The defensive player should know that he cannot impede the progress of any runner between bases in any way, by touching, holding, brushing against him, or in any way attempting to slow his progress. The only touching allowed in baseball by a defensive player to a runner is the application of the "tag," touching a part of his body with the baseball for an out.

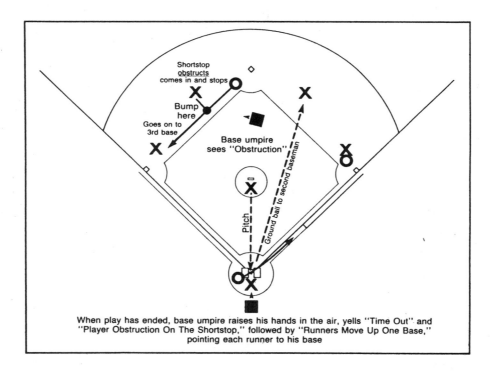

Shortstop obstructs comes in and stops

Bump here

Goes on to 3rd base

Base umpire sees "Obstruction"

Ground ball to second baseman

Pitch

When play has ended, base umpire raises his hands in the air, yells "Time Out" and "Player Obstruction On The Shortstop," followed by "Runners Move Up One Base," pointing each runner to his base

PLAY 49:   AWARDING BASE RUNNERS THE NEXT BASE OR BASES AFTER A PLAY

After any play in baseball in which the awarding of a base or bases to runner or runners is called for in the official rule book, the umpire will throw his hands up into the air, yelling "Time out," then proceed to face each runner in turn, *pointing to him with the left hand,* directing him with that hand to the base he wishes him to go ahead and occupy. He may face a first base runner, for example, point to him, and say "Runner on first, take second base."

Special Instructions and Notations

Umpires and players alike should remember that, if a base runner has advanced more than one base, such as from first to third on a play, and is called back to first base by that umpire, it is not necessary to retouch each base on the way back to the original one. Players may cut across the diamond to save time, since time has been called.

This same rule pertains to runners who have stayed on bases and on a play are entitled to advance two bases. If the runner on second is entitled to home by virtue of an umpire's decision, or, if the runner on first is entitled to third by an umpire's decision, then he may cut across the diamond to take those bases awarded.

However, runners usually either don't know this rule or they play it safe, for you usually see a runner, on a two-base award, touching the next base before going on to the one awarded. Touching and retouching each base in order, in baseball rules, is only required during a play, when the ball is live, or after each foul ball caught or not caught, if the runner has advanced.

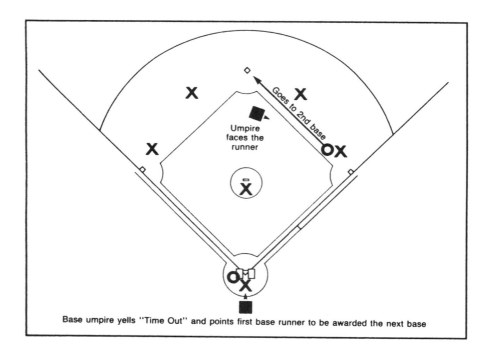

Base umpire yells "Time Out" and points first base runner to be awarded the next base

PLAY 50:   CALLING THE BALK ON THE PITCHER

If the pitch has not been delivered, the umpire calls the balk by pointing to the pitcher and yelling "Balk." He then tells all runners to move up one base, directing them with hand signals.

If the pitch has been delivered to the batter after "Balk" is yelled by the umpire, he waits for the play action to cease. The umpire then yells "Balk" again, points to the pitcher. The umpire must then go to all runners and award them their bases.

If, however, the ball was hit and the team at bat drives the runners at least one base each, then the balk is ignored by the umpire and the hitting team.

It is conceivable that, after the balk has been called after the pitch has been delivered, such an unusual play may occur that the ruling umpire may have to return all the base runners to their original bases first, then award each a base for the balk committed.

Special Instructions and Notations

The umpire calling the balk must be certain to inform the pitcher and his manager the reason for the balk being called. All runners on bases will be advanced one base on the balk call. The third base runner scores a run on the call.

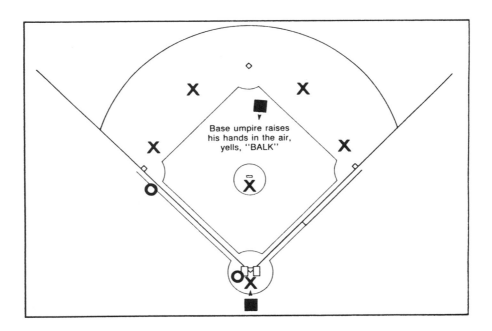

PLAY 51:   CALLING "OUT" OR "SAFE" ON STEALING PLAYS

The umpire quickly moves to an outside position, *not* an inside one. He gets right on top of the play as ball and runner both approach that base. The umpire looks for the part of the body that should reach the base first. He watches the ball as it is applied to that part of the runner's body. He sees if any part of the runner's body touched the bag before the ball touched another part of the runner.

It is imperative that the umpire not make too quick a decision on close plays. First, he may need a second or two to think about what he saw. Second, it will appear to all watching that he is more deliberate (*not hesitant*) if he takes some time before making the call.

The umpire raises the right first in a short jabbing motion for the "Out" call, accompanied by the oral signal "Yer out." The umpire bends low and lowers both hands parallel to the ground, making several sweeping motions, for the "Safe" call.

Special Instructions and Notations

Umpires do not call "Safe" or "Out" immediately for the reasons listed above. Another warning to umpires in making these close calls at a base is that of the possibility of the infielder's juggling the ball and not having full possession when the tag is applied. The umpire must be certain that the infielder held the ball long enough to have full possession at the time of the tag. If he does not, then this is not a tag and the runner is safe.

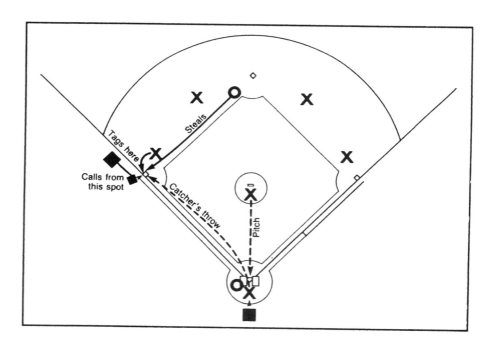

PLAY 52:   CALLING THE FIRST BASE PICKOFF PLAYS

This is probably the most difficult play for a base umpire to call. It is so sudden that the umpire has little time to move closer.

When the runner dives back to first base, the umpire watches the outstretched hand that will first contact the base, as he watches the ball. If the first baseman tags higher on the runner's body, then the umpire has a more difficult call to make.

When the play is too close to call, virtually a "tie" between runner and ball, the umpire should give the runner the advantage of the call.

"Yer out" is called with the right fist jabbed up into the air. "Safe" is called with the low parallel motion of both arms.

Special Instructions and Notations

Umpires must be alert around first base for pickoffs coming from several places on the diamond. *Pickoff's do not occur from the pitcher's stretch.* Most pickoff plays do originate from the pitcher, but there are other situations leading to pickoffs.

Catcher pickoffs can occur after any pitch. The hidden ball play could be thrown to first base from any infielder holding the hidden ball. And the runner could overrun a base, round a base too far, or be picked off by a return throw from an infielder or outfielder at first base. There are also examples of pickoffs in which the runner is caught unaware and diving or stepping back onto a base.

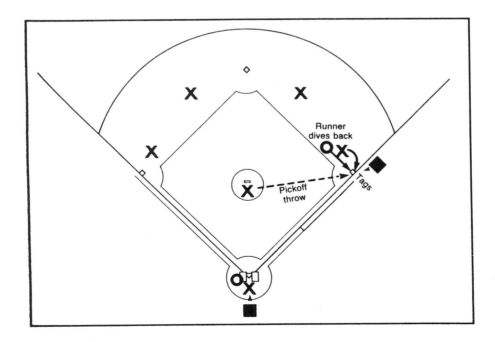

PLAY 53: CALLING THE SECOND BASE PICKOFF PLAYS

Second is a very common pickoff base. It is one of two bases where pitchers can fake a throw. The throw does not have to be completed.

Umpires must constantly be on the lookout for this play to occur. Be alert to move into position quickly, for this play is usually a close one. The umpire's normal position around second base area should give him a good angle.

As the runner dives back to second base, watch his outstretched hand and the ball. One hand will be reaching to touch the base. If the baseman tags higher on the body than the outstretched hand, the umpire will find it more difficult to judge this play. When close enough to be in doubt, give the baserunner the edge on the call.

The umpire will use the usual "Safe" or "Out" calls. He should take extra time on the calls to be certain that he analyzes what he saw.

Special Instructions and Notations

The umpire must anticipate this pickoff attempt. Teams are notorious for using it when the team at bat has rallied, scored many runs is loose and relaxed—*and off guard*. The defense may pull this play with two outs and bases loaded to get out of an inning the easy and tricky way.

In situations where all the runners must go on to the next pitch, be wary of the pickoff at any base to get out of that inning.

Of course, defenses will be using this play against any "hot dog"—a speedy runner who is daring and fast and takes a lot of lead.

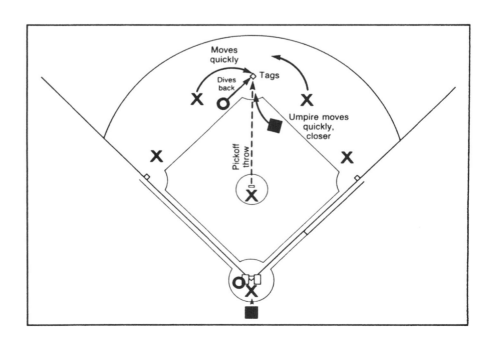

PLAY 54:   CALLING THIRD BASE PICKOFF PLAYS

A pickoff play at third base is rare. It will occur when the official least expects it. As in any other pickoff play, the umpire tries to be in a good position if he anticipates the play.

Watch the runner's body and that part which reaches third base first. Umpire determines if the foot or hand touched third base before the tag was applied. The same umpire's cautions apply here as were listed under first base and second base pickoff plays.

The umpire's signs here are the usual arm gestures for "Safe" or "Out."

Special Instructions and Notations

The umpire must anticipate this very rare pickoff attempt. Teams are reluctant to use the third base pickoff attempt, for an error by the defense could cause a run to score.

Teams are notorious for using second and third base pickoffs, *for a pickoff at first base is more expected,* when the team at bat has rallied, scored runs, is loose and relaxed—*and off guard.*

The defense may pull this play in the following situations: (1) two outs, bases loaded, desperate to get out of an inning; (2) bases loaded or men on first and second only, full count on the batter, runners must go on the pitch, runners usually take more lead off each base than usual; and (3) against daring and very good and fast base runners—they go "down the line" on each pitch, far exceeding the usual lead.

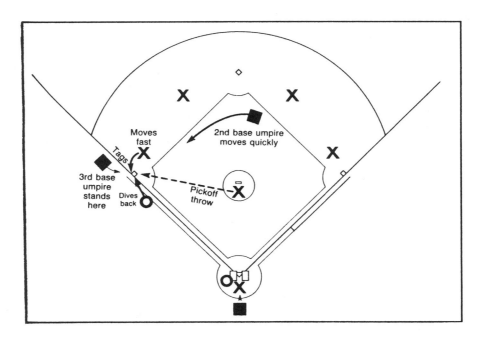

PLAY 55:   CALLING OVERTHROWS AT FIRST OR THIRD BASE

In making the calls on overthrows which may result in all base runners advancing either one or two bases, the most important two things to remember are: (1) where the base runners were before the overthrow occurred; and (2) where the base runners were at the time of the pitch or the release of the bad throw by a fielder.

The umpire calls "Time out" after all action is stopped. *Nothing is said by an umpire during the action of the play.*

All runners are awarded one base if the pitcher overthrows while he is standing on the rubber. On all other overthrows (into the stands or dead ball areas) all runners get two bases from either the time of the pitch or the release of the bad throw.

While the umpire is awarding one or two bases to each runner involved, he will hold up one or two fingers to indicate the number of bases awarded, and will orally direct the runners, as well, with the left hand.

Special Instructions and Notations

This is often called in baseball "the one and one rule." This is actually a misnomer.

Another point to remember about overthrows is that an "overthrow" is not the same as a ball thrown to the first or third baseman that goes down in the dirt and beyond the fielder trying to glove it. It also does not include wide throws no higher than the baseman's body. Throws of "overthrow" type must be those that cannot be fielded because they are too high, or those that might require a superhuman effort to reach.

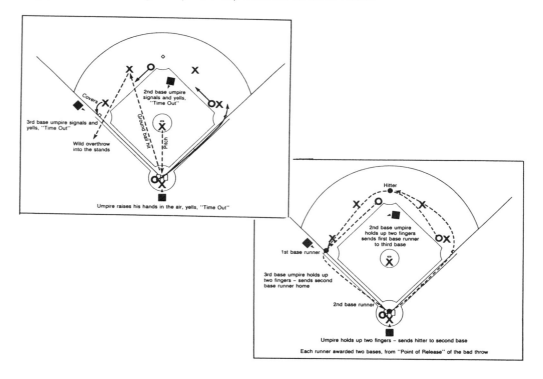

PLAY 56:   CALLING THE GROUND RULE DOUBLE

First, all umpires must know the rules for ground rule doubles in each ballpark.

When the ball is hit in such a way that it bounces over a fence, or into the crowd on the sidelines, or rolls into equipment, or under a fenced area, or into any area designated a "dead ball area," the umpire nearest the play runs out as far as possible and determines that the ball is a ground rule double. He throws his hands into the air as he would for "Time out," then yells "Ground rule double." This is followed by that umpire holding up in the air, so that all may see clearly, two fingers of the right hand.

The second phase of this rule application is that the umpire runs into the diamond area, directs each runner, including the batter-runner, to advance two bases from the base occupied at the time of the base hit.

Special Instructions and Notations

This play is clearly different from the spectator interference play, which involves a spectator preventing a play by defense and *trying to field the ball on a fly or a bounce,* even though it does carry with it an automatic two bases from the original base where runners and batter were at the time of the hit.

The ground rule double carries with it the same two-base advancement of runner and batter, but it is a rule covering balls the defense has no chance to field.

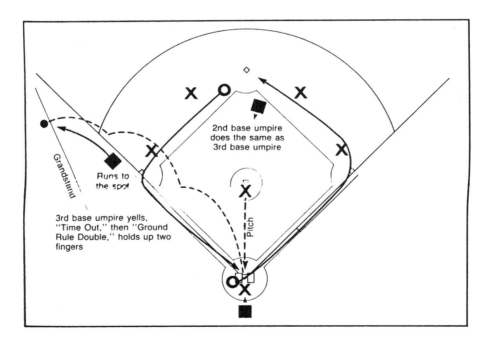

PLAY 57:   CALLING THE HOME RUN

This may sound very easy to do, but some strange events may occur, producing the home run. By far the happiest signal the offensive team likes to see is the umpire holding up the right arm with the index finger held up high and moving in circles. This indicates the sure home run.

The umpire should signal this movement of the hand and index finger *only* after he is certain the ball cleared the fence with no question that it was in fair territory.

It is a home run if a fielder tries to catch it and deflects it over the fence. It is not a home run if the ball hits the fence, then comes back and hits a fielder, then rebounds over the fence.

Many years ago it was ruled illegal for a base runner to circle the bases in reverse order. If a player does this, he is called out for making a farce or travesty of the game. His hit, his home run, and his RBIs are all taken away from his records.

Special Instructions and Notations

Some strange things can occur when a sure home run is hit. In fact, it may not be so sure.

First, if it is a solo homer, the home run and the RBI can be nullified if the home run hitter fails to touch any one of the bases on his circuit, and the defense appeals in the proper manner.

Second, if there are runners on any other bases when the home run is hit, and there are two outs, if one of those base runners fails to touch a base on the completion of his circuit of the bases, the inning is over and the home run is not counted, for it would be scored after the preceding runner should have scored but did not. So a preceding runner can nullify a home run hitter's hit, home run, and RBI. This would all be assuming that the defensive team saw the failure to touch the base and worked the appeal play.

Umpires will observe all base runners touch the bases in their area, watching to see that each runner in turn touches every base.

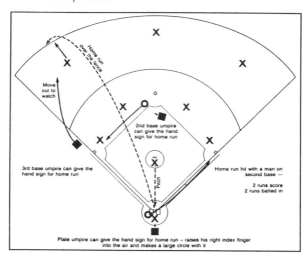

PLAY 58:   FOLLOWING THE HITTER ROUNDING ALL THE BASES ON A DOUBLE, TRIPLE, OR HOME RUN

On every hit ball when there is the possibility of base runners advancing more than one base, the umpires must observe whether the runners touch all the bases in correct order. The umpire must train himself so that he is conscious of this responsibility and looks at the runner's feet as he touches each bag. When more than one runner is on base, this is not a simple job, especially if a long hit has occurred. The duties of the umpiring crew are divided so that total coverage of bases may be handled easily. The plate umpire will watch home plate, and the field umpires will watch first, second, and third bases.

Remember that this is an action which the umpire observes but does not rule on unless an appeal is made by the defense.

In the case of there being only two or three umpires working the game, the first base umpire would do this very easily, for he really has no other duties after the hitter has hit the extra base hit.

If there is just one base umpire, however, that umpire can station himself inside the second base area, following the hitter after he passes first base. This way, the one base umpire can cover all bases while the plate umpire can cover all runners coming home. In this manner, all runners are covered at all bases in case of a later appeal at any base by the defense.

Special Instructions and Notations

If there are three or four umpires working an important game, this duty can be performed much more easily. The umpires at each base can simply watch each base and the feet of each runner as they cross that base to make certain that all bases are touched in order by every runner.

First and third base umpires can stand outside the lines and see this easily. The second base umpire should be inside the diamond area between the pitcher and second base. The plate umpire checks the runners on this play from his position back of the plate.

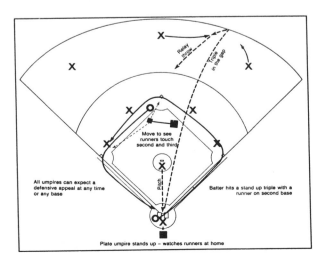

PLAY 59:   CALLING THE REVERSE DOUBLE PLAY

Umpires must be alert for the reverse double play, especially when the first throw is to first base or the ball is hit to the first baseman to start the play. It is common for umpires to be moving in the opposite direction and be out of position for the second out call, which is always a tag, not a force play.

As the ball is thrown or a tag is made on the back base, a throw always follows to the lead base. The first out is a force. Umpire calls that play, then he must quickly turn to the best position to judge the tag at the lead base. If there are three or four umpires working the game, then the first base umpire is relieved of this problem of bad position. Whoever calls each of these plays should give a quick, decisive call.

Special Instructions and Notations

This is a difficult situation to cover correctly when there is but one base umpire. With bases loaded, this reverse double play could start at first base, second base or third base; a lot to cover if the umpire wants to be right on top of the play.

With two or three base umpires this play becomes much more easily covered. No umpire should be out of position on this unusual play.

Reverse double plays do not occur often, but they are also not a rarity. It depends entirely on where the ball is hit to the infielder—and how hard it is hit.

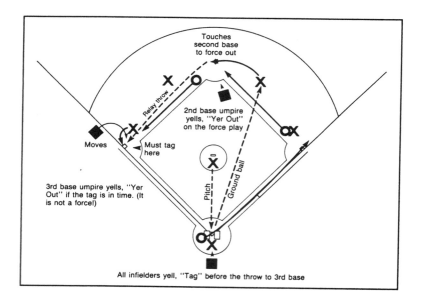

PLAY 60:   CALLING THE BATTED BALL THAT HITS A BASE RUNNER OR UMPIRE

If a batted ball passes the line between infielders (at the positions they are playing at the time), *and then* hits an umpire or a runner on its way into the outfield area, the ball continues in play, the fielders must retrieve and play the ball, and all runners may go as many bases as they dare to try for.

However, if a runner should be hit by a batted ball *before* the ball crosses this line between infielders, the umpire will immediately throw his arms into the air and call "Time out," yelling "Interference, the runner is out" and pointing to the runner who was hit by the ball. That umpire will then send all base runners back to their original bases before the ball was hit. The batter is awarded first base.

If the umpire is hit by the ball before it reaches the infield line, *the ball is dead.* All runners return to their original bases. If the umpire is hit by the batted ball *after* it passes the line of infielders, the ball is live and must be played by the fielders. All runners may advance as many bases as they dare to try.

Special Instructions and Notations

The important thing to determine here is *just where the infielders were at the time the ball was hit.* This is what makes the difference between a live ball and a dead ball, between an out and a base hit, the difference between runners moving up or runners being sent back to their original bases.

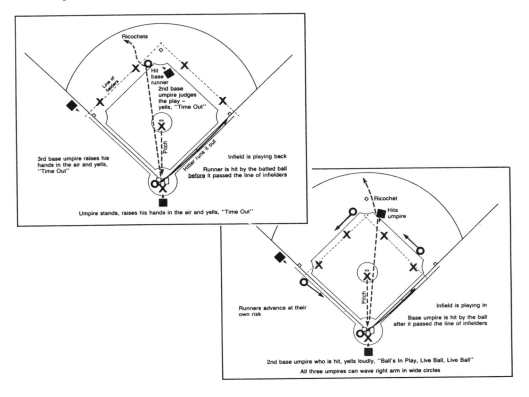

PLAY 61:   CALLING THE OLD "HIDDEN BALL TRICK"

Umpires are always on the lookout for this trick play. The play involves one fielder who pretends that the does not have the ball. It is hidden in his glove or under his armpit. That fielder tags a runner who is off base (thinking that the pitcher has the ball).

Umpires must know two things when this trick play is tried. Who has the ball? Is the ball dead or alive? *The pitcher cannot be near the rubber or the top of the mound.*

Usually the defensive man who has the ball will tag the runner off the base—and yell at the umpire as he tags and holds the ball up in the air to show the umpire.

If the umpire clearly sees the runner off base, having been tagged, and the fielder holding the ball, umpire should call "Yer out."

Special Instructions and Notations

Umpires should always be alert for this to happen in the following situations: (1) by any team that is behind in score and is desperate to pull any trick in the book to get an out or get an out of an inning; (2) by a team on defense which is trying to cut off a rally by the opponent; and (3) at any time in the ball game when the umpire sees more than one person go up to the pitcher and have a conference, and more so if the players gather in a tight huddle near the mound with the pitcher in the middle of them.

When an umpire sees any of the above, the next thing he watches carefully is whether the pitcher is near the rubber or in the dirt area. It is illegal for him to be off the grass near the mound.

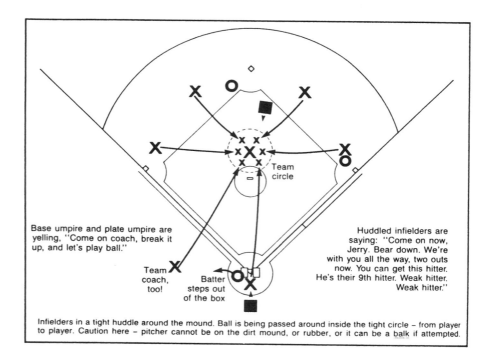

Base umpire and plate umpire are yelling, "Come on coach, break it up, and let's play ball."

Team coach, too!   Batter steps out of the box

Team circle

Huddled infielders are saying: "Come on now, Jerry. Bear down. We're with you all the way, two outs now. You can get this hitter. He's their 9th hitter. Weak hitter. Weak hitter."

Infielders in a tight huddle around the mound. Ball is being passed around inside the tight circle – from player to player. Caution here – pitcher cannot be on the dirt mound, or rubber, or it can be a balk if attempted.

PLAY 62:   CALLING THE DEFENSIVE APPEAL PLAYS

The base umpires will be the officials usually appealed to in this play. At any base, the umpire watches runners touch each base in order, or tag up on a fly ball, or see if a third out is made at a back base while a runner is scoring. Umpires are always looking for the defense to appeal. Umpires will not call runners out unless an appeal is made.

The pitcher takes his stretch on the rubber, then steps off the rubber and tosses the ball to the base where the appeal was made. Umpire then yells "Out" or "Safe," at the same time giving the arm gesture for his decision.

The umpire will watch for the following situations: (1) runner leaving a base too soon on a fly ball catch; (2) runner not touching a base as he proceeds around the bases; (3) runner not retouching bases in correct order if he must go back; (4) runner sliding home or standing up in crossing home plate, but missing home plate on the slide or the stepping across; and (5) runner crossing home plate in a scoring attempt, with two outs, if an out was made at a back base before the runner touched home.

Special Instructions and Notations

When the appeal is made by the defense, the umpire must be certain that the appeal play is executed correctly by the pitcher and baseman. While the appeal play is being executed, no throw can be made to any other part of the diamond but that one base. Other runners may attempt a steal while the appeal is being done.

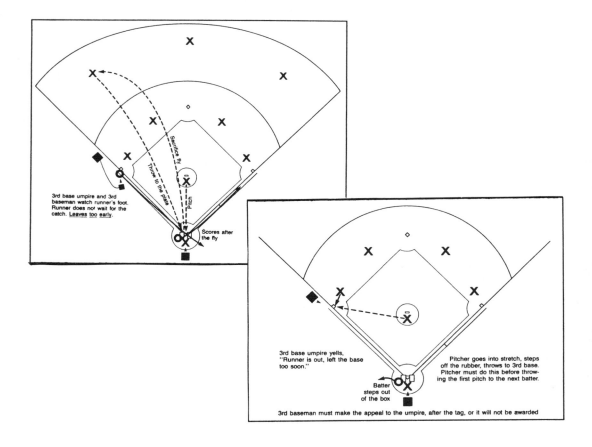

PLAY 63:   CALLING THE OFFENSIVE APPEAL PLAY, THE TRAPPED THIRD STRIKE

This unusual offensive appeal is really the responsibility of the plate umpire, but the base umpires must be aware of it, and they may be asked to assist the plate umpire in awarding the appeal.

This will be the trapped third strike with two outs play. The plate umpire is the official who must deal with this situation. This will occur rarely. The appeal will be made if, on strike three, the catcher fails to either tag the batter who struck out or throw down to first base for the final out.

This play conceivably could cost the defensive team four runs, a costly mistake. If the appeal is allowed by the plate umpire, all runners, including the batter, must touch every base, in order before scoring.

The plate umpire might consult a base umpire as to how to award the appeal. Even on this strange appeal play, base umpires must watch every runner to be certain they touch every base in correct order.

Special instructions and Notations

The official rules of baseball state that, with two outs, any third strike by the batter must be caught by the catcher and held. The rule also states that, if the ball is not caught and held, but is dropped, or is a passed ball, or is "trapped," the catcher must either tag the batter who has struck out or throw down to first base and let the first baseman touch the bag with the ball in his possession.

If the catcher does not catch the ball cleanly, and does not either tag the batter-runner or throw down to first base for the out, all runners, including the batter, may take as many bases as they can, at their own peril, and the inning is to be continued.

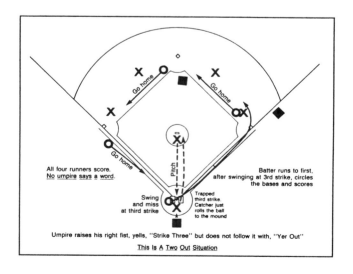

All four runners score. No umpire says a word.

Batter runs to first, after swinging at 3rd strike, circles the bases and scores

Swing and miss at third strike

Trapped third strike. Catcher just rolls the ball to the mound

Umpire raises his right fist, yells, "Strike Three" but does not follow it with, "Yer Out"

This Is A Two Out Situation

PLAY 64:   CALLING A SCORING RUNNER SAFE OR OUT WHEN THE THIRD OUT OCCURS AT ANOTHER BASE

This play involves a runner crossing the plate to score while the third out of the inning is being made on another part of the base paths. The plate umpire is usually responsible here, although he can be greatly assisted and backed up on his call by base umpires who are watching the plate and the last out.

This unusual play requires peripheral vision, for the umpire must see if the runner's foot hit home plate *before or after* the third out was executed. This will be difficult to do because of the angle of view.

The plate umpire will signal the final decision by using the "Safe" sign if the run counts and by using the "Out" sign if the run does not count. The umpire should also yell loudly "Yes [or no], the run does [or does not] count."

Special Instructions and Notations

This call comes up as a result of several types of situations.

There can be runners on first and third. The first base runner gets into a rundown, intentionally or unintentionally. As he is tagged for the third out, the third base runner has hustled toward home plate to score before the third out. Did he make it?

Or, a runner can be rounding third base either hustling or loafing somewhat, thinking that his run will score no matter what happens back at the other bases. This usually occurs on an outfield throw coming in to second or third bases to try to get a runner stretching an extra base hit. The outfield throw beats the runner rounding third base.

These are always judgment calls. Did he make it home—or did he cross the plate too late?

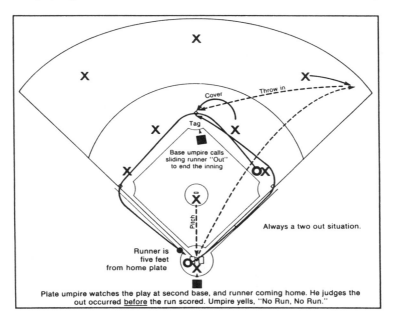

Plate umpire watches the play at second base, and runner coming home. He judges the out occurred <u>before</u> the run scored. Umpire yells, "No Run, No Run."

PLAY 65:   CALLING THE PHANTOM TAG AT SECOND BASE

The phantom tag is illegal during the double play on a ground ball to shortstop or second base. The fielder at second base does not actually touch the base with his foot, but he glides by it to avoid the sliding runner and to prevent injury to himself. Many leagues in baseball accept this as legal. This is a judgment play on the part of the umpire nearest to second base. The umpire must be sure that the baseman is on or near to that base and in possession of the ball before the out there is allowed and before the relay goes on to first base.

The phantom tag play does not pertain to a play in which the infielder cannot take an ordinary throw, one which pulls him off the bag to take the toss and relay to first base. It is reserved only for standard plays: easy to make, easy to handle, easy to relay.

Special Instructions and Notations

On this play, the second base umpire must be certain that the baseman handling the ball has full possession of the ball as he crosses the bag or near the bag. Umpires must also watch to see that the ball has reached the pivot man *before* he crosses the bag or near the bag. On a slow or delayed throw, the foot can often be dragged across the bag *before* the ball is received, making the sliding runner safe.

Various levels of baseball, from Little League to the major leagues, have different interpretations of the action around second base on double plays. The lower the level of baseball played, the more restrictive the rules are on the sliding man taking out the pivot man to prevent the second out of the double play. This would also apply to the leeway given the pivot man in executing the phantom tag.

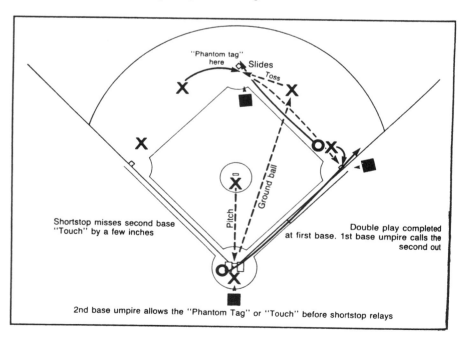

PLAY 66:   CALLING A PLAYER OR COACH EJECTED FROM THE BALL GAME

As the game goes on, there's bound to be a controversial call or two, which will usually bring out the coach to discuss the call. If the umpire's face turns red and both mouths start talking faster and faster, we can be sure a heated argument is developing. Sometimes the umpire will turn away from the arguer to say in effect that he has heard enough. But if it appears that the official is mimicking General Custer in his "Over the hill, men" directive, we can be certain the man has overstepped his bounds with the official and has been thrown out of the ball game.

The umpire will point out and up.

Special Instructions and Notations

Generally speaking, as we go from the lower to the higher levels of the game of baseball, more and more argument is tolerated, more derogatory remarks are tolerated, and wilder actions and mannerisms are tolerated. However, even at the level of major league baseball, certain actions, gestures, and key obscene words by the player are call for automatic ejection from the baseball game.

At all levels of baseball, also, we must realize that some umpires are more tolerant of actions and arguments, and that other umpires have a very short fuse. Baseball teams and coaches soon learn the differences in what an umpire will tolerate.

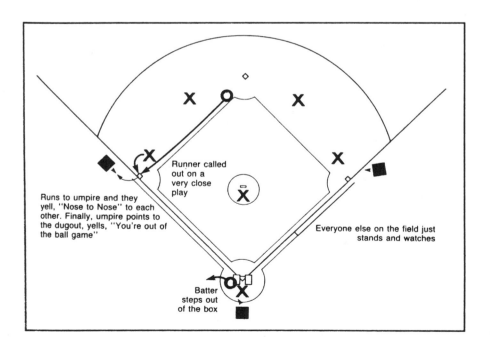

Runner called out on a very close play

Runs to umpire and they yell, "Nose to Nose" to each other. Finally, umpire points to the dugout, yells, "You're out of the ball game"

Everyone else on the field just stands and watches

Batter steps out of the box

PLAY 67:   CALLING A TIME-OUT ON THE BASES

Before the pitcher delivers, or after all action on a play stops, the umpires, any one of them, can throw both hands up in the air and yell "Time out." A timeout can be called at any time for any reason by the umpires, but players or coaches must request the umpire to call one. He may not grant the request in every case.

Umpires never call a timeout during play action; action must first stop completely.

If a timeout is called before a pitch is delivered, all action resulting from that pitch is nullified. It is declared "no pitch." The count remains the same.

Special Instructions and Notations

Any umpire may call a timeout for a good reason.

Any player, coach, base coach, or other game participant may *ask for* time to be called, at any time, for a good reason. However, this may not be granted, for various reasons, by an umpire. He may tell the person requesting the timeout the reason later.

All play must stop before a timeout can be called. It would be illegal for a player to ask for it or for an umpire to grant it.

"Timeout" should always be called if there is a condition on the field which could affect the next play on the field. Of course, "Timeout" is always called if a condition on or around the field exists which could be a danger to the safety of anyone on the field, in the dugouts, or in the stands.

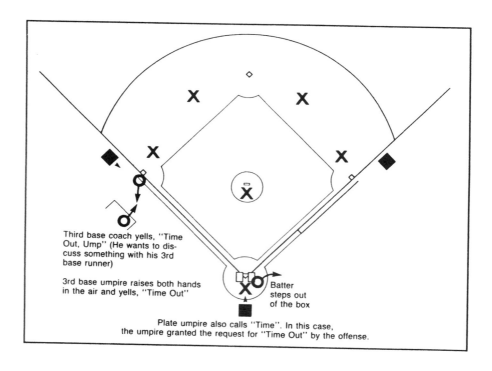

Third base coach yells, "Time Out, Ump" (He wants to discuss something with his 3rd base runner)

3rd base umpire raises both hands in the air and yells, "Time Out"

Batter steps out of the box

Plate umpire also calls "Time". In this case, the umpire granted the request for "Time Out" by the offense.

PLAY 68:   CALLING TIME IN ON THE BASES

First, the umpire yells "Time in" or "Play ball." He also drops his hands down from above his head and points one hand at the pitcher.

Special Instructions and Notations

Actually, the plate umpire is the only one who can get the game going. He does this by yelling "Play ball" and signaling with his right arm to the pitcher. Usually he will point the right index finger at the pitcher to make the next pitch. The plate umpire stands and watches until his base umpires drop their hands to show that their timeout is terminated.

In the strictest sense, "time in" begins only with the ball being delivered to the batter on the next pitch. There are exceptions to this. Actually, as soon as the ball (or a new ball) has been thrown to the pitcher and he has stepped on the rubber (for either a stretch or a windup delivery), then action can begin. A good example would be: runners on first and third, pitcher on the rubber in a stretch. The first base runner tries an early steal (he has initiated action before the pitch). In this case, this is OK.

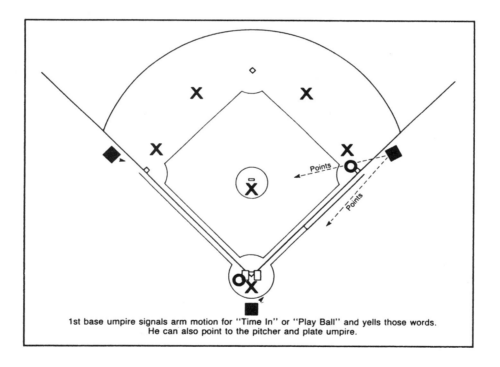

1st base umpire signals arm motion for "Time In" or "Play Ball" and yells those words. He can also point to the pitcher and plate umpire.

UMPIRES' SIGNS TO EACH OTHER

PLAY 69:   "I NEED YOUR ATTENTION"

By patting the top of his cap, an umpire attracts the others' attention for a meeting, *after the half inning is complete,* for any number of reasons.

If an umpire needs the immediate attention of another umpire, he calls "Time out" and goes over to him and makes his point.

Special Instructions and Notations

This can be used between any two umpires, but usually goes from the base umpires to the plate umpire. It is often used to ask the plate umpire for the correct count on the batter.

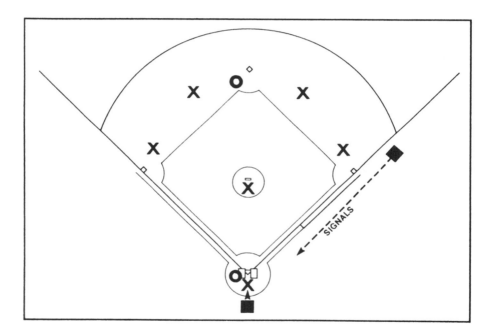

PLAY 70: "I AM ASKING FOR YOUR ASSISTANCE IN CALLING THE BATTER'S LAST SWING. DID HE COME AROUND? I AM NOT SURE FROM MY POSITION."

The first signal, the plate umpire pointing to the umpire on the first base line (if the batter is a right-hander), is a silent one. The plate umpire merely points directly at the umpire on the line. If the batter is a left-hander, the plate umpire will point to the umpire near the third base line.

Either umpire called upon to express his opinion will then raise the fist *quickly* to signify "Strike" or lower both arms parallel to the ground to signify "Ball" or "No, he did not go around." While giving these arm signals, those umpires may or may not add various verbal signals such as "Strike" or "Ball" or "Yes" or "No."

Special Instructions and Notations

At the lower levels of baseball, college and below, the catcher must ask the plate umpire to point to the base umpires for assistance. The base umpires will render a decision *only* when asked to do so by their plate umpire. In professional baseball, you will see the catcher often doing the pointing for the opinion. It should still go to the plate umpire first, for he is in charge of the game.

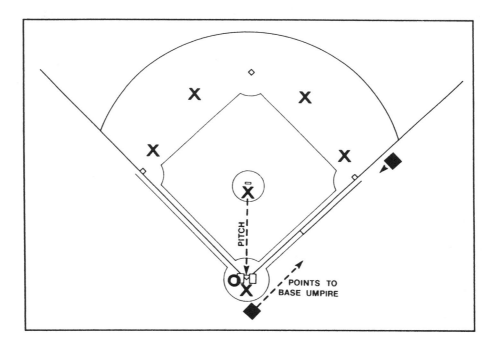

PLAY 71:   "THE INFIELD FLY RULE IS IN FORCE NOW. BE PREPARED FOR THE FLY BALL HIT"

Before the first pitch to the next batter in any infield fly situation (bases loaded, or men on first and second bases with less than two outs), one umpire reminds the others that the infield fly will apply if the ball is hit on the fly to that part of the diamond. The umpire who reminds the others will point up into the air with the right index finger and be looking up into the air, too.

When the ball is hit into this infield fly region, any of the umpires should yell "Infield fly, batter is out." If the infield fly is hit close to either of the foul lines, the plate umpire *only* will yell loudly "Infield fly, if fair."

Another signal given for the possible infield fly is the rubbing of the right hand over the belly.

Special Instructions and Notations

Runners must remind themselves that if the ball is dropped by an infielder, intentionally or not, the batter is still out. The runners, therefore, may advance after the catch, or the "muff," at their own peril. They are not forced to the next base if the ball is dropped.

Another signal umpires often use for this situation is to pat the top of their head with the right hand. Although this means "I need your attention," in this case it would remind the other umpires of this special situation.

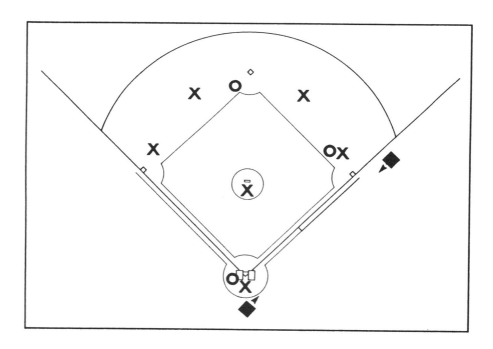

PLAY 72:   ASSISTING EACH OTHER IN THE RUNDOWN PLAYS

If one umpire is near the baseline, he should yell "I've got it." If more than one umpire gets into the rundown play, he yells "I've got this end." Thus the play can be covered from the middle and both ends. If there are two umpires in on the play, they get on opposite sides of the baseline and move back and forth with the runner.

Special Instructions and Notations

When two umpires yell "I've got this end" on the rundown play, each heads for their respective points that are "the cut of the grass." They then move with the play, going with the runner as he moves.

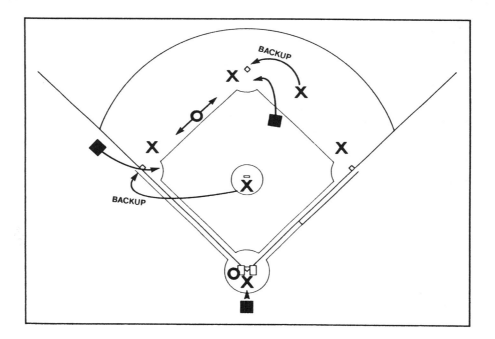

PLAY 73: TAGGING UP AFTER THE CAUGHT FLY BALL

Umpire goes out to the outfield when it is obvious that a runner will tag up on a deep fly and probably advance after the catch, but he also views a base. He will be the umpire to whom any appeal is made. Other umpires should also watch the catch and tag. They could be consulted if the nearest umpire is uncertain.

Peripheral vision and the "camera angle" are important here. Every umpire on the field must position himself in such a way that his "split vision" allows him to view the ball disappearing into the glove of the outfielder and, at the very same instant, see the foot of the nearest runner on the bag for which that umpire is responsible. This is easier if there are four umpires, of course, for they must check only one runner at one bag.

Each umpire on the bases, positioning himself correctly, will make a loud verbal signal to the other umpires, yelling "I've got it here," meaning at that bag near him (or perhaps two bags near him). Every base on which a runner is tagging and perhaps advancing should be covered.

Verbal signals merely help umpires know that all runners' bases are covered for any infraction by those runners.

Special Instructions and Notations

Remember—*umpires do not call runners out* for not tagging up, nor for leaving too early, nor for not returning to a base after a foul ball has been hit. The umpire awards the defensive team the "Out" call on an errant runner *only after the defense has appealed* in accordance with correct procedure.

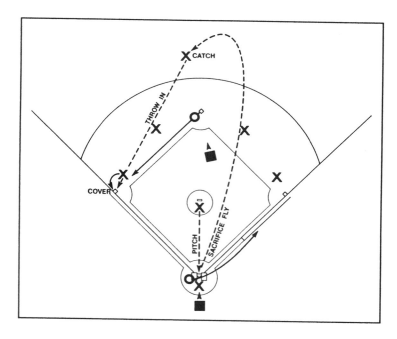

PLAY 74:   COVERAGE OF A DIFFICULT OUTFIELD PLAY

When it is obvious that a field umpire must run out toward the outfield to judge a fly ball caught, etc., the other base umpires move into positions to call the next play on a throw to a base. They must judge which base the throw will go to and be in proper position for either a tag or force play at that bag, or an appeal play later. Each umpire yells to the others, "I've got it here."

Special Instructions and Notations

The only instruction to any umpire in the case of an umpire's having to leave the infield area and move into the outer playing area is that all other umpires move to positions to see the catch or ground ball played, then be in the best possible spot to make the call for a relay throw and tag or an appeal play by the defense later.

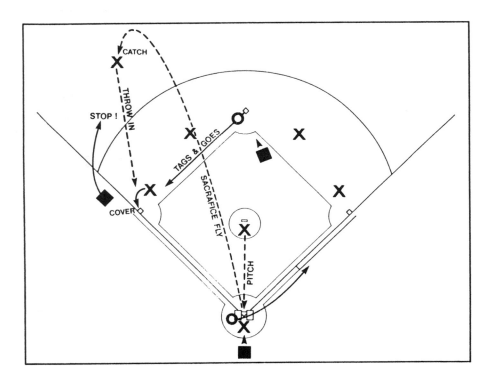

PLAY 75: "I'M GOING TO COVER ANOTHER BASE"

If the plate umpire is seen raising a finger in a clockwise circle, with a man on first base, he is telling the field umpires that he will go down to third base to cover plays when the ball is hit. This tells the field umpires to come in and watch plays at home plate.

Special Instructions and Notations

As the play develops, and the plate umpire removes his mask and hustles toward the third base area, the first base umpire will dash toward home. When he gets forty-five feet from the plate, he yells, "I'm at home" so other umpires can hear.

Another umpire, say the second base umpire, may be occupied with a call near second base.

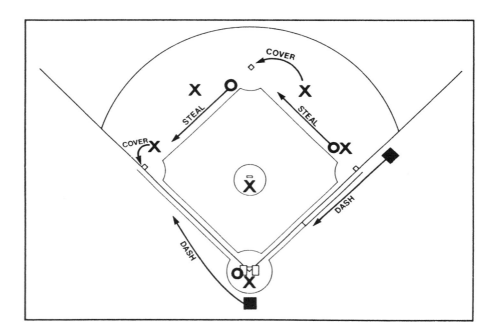

PLAY 76:   "I'M STAYING HERE TO WATCH A POSSIBLE PLAY"

If the field umpires see the plate umpire step out and point down to home plate with his right index finger, this sign tells all the others that the plate umpire will not move from the home plate area to help make a call at another base. He anticipates a possible close play at home plate.

Special Instructions and Notations

The plate umpire may use the "I want your attention" signal first but usually the umpires on the bases are watching the plate so intently that this is not necessary.

As soon as the other umpires see that the plate umpire will not leave home plate to make a call, they must check the runners (and their positions on the field at that moment), *anticipate* what play may develop, *then be prepared to cover a play at any of the three bases.*

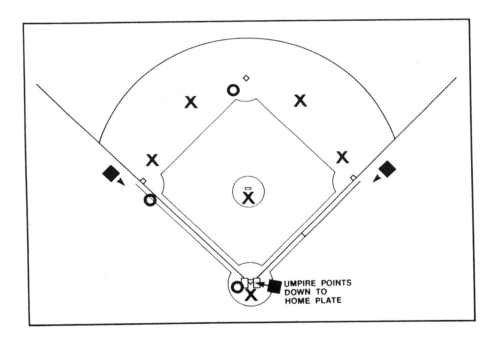

UMPIRE POINTS
DOWN TO
HOME PLATE

PLAY 77: "WATCH FOR A POSSIBLE BUNT"

There should be a subtle sign among all umpires to alert them to a possible bunting situation on the next pitch. It alerts all umpires to be in position at the bases where throws might occur. A possible sign would be two fists close together and pushing outward, as the batter's hands are on the bat as he bunts.

Special Instructions and Notations

This sign should be given any time in the ball game when any kind of a bunt is suspected, whether the defense is alert and preparing for it or not. The umpires must be anticipating the offensive coach's moves—the sacrifice, suicide, safe squeeze, fake bunt, fake bunt and slash, etc.

Any umpire on the field can initiate this signal and relay it to any or all other umpires.

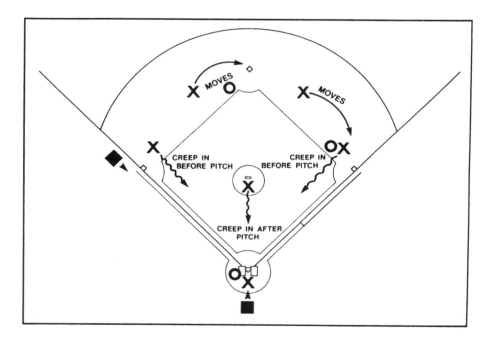

UMPIRE'S POSITIONING ON THE DIAMOND

There is a school of thought that feels that when there is only one umpire for a game of baseball, he should stand behind the pitcher and make all decisions from that vantage point. The reasoning for this is that there will be more consistency throughout the game because all decisions are made from the same spot.

This school believes further that any mistakes on close pitches where depth perception is involved would be equal for both teams.

Thus, the team that was unable to get men on base would receive the same treatment as the other team, which, because of baserunning situations, was forcing the umpire to rule from behind the pitcher.

One must recognize a certain validity in this line of reasoning. Since there is no rule that dictates that either technique be followed, the practice an umpire adopts should become a matter of personal preference.

This author prefers his one umpire to stand behind the catcher in such a situation, for he believes that being able to call the pitches more accurately far outweighs any calls made at the bases. Also, the umpire behind the catcher is at home plate and can call close plays there. *Home plate is the only base where scoring occurs and should be well covered.*

The umpires who officiate C.I.F. (Southern California Interscholastic Federation) baseball games assure the author that when one umpire is used, it is the rule to use him behind the catcher, not the pitcher.

The following pages show the positioning of umpires in various situations where there are one-, two-, three-, or four-man umpire teams.

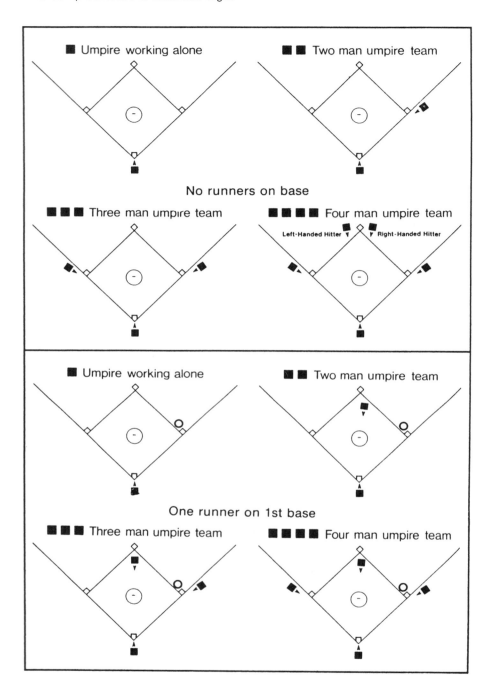

Umpire working alone   Two man umpire team

No runners on base

Three man umpire team   Four man umpire team

Left-Handed Hitter   Right-Handed Hitter

Umpire working alone   Two man umpire team

One runner on 1st base

Three man umpire team   Four man umpire team

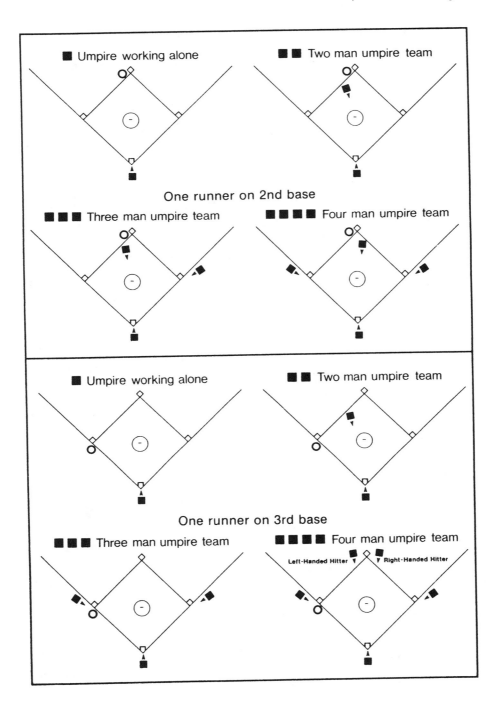

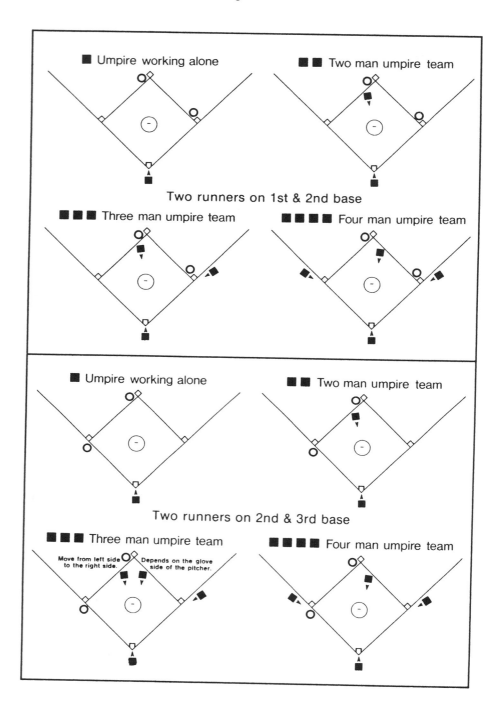

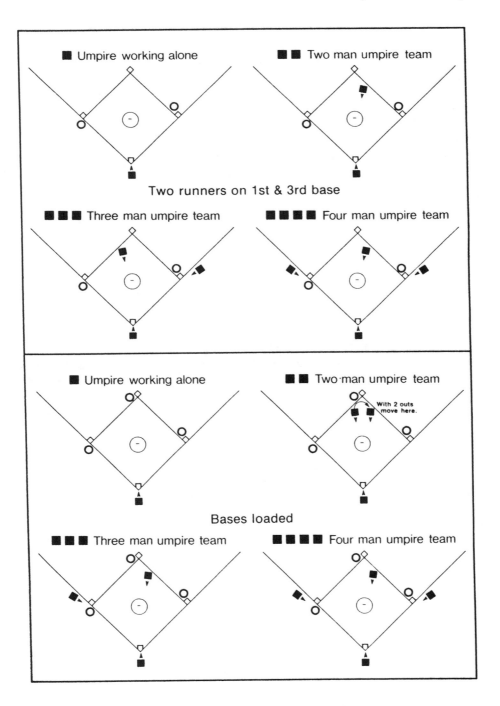

■ Umpire working alone

■ ■ Two man umpire team

Two runners on 1st & 3rd base

■ ■ ■ Three man umpire team

■ ■ ■ ■ Four man umpire team

■ Umpire working alone

■ ■ Two·man umpire team

With 2 outs move here.

Bases loaded

■ ■ ■ Three man umpire team

■ ■ ■ ■ Four man umpire team

CONCLUSIONS

When the author sat down to write this chapter on umpires' plays, calls, and signs, he was not prepared for the complexity of the rules and the vast amount of knowledge required to work a game of baseball. The author had not umpired even one game in his experience.

The teamwork between umpires was quite a surprise. There are actually three teams on the diamond during a game. The umpires comprise the third team. Baseball officials must always be ready to assist their fellow umpires in making the correct calls. Umpires must also be detached from either of the playing teams, becoming totally oblivious to the score of the game and to the personality of any player on either team.

As with the offense and defense, the umpires must learn a set of signs, both verbal and gestural (usually the umpire is yelling out his call as he gestures on a decision). Plus, there are more signs for him to learn and execute instantly than either the offensive or defensive player or coach must learn.

Amazing to both player and spectator is the quickness of many of the umpire's decisions, based on instant knowledge of the rules, the game, what he sees, and his confidence in his decisions. The author is further aware of the businesslike manner in which the umpire carries on, exhibiting his ability to be extremely patient, to think ahead, to apply the rules impartially, to explain to players and coaches his decisions, to control the game, and to realize that no play is so insignificant that it might not change the complexion of the game.

Chapter 5

STEALING OFFENSIVE AND DEFENSIVE SIGNS

As the previous chapters of this text have shown, the business of transmitting signs and signals is one of baseball's truest art forms silently performed before the unknowing opponent and the crowd in the grandstands.

Far more difficult than sending and receiving signs in the game, however, is stealing the opponent's signs and relaying that information in time for it to be to your team's advantage.

As in military intelligence, there is no system of signs in this game of baseball that another "sharpie" somewhere cannot decode. Coaches who have both given and stolen baseball signs for many years look upon this type of communication as their "second language."

The higher the level of competition the more apt we are to find "sign stealers" on the opposing bench. Coach Tom Petroff, of the University of Iowa, in his 1986 *Baseball, Signs and Signals,* mentions two men who played professional baseball and later were hired as specialists in decoding sign system. Their names are Joe Nossek and Peanuts Lowery. These men, and others very skilled in this art are paid handsomely to sit in the dugout and watch, decipher, and inform the team manager so he can relay to his players the next move of the opponent.

Before we set out to become effective sign stealers, let's review some basic facts about most opponents' sign systems.

- Batters and runners will watch for their sign *immediately after each pitch.*

- It is usually the third base coach who relays the offensive signs. *But you can be fooled on this.* Look around the vicinity of the coach on the bench. The head coach may have someone else relaying the signs, and the coaches on the third base line and in the dugout may merely be decoys. This is occurring more and more in baseball. Carefully watch the eyes and head of the batter when he looks for signs. Does he look beyond or to either side of the coach giving signs?

- Many more signs are *missed* than are ever stolen by an opponent, possibly causing a strategy to backfire.

- Most teams use signs for five basic strategies: take, sacrifice bunt, suicide squeeze bunt, steal, and hit-and-run. (Most coaches believe in keeping the signs *too simple,* thus not covering the fake bunt, the fake steal, the fake bunt and slash, safe squeeze, double and triple steals, and all of the delayed steals.)

- If an opponent has devised a system that covers every possible play on offense, has another person other than the third base coach giving the signs, and uses other coaches giving signs as decoys, a team's chances of intercepting, decoding, and passing on to the right player in time that opponent's signs are extremely slim.

- Most teams do not know when their system has been intercepted, to be used against them. Also, most teams stay with one system all season. If another team plays such a ball club very many times, it should not take too long to break some of the key signs. Most baseball teams are not prone to change (at all levels other than professional ball). When a team steals a sign it should act in a nonchalant manner. Don't give it away.

- To decode a set of baseball signals, the sign stealer must first pick up his opponent's indicator sign. Nearly all teams will use an indicator if they are giving multiple signs.

(NOTE: The author, in his thirty-seven-year career, had both a single holding sign and a multiple five-sign series. He covered the possible plays, but required players to learn only ten to twelve signals. The important thing to note here is that most of the teams he coached *had every play ready to execute.* All of them had good sign memorization. The more signs and plays you have, the wider can be your selection in choosing the right play at any given moment in the game.)

A prominent coach in the college ranks today uses the following system to simplify the signs to his players:

- Right hand to the *h*-at is his hit-and-run.

- Right hand to the *b*-elt is the bunt.

- Right hand to the *s*-hirt is the steal.

- Right hand to the *t*-ip of the nose is the take.

- Most signs are missed because the player does not look at the right time. The hitter and all runners should be looking at the signgiver *just before the hitter steps into the batter's box or just after a pitch has been delivered and not hit.*

- Base runners must be looking at the signgiver at *exactly the same time as the hitter.* Watch the opposing runners as they take signs. Some runners take signs while standing off the base. Note this and use it later for possible pickoff plays on that runner.

- Many hitters, looking at a five-or-more sign system of signs, do not look at the entire series of signs. *They turn away just after the hot sign has been given.* Be alert to see which sign was the last one given before the batter turned away. This can be used later.

Coach Tom Petroff included the following humorous tale in his book on signs and signals. He was trying to persuade baseball coaches not to let any person give the batter and runners signs except himself:

CAP THAT

The late Jack Coombs, one of college baseball's greatest coaches, who also had a superlative pitching career with the Philadelphia Athletics and the Brooklyn Dodgers, gave sage advice on the vagaries of giving signs and signals. '"I once requested my freshman coach to use a very simple set of signals that could be given by some player on the Duke University squad— a player who was not actively in the game. This young coach decided that a boy with bright red hair would be the proper boy to flash the signals' as he was very easy to see. The coach decided that the redhead should take off his cap for the steal signal. His cap held in his left hand was the sign for the hit-and-run play. These were very conspicuous signs, very easily seen by everyone on the team. With the score tied 2-2, in the sixth inning, I was suddenly treated to some of the most unorthodox baseball I had ever witnessed, from an offensive standpoint. The first batter took first base when hit by a pitch, and then he stole second, third, and home on the next three pitches. The next batter singled and then stole second and third on the next two pitches. He scored when the batter hit a sacrifice fly on the third pitch. Then came two out, and the fifth batter was safe at first on an error. On the next two pitches, just as before, he stole second and third bases.

I couldn't stand it any longer, and I rushed from my seat in the stands to the bench to find out why such offensive tactics were being employed. The answer came quickly when I was told that the red-haired boy had taken his cap off his head and forgotten to put it back.

The moral of the story? From that day forward, I never asked any of my players to take the responsibility for giving the offensive signals; for an older man is free from that mental attitude which often causes a younger person to forget himself."

The author coached for years on the high school and American Legion levels of the game, working in Washington, Oregon, and Southern California and being in many types of communities, from rural to heavily populated urban. And competing in baseball leagues in these environments from 1947 to 1984, in his nearly seven hundred games as coach his teams had signs stolen three times that he knew of. This is remarkable.

During most of his career the author used a simple system of signals. However, opponents never did realize *who it was who was giving the signs*. (You see, I do not agree with the story about the red-haired boy. I have had real success training other persons, sitting on my bench or in the stands, to relay my signs. As I recall now, I don't believe that any of my squads had any trouble adjusting to someone else giving signs.)

The point here is that the author was very lucky. He found that most teams either didn't care to steal signs or didn't know what to look for. The author realizes that this is not the case everywhere. Many teams are spying on other baseball teams the minute they get off the bus. They may have extensive scouts; they may watch the bench, base coaches, all players; and they are very adept at picking up clues and intercepting signs. From high school level up, coaches should expect this and be ready to adjust to it.

Of course, it is impossible to gather in one volume (or in one chapter) all of the usual and ethical tricks employed in baseball in the skill of stealing the other team's signs. How many unethical methods were used during the past hundred years is hard to say. We do know that the illegal methods increase with greater pressures to win, more money involved in the sport, and the advance in electronics.

OFFENSIVE TEAM STEALING DEFENSIVE TEAM'S SIGNS

First and Third Base Coaches Steal the Catcher's Sign and Relay It to the Batter Before the Pitch

Catchers are not too careful to close their legs while giving signs to their pitcher. If the third base coach and the first base coach will step out of the coaching boxes and toward the foul line, they can get a better view of the catcher's hand giving all the signs. After an inning or so, these base coaches can be giving the batter signs as to which pitch is coming.

Catchers have a tendency to open the right leg more than the left leg, so often the first base coach sees the sign better than the third base coach.

Signs to the batter can be simple hand signs or verbal signs. Do not use first and last names of the batter, that is too obvious.

Runners Leading off Second Base Steal the Signs that Catcher is Giving to the Pitcher and Relay Them to the Batter Before the Pitch

Each runner who arrives at second base may be on that base for many minutes. As he leads off, he can see directly the signs that catcher is giving his pitcher. After seeing the sign and the type of pitch a few times, the second base runner can decipher which sign signals which pitch. In very few pitches, the batter will then know every pitch before it is delivered.

Second base runners and the batter can use simple hand signals or verbal signals.

Do not use first or last name of the batter when the second base runner is verbally giving the sign. Names of the batter are too obvious.

Batter Is Able to "Peek" at the Catcher's Hand Signal to the Pitcher or He May Look Back and Down as He Takes His Practice Swings Before the Pitch

It is possible for a batter with very good peripheral (split) vision to stand up fairly far in the batter's box and, while appearing to watch the pitcher, pick up every sign that the catcher gives. With this kind of vision it does not take the batter long to know if a fastball, a breaking pitch, or a change-up is coming.

Intercepting and Decoding the Signs to the Catcher (or the Pitcher, or Even an Infielder) by the Coach and Relaying These Signs to the Batter Before the Next Pitch

Many coaches call every pitch from the dugout, and the catcher will look over to his coach after every pitch to get the next sign. After seeing which pitch comes after each sign given, the opposing team coach soon has the pattern. He will send a hand signal or a verbal sign to the batter before the pitch.

Do not use the first or last name of the batter as your signal. It is too obvious.

Intercepting Any Kind of Sign From One Infielder to Another

During any game you play, if you see a sign given and repeated which always results in the same action, call a timeout and talk to the runners and the batter. Plan a counterplay that will defeat the defensive strategy.

Seeing the Pitcher Grip the Ball a Certain Way for Each Pitch and Relaying the Fact to the Batter Before the Pitch

Sometimes a coach or a spy on the bench or in the dugout will study a pitcher's deliveries and his grip on the ball before the pitch or an unusual movement he makes prior to throwing that type of pitch. As soon as the spy has determined the pitches by these actions, he relays a verbal or hand signal to the batter. Batters are all alerted before a game, or in a huddle between innings, as to what these signs will be.

Do not use the first or last name of the batter. It is too obvious.

Guessing or Stealing the Bunt Sign or the Steal Sign or the Hit-and-Run Sign and Relaying the Pitchout Sign to the Catcher

When an opponent has a man on first or men on first and second, look for their bunt sign or their steal sign or their hit-and-run sign. As soon as you see the sign, or really suspect that one of these plays is on, flash the sign to your catcher for the pitchout. If the runners were not going on that pitch, perhaps call for the pitchout on the next pitch.

Your catcher should be able to throw out the lead runner on one of the two pitches.

Relaying to the Proper Infielders that the Offensive Signgiver Is Giving Away the Sign by Being Too Slow or Deliberate When He Shows the Hot Sign

Signgivers, in order to be certain that they are giving the hot sign long enough for the batter or runners to see it well, tend to slow down and perhaps overexaggerate that sign more than the others in that series.

This fact gives the sign stealer a good clue. Not only does this enable the stealer to get the hot sign but also he will see the indicator sign, for it usually precedes the hot sign. Knowing the indicator then enables the spy to pick up many more signs later in the game.

Team Members Who Have Played For or Against the Opponent Can Give Stolen Signs During the Game or in a Pregame Meeting

Many times a player will have either played for that day's opponent or played against them several times. He has seen that opponent enough to know some of their important signs. When your team's player sees one of these familiar signs, he can call a time-out and inform the key defenders.

Now the defensive team can have the fun of watching the opponent's plays backfire on them.

The Batter Turns Away From the Signgiver as Soon as the Hot Sign Is Flashed, Relaying the Sign to Your Defensive Players

When players, batters particularly, are looking at a series of signs they have a bad habit of watching all the signs in that series until the hot sign is given. You can then often see that player turn his head away from the signgiver. This provides an excellent clue as to the hot sign.

A good example would be a poor-hitting pitcher coming to the plate with a man on first base or men on first and second. The pitcher will probably be given the bunt sign here. This is a good place to steal the bunt sign. (Be certain that all players on your team who receive signs from your signgiver watch every sign in the series.)

When your team has stolen a sign in this manner, relay it to the proper infielders.

Stealing Signs From the Opponent Who Teams Up Two or Three Coaches on the Bench

Some coaches and managers tip off their signals. They never quite seem to get the knack of giving them properly. Perhaps they are not good enough actors, which really is what top-notch signal callers are. Many coaches have a habit of being too deliberate when they give a sign. Although their decoying tactics are nonchalant, when they flash the hot sign, they overemphasize it, thus giving away most of their signs.

The deciphering process begins in the dugout and usually involves three people—one to watch the coach, one to watch the batter, and a third to watch the manager in the dugout or on the bench. To begin with, the manager is usually the one who initiates a play, and he flashes a sign to the coach. To decoy the initial sign, he may have someone sitting or standing next to him. This person will be giving the actual hot sign while the manager is flashing fake signs.

The following was found in Coach Tom Petroff's 1986 *Baseball, Signs and Signals*:

If three people are involved in trying to steal the signals, the one watching the manager will concentrate on the upper half of his body, for the depth of many dugouts in baseball fields is too deep to give signs below waist height.

Many sign stealers believe it is smarter to concentrate on the opposing manager and his first signal than it is to zero in on the third base coach. This is because of the fact that the manager's signs are much more simplistic than are those given by the third base coach. The manager's actual sign may be something as simple as whether or not he is standing up straight or is leaning against a post.

The second coach of the "spy team" will watch the third base coach or whoever is giving signs, and the third man looks at the batter as the signs are given. It is here that the sharp-eyed spy will catch the clue if the process from coach to batter is not smooth from start to finish.

Quite often the procedure is as follows: The person watching the base coach will watch every sign given until the person watching the batter says "Stop." The last sign that he sees before he hears "Stop" is the "hot sign," the one that counts.

How will the man watching the batter know when to say "Stop"? Well, there are a number of good keys here:

- The batter may turn his head away as soon as he gets the sign, often unaware that he has done so, because it is a reflex action.

- The batter may make an unnatural movement of his body or perhaps hitch up his trousers or grip the bat a different way than he usually does, maybe just for a moment, again just a reflexive action, but nonetheless, a big tip-off. Also if a base runner gets the sign to steal or a hit-and-run is coming, he may give the sign away by his lengthening the lead beyond the point where he would normally stand as he leads off. Or he might look away from his coach toward second base, or he might adjust his uniform in a different manner—all of these are tip-offs.

- A third base coach may become too deliberate when he gives a sign, slowing down or exaggerating the sign that is "hot" in the course of his body rhythms, then picking up the tempo once he has flashed the signal. The overemphasis is another tip-off.

- A team's strategic move also can be a tip, such as a weak hitter coming to bat with men on base and less than two outs. Obviously the pitcher will attempt to sacrifice the runners over. Now the corps of sign stealers on the bench will all look for the bunt sign to be called. Stealing this sign could be a key to other strategies, such as the squeeze bunt.

- Often an opposing coach will see a batter hesitate for a moment, during the process of sign taking, and the spy will make a mental note of just where the hesitation occurred and after what sign, and then watch what the batter did on the next pitch. All three actions can provide an answer.

CONCLUSIONS

Stealing signs takes a tremendous amount of concentration to the exclusion of all else in the game. The moment that your attention wanders to the game events is the moment when a key to breaking the code might be given. Managers usually assign coaches to be their spies, because they have to concentrate on the game as a whole.

UNETHICAL AND ILLEGAL METHODS USED TO STEAL A DEFENSIVE TEAM'S SIGNS

The man who was credited with starting this sign-stealing business was an outfielder named Dan Murphy, a man who couldn't make it with the old Philadelphia Athletics three quarters of a century ago. Connie Mack, the venerable A's manager at that time, installed Dan Murphy on a rooftop across the street from the A's ballpark and gave him a pair of binoculars. After two innings had passed, Murphy could decode the catcher's signals for each pitch. He then flashed the upcoming pitches either by crossed-arm signals or by twirling a large weather vane. One direction was a fastball; the other direction was for the breaking pitch. One day his weather vane was completely out of control due to a sudden violent windstorm. And so, for a brief time, was the A's' sign stealing stopped cold.

One of the favorite vantage points from which to see a catcher's signs is the bullpen. Binoculars are quite often a favorite piece of bullpen equipment, especially if they afford a spy some good cover where he can peer in to home plate. When Al Lopez was manager of the Chicago White Sox, he had the club purchase a World War II submarine periscope from a surplus store. It was put in the scoreboard.

Signs can be stolen from:

- The centerfield clubhouse.

- A sentry box built into the centerfield wall.

- A person sitting in the centerfield stands.

- A person hidden in the centerfield scoreboard.

- A person sitting in a high building across the street from centerfield.

Then, too, some major league clubs have been accused of posting a man with strong binoculars inside some of the centerfield scoreboards. According to the accusations, including one against the Chicago Cubs, the man with the binoculars relays his findings electronically to someone in the dugout who, in turn, relays the next pitch to the batter through a verbal signal system or a hand signal.

By far the most entertaining of these stories occurred in a game in 1900 in which the Philadelphia Phillies were entertaining the Cincinnati Reds. Our tale begins with Tommy Corcoran, third base coach for the Reds, whose actions baffled everyone in the ballpark. Tommy suddenly dropped to his knees and actually took on the look of a canine trying to locate a bone it had buried some time ago. This major league player began to dig in earnest, right in the middle of the third base coaching box. He let out a big war whoop and dug away. The game was halted momentarily as players and security guards came to his side to ask him what he was doing. Corcoran never stopped to answer their questions, but in a few minutes he had excavated a long board. Beneath the board was a small hole, and from this small pit he dragged out some kind of mechanical gadget connected to several wires.

The Cincinnati team claimed that Philadelphia had rigged up a device for the sole purpose of stealing the signs from their opponents. The Cincinnati manager even claimed that the Phillies had stationed Morgan Murphy, one of their spare catchers, in a clubhouse window located in dead centerfield. Murphy would sit there with high-powered binoculars, reading the catcher's finger signs to his pitcher.

These signs were decoded by Murphy and relayed by an electrical system to that board dug up in the third base coach's box. The impulses sent over the wire to that spot were felt by the foot of the third base coach, who kept one foot directly over the board. Of course, that third base coach decoded the number of vibrations sent from centerfield and quickly signaled the batter as to which kind of pitch to anticipate.

The Philadelphia management denied all charges. The president even claimed that the device and its wires were left over from a recent carnival which had played at the ballpark. But the discovery of the device that day set off a whole series of charges and counter-accusations between ball clubs.

One of the most common contrivances discovered in ballparks is a form of sentry box or enclosed house resembling a small outdoor toilet. The designated sign stealer would enter that house long before the game started. Through a hole in the centerfield fence he would train his binoculars on the catcher. This spy would communicate with the batter in a very subtle manner.

One sentry box system uncovered in a major league ballpark used the billboard of a New York hatter. The man inside the sentry box would sight the catcher's sign, then he would use a handle to move the crossbar in the middle of the "H" of the word hat. When that crossbar was turned a certain way, it meant a fastball was coming, and the straight crossbar of the "H" meant a curve or breaking pitch was due next.

CONCLUSIONS

When the author set out to write this text on the topic of stealing signs, he knew a very limited collection of facts and had heard a great deal of hearsay. Did any of us realize how much of this activity was really employed in each game? After seeing the examples brought out in this chapter, the coach, the player, and the fan in the stands will have a new appreciation for the participants in a ball game. Take this knowledge and try spotting the signs yourself.

There seem to be many more ethical means for the defense to steal offensive signs than the other way around. Perhaps the reason for this lies in the fact that the offensive signs are laid out in front of the whole world to see, and they are constantly given. Not as many defensive signs are given during a ball game, which may make them more difficult to recognize.

The higher in level that we go in baseball, the more signs there are to learn and the more signs are given.

The author was also surprised to learn that the art of stealing opponents' signs is not nearly as difficult as he had imagined. To be successful in this endeavor merely requires a systematic approach and a great deal of experience.

Chapter 6

TWELVE HUMOROUS
BASEBALL TALES

This, the reader will find, is a unique chapter in baseball literature. It contains stories about the grand old game's most unusual and/or funniest characters and events. No game has seen such a wide variety of humorous incidents, both on and off the field. Some are so famous to this day that they are actually legendary. This collection of adventures and misadventures is mainly centered on signs given to players, or signs missed, ignored, misunderstood, or stolen. It is selected to amuse, but also to teach a hard lesson in the playing of baseball—each story has a moral.

It would not be proper to introduce the player or fan to this section of the text and fail to mention the agony with the humor—the painful results of some of baseball's miscues.

Amazingly enough, these stories are true. It is strange to hear, as these tales are passed down from person to person, the number of ways in which each can become embellished and somewhat distorted, and how each hero can become overglorified in our minds.

Unlike so many of baseball's collections of humorous tales, these twelve stories are not taken from incidents in major league baseball. Instead, these misadventures and adventures are taken from the lower levels of the game—Little League up to the various college levels, where the incidence of unusual occurrences relating to signs and baseball communication in general are more frequent. These younger ball players are portrayed as performing the most unorthodox acts in rare moments of baseball games.

A few words now concerning each of the dozen stories.

- "Gordo's Long, Long Bunt." The tale shows an example of the perfect execution of the push bunt in baseball. The results of this beautifully executed play were far beyond the wildest expectations of either the coaches or players of the Pacific High School team of 1956.

- "Mike Stipes's Measly Home Run." This story brings us an account of a high school player in 1962, whose will, determination, and acute skills, learned over a period of many years, all came into play. Mike had climbed out of a sickbed, but his long pinch hit saved his Eisenhower High School team from defeat.

- "Pacific High School's Wet Blanket." This story of a Junior Varsity baseball team recalls the most unexpected event at the critical moment in the championship game—a situation completely out of the hands of any umpire, player, or coach on the field that day. The game was brought to a screeching halt when it was learned that someone on the baseball ground crew had failed to set the timer correctly for the watering of the diamond.

- "Bunter Turns Home Run Hitter." This baseball contest in Riverside, California, shows the reader how dangerous the game of baseball can really be, and it illustrates how wrong the defensive coach can be in his attempt to figure the strategy of the hitting team. This incident could easily have resulted in death or serious injury to an infielder.

- "Davenport's Batter With the 'Coke Bottle' Glasses." The author has chosen this one incident, of all the moments in his coaching career of thirty-seven years, as perhaps the most unusual act he ever saw any baseball player perform—but also be reminded that humorous moments can turn into tragic ones. The small batter in 1953 to whom this happened was not aware of the danger he was facing.

- "My Most Hilarious Day in Baseball." This inning from a high school baseball game should be made into a movie or TV show. It would bring the house down. True, it is funny—but it was only funny for the winning team that day. This is the author's personal favorite memory, a 1967 story of his high school's unusual encounter on the diamond with a league opponent. It is really doubtful whether the feat performed on that afternoon has ever been duplicated in the history of the game—at any level.

- "The Superstar Who Refused to Be Walked Intentionally." Superstars in athletics often cross the line into several sports, especially in high school. They prove their almost magical abilities in any event they try. Enjoy this account of the California high school player, a senior in his last high school athletic contest. This same superstar became a quarterback for UCLA and later for the New Orleans Saints and the Washington Redskins.

- "The Upland Game—the Trapped Third Strike." An unusual umpire's call at the most crucial time shows the baseball reader, coaches, and players that failure to know one of the least known official rules from baseball's rulebook can cost a team as many as four runs. Ignorance is no excuse, determined the umpire.

- "An Experiment in Bunting." A Eugene, Oregon, American Legion team in 1950 calls for a bunt from every one of its men in the lineup the first inning. This daring experiment netted a quick five runs.

- "The Grand Slam Triple Play." An incredible story of California Junior College ball clubs on a day in 1968. How could the most devastating offensive weapon in baseball suddenly be wiped out by the most devastating defensive baseball weapon? It happened in a game-ending play in a J.C. tournament.

- "The Little League Rundown Play Between Home and First Base." A sudden performance in Midland, Texas, which could only have happened at the Little League level of play. This amusing misplay shows us not only how some rules of the game of baseball might be interpreted to contradict each other, but also demonstrates how the young mind of a ball player could easily misinterpret those instructions during a tense moment in a game.

- "The Perfect Play Backfires." A most amusing occurrence in a game played in Chicago's Catholic High School League one day in 1988. Two baseball coaches, the author and another author/coach who is actively coaching now, had agreed that a certain running play was practically perfect. Practically. The play worked like a charm. But the runner nullified its success in the only way possible.

GORDO'S LONG, LONG BUNT (1956)

Pacific High School, San Bernardino, California, was in its second year of existence in the spring of 1956. I had just been appointed head coach of the varsity squad, and we were in the thick of the league race.

Our first meeting with Colton High School in the AAAA Citrus Belt League was on our home diamond. The diamond had been prepared for the game after a couple of days of rain and overcast weather.

We played the game on a threatening day. Rain clouds hung low and thick over the field. Occasional sprinkles fell all afternoon. It was a close ball game until the bottom of the fourth inning. Then the dam burst on one unusual play.

We had the bases loaded with one out, score tied 1-1. Up to the plate stepped my third baseman, Gordon Sloan, nicknamed "Gordo." He was a fine bunter and an excellent switch-hitter and our team captain.

When bases are loaded, sometimes the two infielders "peel out." They leave the second base area open, covering first and third for a pickoff attempt on a missed bunt on the first pitch. Gordo was batting from the left side of the plate. Sure enough, the right fielder was dashing way over to the right field line behind first base to cover an overthrow at first base. The center fielder was playing straight away. The second baseman dashed to first base to cover the throw there. I called a timeout and told Gordon to push a hard bunt past the pitcher, just out of his reach to his left, to roll out near second base.

Gordon Sloan was an athlete who took great pride in following directions to the letter. On the next pitch, Gordon did exactly what I had asked. *His bat was in bunting position, but he pushed the bunt harder than usual, more than a bunt.* I had signaled all runners to steal on the pitch. Runners were going hard!

The ball was pushed just outside the reach of the pitcher; it rolled hard out to the spot the second baseman had vacated. It kept rolling hard, for our diamond was hard and the grass was cut low. Would you believe the center fielder and right fielder had to go get it *out in medium right field?* But both outfielders were shifted wrong, and they were both surprised. It took them a *long time* to get the ball. All the runners scored, and Gordon was on second base before you could bat an eye. As the outfield throw came in from the center field to the catcher, Gordon watched the throw go through, and then he was sliding into third base, safe.

When the dust cleared on this play, everyone was in a state of disbelief—here a baseball player had bunted in three runs and ended up on third base on a long, rolling bunt through the infield.

The score was now 4-1. We scored three more times in that inning going away the winner 7-1.

MIKE STIPES'S MEASLY HOME RUN (1962)

Once in a coach's career he has a player like Mike Stipes. You know it during the season you have him. You keep waiting for another one, but you know he will never appear. And he hasn't yet.

In the spring of 1962, at Eisenhower High School in Rialto, California, I first saw Mike Stipes at spring tryouts. He not only made the team, he was to become, in a few short weeks, all of these: switchhitter, best bunter, best pitcher, team captain, inspirational leader, best hitter for average. I could go on and on and on....

Our team was so good that year (we won eighteen, lost one, won our league three games ahead of the second-place team) that we could have won nearly all the games without Mike. But, man, what a difference when he was in the lineup. Alas, measles epidemics knock down the best specimens of humanity. About mid-season, Mike got the measles. Two weeks out, the doctor said. No buts about it! What a competitor he was; it was all they could do to keep him in bed

About four days before we traveled away to play Chino High School, Mike started showing up each day and watching practice longingly. I told him to get on home toward evening before he got chilled. Mike was most obedient. The doctor examined him two days before the game and said, "You can go to the game with the team, but do not play until a week from today." Mike's face brightened, and he came to school and dressed in his uniform. He said he wanted to sit in the stands with his mom, but with his uniform on. As his coach, I relented. There he was, next to his mom, with a warm jacket on, watching his team play.

Chino was tough that day. They hit the ball and defensed well. We were undefeated, but, in the fifth inning, it looked as though we might get beat. Down by a 5-4 score, we had men on first and second, and the next two batters weren't strong hitters. There was one out.

I heard a commotion in the stands behind me. It was Mike running down to me. Through the fence he said, "Let me pinch-hit. If I get on, just put a runner in for me right away." He had been in bed for two weeks, remember. With a right-handed pitcher up, I let him take his practice swings. He chose to bat from the left side of the plate. He must have been hitting over .500 from both sides of the plate at that time in the season. *Mike hadn't seen a pitched ball for over two weeks*. Mike stepped up to the plate. Ball one. He fouled off strike one. On the third pitch, the whole ballpark dropped their teeth. Mike Stipes hit a hard, high fastball dead center field, completely over the high tennis court fence, almost hitting a tennis player—*his longest home run of the year*. It was a tremendous blast that jumped off the bat and carried forever.

I ran to the foul line and yelled, "Walk around, Mike." They all waited for him to walk slowly around. I told the umpires he had had measles and I didn't want him to get a sweat up. Mike crossed home plate, winked at me, smiled, and said that he had known he was going to get a good hit. But a pinch homer?

The score was now 7-5. That's the way the game ended. Mike got bundled up and sat in a car the rest of the game—then went home to bed early.

Mike Stipes, two years later, went to Cal Poly College at Pomona and had a good college career in baseball under Coach John Scolinos.

PACIFIC HIGH SCHOOL'S WET BLANKET (1965)

Have you ever seen a game of baseball tied in the bottom of the last inning and called because of sprinklers going on? That is exactly what happened one day late in the 1965 season during a classic Junior Varsity duel between the two powers of the league that year.

Coach Larry Mercadante was the coach for Pacific High School. The score was tied, and Pacific, the home team, was batting last. Somehow, Pacific High got a man to second base.

At that moment, I walked up to the game. I had been doing some work for the next day's classes. Wouldn't you know that just as I walked over and put my hands on the fence behind the home plate, *it* happened.

Up to bat stepped the good hitter for Pacific High School. After a pitch or two, the pitcher released the next ball to the batter. Just after the ball left his hand, the umpire behind the plate stepped back and yelled, "Time out." The sphere sailed toward the plate. The batter swatted the ball for a base hit. The hit ball went out between left field and center field. One of the outfielders picked up the ball and fired a good throw home. But the runner from second base was fast, and he slid in way ahead of the throw.

The game was over! Pacific High had won this crucial game by one run. Hurrah! But wait! The sprinklers all over the field were getting everyone wet. People hurried to get off the field. They were getting soaked out there. But Pacific High players were delirious! The umpire yelled, "Game called a tie. The hit doesn't count, the run doesn't count, the field is too wet to continue. Good-bye."

Someone had forgotten to adjust the timing on the automatic sprinklers.

I actually collapsed on the ground, laughing so hard that my sides were aching. If I live to be 214 years old, I doubt if I'll see anything funnier than Coach Larry Mercadante standing near home plate with hands on hips, facing the building where the sprinkler controls were housed, saying very plainly and loudly, "This g___ d____ school!"

I can sympathize with him. How many baseball coaches have ever been beaten in the "big game" by a set of automatic sprinklers *after* the winning blow was delivered?

BUNTER TURNS HOME RUN HITTER (1966)

During the 1966 season, I was coaching the Junior Varsity baseball team at San Gorgonio High School in San Bernardino, California. One afternoon, late in the season, we were locked in a crucial struggle with Riverside Poly High School at Riverside.

I distinctly recall it being the top of the sixth inning. San Gorgonio High had runners on second and third with one out, and we were behind 4-3.

Jim Charles was the right-handed hitter up. Everyone in the ballpark knew that Jim was a great bunter. He had laid down a good bunt earlier in the game and beat it out for a hit. So they thought we were going to bunt. They didn't know that Jim also was a very good long ball hitter. His home run potential was great.

Riverside Poly's coach, Orrin Rife, then did something that I have never seen a coach do. He called a timeout, went out onto the field, and told his third baseman and his first baseman to come in and stand ten feet from the batter. I guess he thought that this would upset the bunter so he would miss the ball or pop up the bunt so it could be caught.

I yelled at both the infielders who had been moved in, "Hey, you guys better move back. One of you is going to get beheaded. I have no intention of bunting." The two infielders just ignored me, and the Riverside coach came storming onto the field. He told me to leave his infielders alone and to quit telling them what to do. I warned him that he was endangering the lives of his players. The pitcher took his stretch and then delivered the ball.

Jim Charles connected with that bat and hit his longest home run of the year. It cleared the left field wall by twenty feet. But the ball took off that bat and whistled by the head of that third baseman, missing him by only three or four feet. I looked over at him, and his eyes were as big as saucers. He just stood there, transfixed on the hit ball. He didn't even have time to react. I calmly yelled at him, "Son, I told you so." Their coach said nothing. Jim Charles made believers of them all.

The score was then 6-4. We won the game 7-5.

DAVENPORT'S BATTER WITH THE "COKE BOTTLE" GLASSES (1953)

Here is a story no one will believe, but it happened just as I tell it. The moral of the story is, "Don't let anyone who has terrible eyesight ever get up to bat in baseball."

One fine spring day in 1953, tryouts were being held for the Davenport Gorillas baseball team. As head coach of that young team situated in a small wheat-farming town in eastern Washington, I was busy that day, watching prospective candidates hit balls pitched by our young batting practice pitcher.

One young freshman, blond and wearing the thickest glasses that I have ever seen, stepped up to the plate. I noticed that he would swing at anything thrown. As the pitcher delivered, he seemed to have no idea where the ball was. I questioned him about his eyesight and he said that he could see the ball all right. I doubted that, but he was fiercely competitive, and

I later learned that his mom and dad were pushing him to land a position on our team, for we had won the league title the season before and we were highly regarded.

After several days of watching this boy perform in the field (he wasn't a bad thrower and fielder) and swing at bad pitches at the plate (and *never* hit one), it was time for our intersquad game. After this game we would decide who to cut for the season.

During the game, we had a very good left-handed pitcher for one squad, when this blond boy stepped to the plate, determined he would get his first hit of the season.

The pitcher fired two pitches so fast over the plate that the boy with "Coke bottle" glasses swung each time after the ball was in the catcher's mitt. Everyone chuckled.

There was a runner on first base. The pitcher had an excellent pickoff move to first base. He took his stretch, stepped toward first and threw a very fast ball to the first baseman. Runner was safe.

Just as the ball was released to first, the little blond batter "saw the blur of the ball" with his poor eyes and swung with all his might. He actually thought the ball had been delivered over the plate and he had struck out, so he walked to the dugout!

The umpire stopped, laughed, and said, "What shall I call that one?" looking at me. Everyone on both teams was stunned by the incident and no one knew what to say or think.

Who had ever seen a player swing at a ball thrown to first for a pickoff? I called the boy away from the plate and let another batter step up, warning the original batter that he was a danger to himself at the plate.

After the day's practice was over, I convinced the little blond boy that baseball was not his game, and he quit. He still did not understand, though, why he couldn't hit a baseball.

MY MOST HILARIOUS DAY IN BASEBALL (1967)

Even as I am sitting down to relate this baseball game of the past to you, I am chuckling to myself. It was not only the most hilarious baseball game I ever coached, but it is also one of the most memorable days I spent in the game. Unfortunately, as with most funny events of this nature, someone has to be the victim of the humor. For this, I apologize.

It was in the spring of 1967. I was Junior Varsity coach at San Gorgonio High School in San Bernardino, California. We had a team that was composed of players who could do everything well, but they especially loved to run the bases. They delighted in pulling the most outlandish plays on our opponents at the most unusual times.

One afternoon in April, during about our fifteenth game of the year, we journeyed by bus to a high school in our league located in Centreville. Both teams took infield and outfield practice, and the game began. We could see that their team was not too sharp, and their tall right-handed pitcher was not too fast. Perhaps this made us overconfident. Each inning, we went to bat and hit the ball hard and deep, but always right at someone. We made an error or two, and suddenly we were behind 3-1 going into the top half of the sixth inning.

The spectators were many, and they were watching a hard-nosed, close ball game. We had had only two scratch hits up to this point, and so, before we went to bat in the sixth, I told them (in a huddle) that we weren't going to play straight "hit-away-type baseball" anymore. I let the team know that they would be going into our "running game" and told them to watch for signs for *unorthodox* plays we had practiced.

The inning began. My first batter walked. I gave him the steal sign, and he broke. The catcher threw the ball five feet over the shortstop's head at second base, and my runner was on third. The pitcher was not too happy, and he threw two balls to the batter. I called a timeout and we had the old "double steal with a man starting at home plate" ready to go. I told my runner that if he walked, he was to trot to first base and stop, count a slow "1001," adjust his belt, then break for second at high speed. The pitcher had the ball when he broke, and he hesitated to throw to second, but he did throw. My third base runner was edging off third. The second the pitcher threw to second base, he broke for home. When the second baseman received the throw, he threw too late and the ball caromed off the catcher's mitt about twenty feet. The second base runner came on to third.

Now the score stood: San Gorgonio, 2; Centreville, 3. A runner sat on third base.

This upset the pitcher so badly that he walked the next batter. Where were my runners then? Again at first and third. I gave the first base runner the steal sign on the second pitch. He broke for second base on the pitch, and the catcher threw to second, but too late. On the catcher's throw, the runner on third base broke for the plate and beat the throw home. Now the score stood: San Gorgonio 3; Centreville, 3. I tried a different tactic with the next batter. We sacrificed the winning run to third, but the pitcher fumbled the ball, firing too late to first.

Again, where were my runners? On first and third. This time, I called a delayed double steal. The batter took the pitch, and the catcher had the ball. As he tossed the ball back to the pitcher rather softly, the first base runner took off for second base, but stopped halfway. The pitcher threw to the second baseman, and he started a rundown. My third base runner broke for the plate when the second baseman was tossing to the first baseman. The poor first baseman was so startled that he threw wide in the dirt past the catcher, and the stealing runner went to third.

By this time, the Centreville team was fuming. Their coach and players were barking at each other. I looked over at the glum expressions on the faces of the Centreville crowd.

We were now ahead 4-3 on *three consecutive first-and-third double steals*, but the timing had been run differently in all three.

I glanced over at our stands, and the spectators were laughing so hard we could hardly hear ourselves in the dugout nearby.

The situation now was man on third base. By this time, their pitcher had gone into shock. He walked the next batter on four pitches. I called a timeout and told the runner to walk off first base slowly to see what the pitcher would do. He did as I bade, and the pitcher was so mad he charged at the runner. He got close to him in the base line and held the ball up and tried to outrun the base runner. The base runner outran him to second. The pitcher never

The score now was 5-3. We had worked the same play four consecutive times for four runs. A runner was then on second base.

I looked at both stands, and people were laughing so hard they were leaning on each other and holding their sides.

My team in the dugout had become completely unglued. Two or three were leaning on the screen fence to hold themselves up from laughing so hard. Some were actually falling off the bench.

If they had only known what was coming next. The Centreville coach went to the mound now and told his team to completely ignore the runner off first base on future plays.

Up to bat stepped our biggest clown of all, Brian Smith, a football player who was a huge left-handed pitcher. I told him if we got the first-and-third situation again to walk off the base and go halfway, but not to go to second base, just to see what they would do.

I had Brian take the first pitch, and the second base runner stole third base. The catcher threw miles late. This upset the pitcher so that he walked Brian. Men were again on first and third. The pitcher was so stunned by all this he was in a trance. Brian walked off the base, got halfway from first to second, and said something to the pitcher. The pitcher ignored him. Then Brian did something I have never seen anyone in baseball do. *To our utter amazement, that clown laid down on the ground, facing the pitcher, cocked his hat over his eyes, and held his head up by one hand.* He resembled a Roman reclining at a banquet, lying on a soft couch. He took his other hand and, with his index finger, beckoned to the pitcher "Come on and get me." You could not hear yourself think, the screaming and laughing was so loud. Everyone in the ballpark was hooting and guffawing. Centreville's bench was also laughing, as was their crowd. But our spectators were gasping for air. Our bus driver was trying to hold up two of our parents, who were holding each other in tight embrace. They were both kneeling on the ground. Another parent was on the grass, rolling over and over, holding his sides, gasping for a breath.

By this time I was hanging on to the cyclone fence in uncontrollable laughter. Just then, the pitcher went berserk. He charged off the mound and, enraged like a mad bull, went after Brian Smith. He had Brian a third of the way to second base and was gaining on him. The third base runner broke for the plate just as the ferocious pitcher tripped and fell flat on his face and the ball shot out of his hand into shallow right field. By the time the ball was retrieved, Brian was sliding into third base. But now the two umpires were laughing. They had to stop the game a few seconds to compose themselves. The situation was now a man on third base, and we led 6-3. We had worked our famous first-and-third double steal five times in a row, and each time something different had happened.

Their coach would not change pitchers. He said they had only one pitcher that day. So he walked our next batter, to the delight of our bench and our fans.

Same situation: *men on first and third.* This time, we repeated our first option of the play. On the next pitch, the first base runner broke for second base, the pitcher whirled and fired to second, and they finally got the first out of the inning. But Brian tagged up, edged off and broke for the plate. He made it under the late throw to the catcher.

The score was now 7-3, and we had executed the first-and-third play six consecutive times for six runs. My kids came over and talked. We decided to take the running plays off, let the batters hit the rest of the inning. Would you believe we scored no more runs that inning or in the seventh inning? Neither did they. Game score was 7-3.

Why am I telling you this story? Certainly not to embarrass the opponent. I merely want you to see what can happen to a tight ball game when you push the button and say "Run." This game became a circus.

A good running team runs a play into the ground until the opponent proves that he can stop it. They never did stop this play!

We would probably not have beaten that team that day by straight hitting. They had the momentum. We took it away from them by the element of surprise.

Running is a spectator sport. I doubt that anyone on that ball field was not entertained by hustle and clever technique.

Why don't more coaches depart from traditional patterns of play and try something innovative? Are we saying that today's baseball coaches are not experimental and are unimaginative? Yes, we find this to be very true.

THE SUPERSTAR WHO REFUSED TO BE WALKED INTENTIONALLY (1956)

This story was told to me the day I played my first 1957 varsity baseball game at Citrus High School in Glendora-Azusa, California. It happened so long ago that I am not going to vouch for names, team members, etc., except to tell the reader that it is a true story.

We had gone to Citrus High School that day in late February 1957. As we were waiting for the field manager to line the field, the Citrus varsity coach told me this tale of his final game *the year before*. His varsity baseball team won the C.I.F. championship that year, but the manner in which they did it will leave the reader speechless. What a finish to a season, a championship game, and to a superathlete's high school career.

Citrus High School was playing El Centro High School for the title that day at the Citrus High School field. Now, in those days, out in right center field there was the corner of a tennis court sticking quite prominently into the outfield area. It protruded enough to make a long fly ball not too long, excepting that it had to be high enough to clear the high fence.

The game had been a nip-and-tuck contest. In those days, all high school games were nine innings, not seven. It was the bottom of the ninth inning, and the score was 5-3 in favor of El Centro, the visiting team.

Up to bat stepped Citrus High School for the last inning. Somehow they got one man on base, on second. El Centro had a great pitcher who had done a super job all day of holding down the strong Citrus lineup. (He later pitched for U.S.C.)

Up to bat stepped a heavy hitter for Citrus High School. He tripled the fourth run in, and the stage was set for the final heroics of our star of this tale. A base hit would bring in the tying run, and the hitter would represent the winning run on base.

Up to bat stepped a heavy hitter for Citrus High School. He tripled the fourth run in, and the stage was set for the final heroics of our star of this tale. A base hit would bring in the tying run, and the hitter would represent the winning run on base.

With first base open and Citrus High School's great superstar coming to bat, the El Centro coach instructed his pitcher to walk the superstar. This star player is, to this day, probably the greatest athlete ever to graduate from the Citrus High School district. Ball one—the catcher stepped out to receive the pitch. Ball two—the batter let the second one go wide. He called a timeout and went to the bat rack and did something. While there, he told his coach that the two pitches thrown were close to the outside corner of the plate. He wanted to know if he could swing on the next one, if it was close enough, get a late hit into right field, and tie the game. The Citrus High School coach okayed it, if it was reachable. The El Centro pitcher had been careless and probably would be again.

The batter stepped back into the batter's box. The next pitch on the intentional walk was again, just a few inches outside the corner of home plate. Wham! The superstrong athlete didn't just poke it out for a base hit. He rifled a double off the tennis court screen, sending in the tying run, and was standing on second base. This star was five for five at that point in the game and had stolen second, third, and home his first time up, and in another inning had stolen another base.

The coach gave him the sign to steal third base on the next pitch. The hitter grounded one to shortstop as the second base runner broke on the steal. As the shortstop threw to first base for the second out, this great athlete just rounded third and headed for home plate. The bewildered infielder covering first on the throw hesitated long enough for the runner to slide under his throw home and score the winning run, 6-5.

The game was over. Citrus won the Southern California Baseball title in the AAA class section!

The great superstar who ended his high school career on this note was none other than Bill Kilmer, eventually the quarterback for the NFL New Orleans Saints football club and the Washington Redskins, as well. He attended UCLA after high school.

Fans, how would you like to win or lose the big game that way?

THE UPLAND GAME—THE TRAPPED THIRD STRIKE (1962)

This is a great baseball tale with all the fun and excitement of the old American game, but it also points out how vital it is to know *every* rule in the voluminous official baseball rulebook.

In 1962, I served one year as Junior Varsity baseball coach at Eisenhower High School in Rialto, California. I happened to be gifted with such a talented squad of eighteen players that I soon realized that: I had two men at each position (*exactly two men at each spot*) and I had such intelligence on the team that I *decided* to "overcoach" and see just how much of a running game could be taught to a high school squad. We sent four boys from this team to top scholarships at the end of their senior years. One went to the U.S. Air Force Academy, one went to Annapolis, one went to West Point, and the fourth became captain of the Dartmouth College baseball team.

The eighteen men were of equal ability. We decided to start nine players and let the other nine sit. At the end of four innings, the other nine came in, *no matter what the score.* In the next game, the nines would switch. At the end of the year, each of the nine-man squads had played the same number of innings. We won nineteen and lost one and won our league three games ahead of the second-place team.

This tale has to do with our toughest game of the season. We were playing Upland High School, and Rollie Fingers, who later played for Oakland, Milwaukee, and San Diego professionally, was a member of Upland's frosh team that year.

It was a warm day in April. Upland and Eisenhower had not yet met on the diamond that year. We were tied for first in our Tri-County League. As it turned out, the winner of this game would win the league.

We played four innings of a seven-inning game. We were behind 4-3. The bases were loaded in the bottom of the fourth. My big catcher, Wayne Haggard, a bad curveball hitter, was at the plate.

Our only umpire was behind the plate. His name was "Scotty," and he was a real good guy—and a character. A clown with a good sense of humor.

Wayne worked the count to three and two. The pitcher, with bases loaded and all three runners going hard to the next bases, threw a hard curve that broke down. The Upland catcher caught the ball after Wayne swung and missed for strike three. The catcher for Upland rejoiced. Yelling and excited, he tossed the ball slowly out on the ground at the base of the mound. All the Upland players were congratulating the Upland pitcher for striking out a man with bases loaded.

Suddenly, my right fielder, Harry Brehm, yelled at all the runners, "Circle all the bases and come home." I looked at him and didn't know what he was doing. All the runners obeyed him and came home, touching every base in order. He said to me, "Coach, that was a trapped third strike. The catcher has to touch the runner who struck out, or throw down to first base. He did neither. The inning hasn't ended."

I told my team to stay in the dugout. No one went out and took the field. I strolled up to the umpire, and I said, "Scotty, I appeal that last play. That was a trapped third strike, not a caught third strike. Therefore, all the runners' runs count. They all touched home plate. The third out of the inning has never been made. The score is now seven to four in our favor. Upland has to return to the field." Scotty said to me at the top of his voice, "Coach, you are absolutely right. The appeal is awarded to you."

About this time, the whole Upland team came out of the dugout to find out just what was wrong. Scotty told the Upland coach that the half inning was not over. I won't repeat the words that transpired among Scotty, the Upland coach, and the Upland players. Finally, the rhubarb ended. My team, sitting in the dugout, was enjoying the scene but not rubbing it in. Would you believe that there were no more runs scored that inning, or during the rest of the game?

We won the game 7-4, scoring four runs on that one play (incidentally, the catcher who missed the third strike circled all the way around the bases and scored too).

We beat Upland again, won the league by three games, and no one came close to beating us from that point on.

I'll bet that wherever those kids are now, they still remember that day, that inning, that good call by Scotty at home plate. He was correct and had the courage to call it.

The moral of this story, of course, is that failure to know even one of the rules of defensive play is costly. The penalty for this was terrible. I happened to have a sharp, alert boy in the dugout who picked up their error. *I didn't pick it up. He did.* But I sure learned a lesson that day.

Finally, I have to tell you readers that exactly the same thing happened the next season—at Colton High School. I again appealed the play; that time, we just got two runs on the appeal. And again, the umpire saw it but was waiting for my appeal!

So, you see, these unusual occurrences sometimes crop up more frequently than you would think.

AN EXPERIMENT IN BUNTING (1950)

The summer of 1950 found me at the University of Oregon, working on a master's degree in physical education. I needed a job, so I agreed to coach the American Legion baseball team for the city of Eugene. The American Legion League in the Willamette Valley of Oregon is made up of eight tough teams. My team was composed of boys from fifteen to seventeen years old, representing three area high schools.

It was apparent, after having played all our practice games, plus three league games, that we were not heavy hitters, but our bunting and running were exceptional.

One evening, we were discussing our bunting game. I remarked to our team, "I wonder if anyone has ever opened the first inning of a game by having every man in the lineup bunt the first time they came to bat." The kids laughed and said, "Let's do it and see what happens." So we practiced very hard on the types of bunts. We had boys bunting for spots on the diamond, making the ball roll right into a circle we drew. We bunted for base hits and sacrifice bunted, and we practiced all of our suicide and squeeze bunts. We worked on fake bunts. The next evening, we played a strong Corvallis Legion team who we knew had sluggers and fair pitching, but poor defense in the infield. Our pitcher got them out in the first inning, and now we came to bat. There was an overflowing crowd in the stands.

In the pregame talk, I told the team that no matter how many outs there were, or where runners were, or what the score was, we were going to bunt nine straight times, just as we had promised each other!

I signaled the first man up to drag bunt for a hit. He laid it down in front of the third baseman. That infielder threw the ball over the first baseman's head. The runner went to second base. No outs. I signaled the next batter to lay down a sacrifice bunt. He laid it down to the left of the pitcher. The pitcher threw too late to first. Men on first and third, no outs. I gave a sign on the second pitch to the next batter to fake a bunt, and the first base runner got the steal sign. The runner stole the base and the third base runner held.

The third hitter was a good bunter. I had both runners steal on the next pitch. The hitter laid down a bunt in front of the third baseman. Of course, the first runner scored easily, as he was stealing home on the pitch. The infielder picked the ball up and threw to first base for the out, but the runner who was on second kept coming and scored on a late throw from the first baseman. Now we were ahead 2-0 with no one on base, with one out.

The cleanup hitter was next. We signaled a fake bunt and slash. He faked the bunt and popped the ball over the third baseman's head. The fifth man up was our best bunter by far. I gave him the sign to bunt to the right side. The runner was stealing, so the throw from the first baseman to second base was too late.

The situation was now one out with men on first and second. Score: 2-0.

By this time, the Corvallis infield was in a state of shock. They really feared a bunt now.

I signaled a fake bunt to the sixth batter in our lineup on the second pitch. He faked it early, and the third baseman came in too far. He couldn't get back to receive the catcher's throw to third, for I had signaled both runners to pull a double steal. The ball went into the outfield, and the man who had been on second scored. The catcher had thrown to third base, trying to get to third to cover. Now there was a man on third base with one out. Score: 3-0.

The Corvallis coach yelled over at us, "Hey, don't you guys know how to do anything except bunt?" Was he in for more of a shock. We still had three more men who would bunt before we had agreed to start hitting the ball. My seventh man in the lineup came up, and I gave him the sign to safe squeeze. He laid it down between the pitcher and first base. The first baseman threw home, but my runner on third had held up to see if it was a good bunt before breaking for home. It was a close play, but my sliding runner knocked the hall out of the catcher's hand and behind the plate. The bunter rounded first and went on to second base.

The situation now was a man on second with one out and the score 4-0 for the home team.

From the time we scored the third run on, the crowd was really having fun, waiting to see what our next move was. (By the time we ended the inning, with the score 5-0, having bunting nine men, they were wild.)

It was time for the eighth man to step up to the plate. He was left-handed. I told him to push the ball on a hard bunt past third base and into the shortstop hole. He did just that. The third baseman was in and the shortstop was shifted to the right, nearer to second base. The hard-pushed bunt rolled out into left field, and the second base runner scored. The left fielder threw to the plate too late. The man who had laid down the great bunt was on second. The score was 5-0 for Eugene.

Up to bat came our ninth hitter. He wasn't a hitter, but he had speed. He bunted to the left of the pitcher, and the pitcher forgot to cover first base. The bunter was safe at first and a runner was at third.

As agreed, we took off the bunt and let everyone hit from that point on. I tried a first-and-third steal again. The catcher made a good throw and nailed the runner sliding into second base for the second out.

The leadoff man, the tenth batter of the inning, was up. He lined a deep fly to right field for the final out.

We finally won the game 9-6, *but we would have been beaten without our wild, experimental first inning.*

Parents, fans, and umpires came up after the game to congratulate us. They all said, "Well, I've seen everything now." They were laughing all the way out the gate.

The point of the story I relate is that a poorer team beat a better team with the bunt; in fact, *with all kinds of bunts!* Of course, we had some luck. The conclusion: The bunt is a very powerful weapon. It is not used enough in the game. Its main effect is one of shaking up the opponent. Do you know that I have never had the guts to do that again with a team. I wonder why? But it was sure fun.

THE GRAND SLAM TRIPLE PLAY (1968)

In 1968, in the consolation finals of the Citrus Junior College Baseball Tournament, John Monger was pitching for Mount San Antonio College. It was the bottom of the ninth inning, with our team leading 10-8, bases were loaded, with Golden West at bat. The count was 2-0, and the batter hit a deep shot to left field that had "grand slam" written all over it.

The runner on third base crossed home plate, the runner on second was about five feet from home plate, the runner on first was halfway between second and third, and the batter was in his home run trot. The left fielder, Kelly Godfrey, turned his back and raced to the fence. Making the catch, he turned and threw the ball to the shortstop, Ron Opatkiewitz, who threw it to the third baseman, Tim Feldhaus, for out number two, who threw the ball to the second baseman, Mike McClure, for the third out—a triple play. Golden West won the game 10-8.

The funny thing was that when the ball was caught, all of the runners stopped in a state of shock, as if their feet were set in cement.

THE LITTLE LEAGUE RUNDOWN PLAY BETWEEN
HOME AND FIRST BASE (1988)

The baseball rulebook declares that any runner (or player, for that matter) is to be called out or "kicked out" if he *obviously* intends to make a farce of the game. If a *team* does this, after a suitable number of warnings by the umpire, the umpire will declare the game forfeited to the other team at that point.

But what if a player, in his anxiety or effort, commits a farcical act unintentionally?

Such a play occurred in a Little League baseball game of several years ago, around 1988, I believe.

Coaches who teach young kids to play baseball often assume that the child knows the rules of the game or the obvious moves of the game in a given situation and will never vary. This particular Little League coach had done his job when he exclaimed one day, in practice, these instructions: "Now, gang, any time you see the ball in the hands of a defensive player and you are running toward that player, *never* allow yourself to run into the ball, or the man with the ball will tag you out. Instead, back up and get in a rundown between the two bases." The coach's word *never* really hit home apparently.

In a matter of a few days, his team was involved in a tough game. Here is an account of the order of events in the fourth inning:

Little Leaguer Jim Walsh hit a slow roller to the first baseman. The ball rolled up near the first base line, about ten feet from the base. There were runners on first and second when the ball was hit. They lit out for their next bases, for it was a force-out situation for them. But Jim Walsh, the hitter, tore out for first base as he had always done since playing baseball. Suddenly, he saw the first baseman coming at him to tag him before he reached first base. (Of course, the first baseman should have gone over and stepped on first base for that one out). Jim Walsh recalled his coach's words: "Never run into the ball that's held by a baseman." Jim put on the brakes and headed back to home plate. This unnatural act so confused the catcher and first baseman that they proceeded to start the rundown play between bases. (Incidentally, this is a good object lesson in how surprise tactics will create panic, error in reasoning, and unnatural moves in the opponent.)

While the rundown ensued, the runner who had gone to third base on the hit scored behind the catcher. On about the third rundown toss between the two defensive men, the first baseman's throw sailed miles over the catcher's head. As the poor catcher ran lickety-split to retrieve the errant throw, the next runner, who had originally been on first base, scored easily, and the hitter ended up on second.

A summary of the damage is: two runs scored, seven bases gained by three runners, no one put out, and "egg all over the faces" of the defense.

In reviewing this strange baseball play, we are lead to believe several things. First, this could only happen with kids who are in their earliest baseball experience. Second, when surprised by a hitter's sudden stop, all first basemen should know enough to automatically go over and touch that base. Third, we would bet our last dollar that such a play would never occur in high school. American Legion. Colt, college, or pro baseball.

In reviewing baseball records, we find that we are wrong on all three counts. There is probably no play that hasn't occurred at least several times, somewhere, before we are exposed to it.

Let's let our imaginations really wander afar for a few minutes. What if, in a World Series game, this exact situation occurred? The runner has every right to dodge being tagged by the ball. The first baseman has every right to go after the runner.

What if the runner ran back toward home plate, hotly pursued by the first baseman? What if he ran past the plate into foul ground? He would be out.

Now the umpire comes into play. According to the rules, the runner cannot make a farce of the game. Also, the infielder, in running down such a runner, could also be guilty of farcical behavior. So which team does the umpire call the infraction against? One or both?

Rules are interesting, controlling factors in a game. The exceptions to rules are even more interesting, aren't they?

THE PERFECT PLAY BACKFIRES (1988)

For years, the author had been touting his favorite running play, the double steal with men on third and at the plate, as baseball's most successful one. In his letters to Coach Cliff Petrak of Brother Rice High School in Chicago, during 1987 and 1988, he had encouraged Cliff to practice this running trick diligently and execute it at *every opportunity*. Coach Petrak wrote the author the following lines in one of his letters during the 1988 season.

> Fortunately, we won the game 10-0, so I can laugh at it. Here's what happened. Runner on third with two outs. The batter is given the signal that says to break for second, in the event that he gets a walk, and to stay in a rundown, if necessary, until we score the run from third. Sure enough, we get the walk; the batter runs down to first, then breaks quickly for second. The lazy catcher, who was still holding the ball then threw it into center field as our runner from third scored easily. The batter-runner tried for third base and made it when the center fielder's throw bounced away from the third baseman. I waved him home. It looked like a typical "Southworth-Petrak ploy." But the umpire said that the inning was over and NO RUNS SCORED because the batter had MISSED FIRST BASE on the "walk." Our coach at first agreed that the umpire was right. *I could have killed the kid, of course,* but what I still haven't figured out is how to score the play. The first baseman (closest to the play) gets credited with the putout, but DOES THE BATTER STILL GET CREDITED WITH A WALK OR NOT? He never did arrive at first safely. Is he 0-0 or 0-1 batting? I've got a call in to the Chicago Cubs' official scorers, trying to get the answers for me. WHAT A WEIRD EVENT!

Well, how about that one? A coach tries, for the first time, baseball's highest "percentage of success" running play (85%), has the opposition suckered into complete surprise and into making two bad throwing errors, scores two free runs on the play, *and his batter-runner doesn't touch first base, after a walk!*

REFERENCES

Alston, Walter, and Weiskopf, Don. *The Complete Baseball Handbook*. Boston: Allyn and Bacon, Inc., 1972.

Baseball Canada, Technical Staff. *Coaching Advanced Baseball*. Champaign, IL: The Leisure Press, 1986.

Bunn, John, et al. *The Art of Officiating Sports*. Englewood Cliffs, NJ: Prentice-Hall, Inc., 1950.

Carew, Rod, and Berkow, Ira. *Carew*. New York: Simon and Schuster, 1979.

Cobb, Ty, with Al Stump. *My Life in Baseball—The True Record*. New York: Doubleday and Company, 1961.

Cummings, Parke. *The Dictionary of Sports*. New York: A. S. Barnes and Company, 1949.

Danzig, Allison, and Reichler, Joe. *The History of Baseball—Its Great Players, Teams, and Managers*. Englewood Cliffs, NJ: Prentice-Hall, Inc., 1959.

Durslag, Melvin. "Will Hustle Beat Muscle?" *TV Guide*, 1982.

The Encyclopedia Britannica, 1968 ed.

Erbe, Ron. *The American Premium Guide to Baseball Cards (1880-1981)*.

Feldman, Sam. "In This Corner." *Sun-Telegram*, San Bernardino, CA, 1956.

Honig, Donald. *The Brooklyn Dodgers—An Illustrated Tribute*. New York: St. Martin's Press, 1981.

Kindall, Jerry. *Baseball*. New York: Harper and Row, Inc., 1983.

Kraft, John A. "Slide, Man, Slide." *The Letterman Magazine*, 1983.

Kuhn, Bowie. *The Official Baseball Rulebook. Rev. ed., Major and Minor Leagues*. Commissioner of Baseball, 1984.

Leib, Fred. *Baseball As I Have Known It*. New York: Coward, McCann, and Geoghegan, 1977.

Litwhiler, Dan. *Baseball Coaches' Guide to Drills and Skills*. Englewood Cliffs, NJ: Prentice-Hall, Inc., 1963.

Menke, Frank G. *The New Encyclopedia of Sports*. New York: A. S. Barnes and Company, 1944.

Moritz, Charles. "Maury Wills." *Current Biographies Yearbook*. New York: The H. W. Wilson Company, 1966.

National Federation of State High School Athletic Associations. *The Official Baseball Rulebook*. Elgin, IL: 1979.

The Official Baseball Encyclopedia. New York: Macmillan Publishing Company, 1976.

Okrant, Daniel, and Lewine, Harris. *The Ultimate Baseball Book*. Boston: Houghton-Mifflin, 1984.

Olan, Ben, and Reichler, Joe. *Baseball's Unforgettable Games*. New York: The Ronald Press Company, 1960.

Orem, Preston. *Baseball from 1845 to 1881, from the Newspaper Accounts*. Altadena, CA: self-published, 1961.

Peterson, C. S. *The Official Baseball Scorebook*. Hollywood, CA: The Scoremaster Company, 1982.

Petrak, Cliff. *The Art and Science of Aggressive Baserunning*. West Nyack, NY: Parker Publishing Company, 1986.

Poe, Edgar Allan. *The Goldbug*. 1844.

Powers, Jimmy. *Baseball Personalities*. New York: The Rudolph Field Company, 1949.

Pullen, John. *The Twentieth Maine—The Story of a Civil War Regiment*. Pleasantville, NY: Reader's Digest Condensed Books, 1979.

Reichler, Joe. *Baseball's Great Moments*. New York: Crown Publishers, Inc., 1979.

Rice, Grantland. "The Midnight Slide of Paul Revere." *Atlanta Journal*.

Schoor, Gene. *The Complete Dodgers Record Book*. New York: Facts-on-File, Inc., 1984.

Siwoff, Seymour, ed. *The Book of Baseball Records*. New York: 1982.

Smith, Ira, and Smith, H. Allen. *Low and Inside*. New York: McGraw-Hill Publishers, 1947.

Southworth, Harold S. *High-Percentage Baserunning*. Champaign, IL: Leisure Press, 1988.

———.*Manual of Baserunning Plays in Baseball*. San Bernardino, CA: self-published, Crown Printers, 1981.

Spalding, Albert G. *Baseball, the National American Game*. New York: The American Sports Publishing Company, 1911.

Stockton, Bragg A. *Coaching Baseball: Skills and Drills*. Champaign, IL: Human Kinetics Publishers, Incorporated, 1984.

Sun-Telegram. "Brock Surpasses Cobb's Steal Mark." San Bernardino, CA, August 29, 1977.

———. "Three Cheers for the Strike. " San Bernardino, CA: 1981.

Tygiel, Jules. *Baseball's Great Experiment,—Jackie Robinson and His Legacy*. New York: The Oxford University Press, 1983.

Webster's Sport's Dictionary "Glossary of All Definitions in Sports. " Springfield, Mass.: G. C. Merriam Company, 1976.

Wolff, Rick. *The Psychology of Winning Baseball*. West Nyack NY: Parker Publishing Company, 1986.

INDEX